TAKING ON
SILICON VALLEY

HOW AFRICA'S INNOVATORS WILL SHAPE ITS FUTURE

by

NNAMDI ORANYE

TAKING ON SILICON VALLEY: How Africa's Innovators Will Shape Its Future

Copyright © 2017 Nnamdi Oranye
ISBN: 978-0-620-77031-6

Written by Nnamdi Oranye
disruptingafrica.com

Edited by Ryan Peter (ryanpeterwrites.com)
Cover design and typesetting by Shane Rielly (lonelyviking.com)

CONTENTS

Introduction: The Disrupting Africa Manifesto

To all Africans who believe in our future
To all entrepreneurs & innovators working
to change our African landscape
To all visionaries bold enough to present
a new African narrative
To young Africans who dare
to have a dream
We keep moving forward
We keep disrupting Africa

THE DISRUPTING AFRICA MANIFESTO

When I launched my 2016 book, *Disrupting Africa: The Rise and Rise of African Innovation*, I included the opening quote (left) on the inside cover and the website. I called it the "Disrupting Africa" manifesto — both a call and homage to Africans who are passionate about their homeland and want to make a difference. I never dreamed that things would take off as they did after releasing that book. It was a whirlwind of a year. In the space of a few short months, I met and spoke to and dreamed with so many amazing people moving this continent forward, listening to their heart, hearing their challenges, and strategising the best way forward.

Little did I know that in writing my book there would be so much attention and focus on it. Perhaps it was my naivety in assuming that everyone was aware of the impressive African innovation on the continent. Having such feedback to my book from peers, investment houses and the media, made me realise that there was huge interest and thirst for African innovation. People really do want to talk about this, know about it and do something about it.

Spending time with the African Innovators and chronicling their journeys, whether through my radio show on Power FM; researching the various industries innovators are involved in; presenting at conferences; as well as writing in various publications; presented new insights that I hadn't previously considered. A fascinating industry that I didn't know was being disrupted by technology was the health industry – with significant strides made in the space of biotechnology and early detection of malaria. It led me to do some unexpected introspection, thinking deeply about what these themes mean above and beyond the technology. Some of these themes bothered me – themes around the unemployment effect of disruptive technologies, lack of access to funding for our innovators, and whether or not the projected working force in 2040 would be an asset of a liability for the continent.

The result of my thinking is that the *Disrupting Africa Manifesto* has matured significantly. Rather than just being a call and a dream it has developed into a strategy, one that I truly believe is needed on our beloved continent. I've learnt a few things. I've found ways to articulate more clearly that mysterious connection I feel to the many Africans I have developed friendships with who serve the same common purpose: to dare to have a dream, to work towards it, to keep moving forward, and to continue to disrupt Africa.

"Disrupting Africa" was meant to be a play on words which works two ways. One, Africa itself needs to be disrupted. We simply cannot go on doing the same thing we've been doing for the last few hundred years—even the last decade. The world is changing, and fast. We must not seek for change for the sake of change, but we need to see our future and grasp it ourselves, otherwise, others will dictate to us who we need to be and what our place in the world is. We must not make that mistake again. My biggest fear is we just allow ourselves to be swept away by the changing tide and future generations will be asking the same questions our grandfathers asked of themselves. That's not good enough.

Secondly, Africa itself is poised to become a disruptor in this world. It is not the "Dark Continent" or whatever other label people want to put on it, but it has the potential to be the "Disrupting" continent. It is the "Disrupting [continent of] Africa" not "Disrupted Africa" — and we need to work to make sure of that. I hope you can see the subtlety here. This is my way of speaking about Africa Rising, that very popular and yet also unpopular narrative that some erroneously want to brush off as nothing but a lot of hot air; a bit of idealism to keep us thinking we're making a difference; a nice phrase to throw around at corporate dinner parties. My own experience with young Africans, in particular, has led me to the firm conviction that Africa Rising explains what's going on at the grass-roots level very poignantly. However, the current gatekeepers do need to make a bit of a move on — which gets back to the reason for why I'm doing what I'm doing in the first place. If we don't move on others will move us on, and the result could be potentially hazardous.

I love my people, I love my continent, I love where we are, and I love our massive potential. For this reason, I've made Disrupting Africa something of my life's work. As I've developed it, thought about it, and wondered what I could do to get things moving, there are three key elements to the Disrupting Africa strategy that I want to highlight. By presenting this here, you will be able to grasp the foundational principles of this book, why I believe all this matters, and hopefully find your place as an innovator in your own field. These are (1) Connect; (2) Classify; (3) Create. Let me expound on each:

1. CONNECT

This has to do with cataloguing innovation, which is what I've been doing and continue to do, and what I did in my previous book.[1] There I looked at the major industries and noted how Africans were innovating in their own context. It covers health, education, transport, finance, digital payment services, power, and more. Interestingly enough, the book was initially supposed to simply speak about how digital payment services (mobile money) could be a major player and game changer in Africa and the world. When I first met with my editor, Ryan Peter to discuss my ideas, we devised a plan of three short eBooks that could be used as supplementary material where I would present mobile money to various executives and convince them there was an opportunity there. But as I continued to meet innovators through my work in its various forms, and I continued to think about our continent, I started to see that much more was going on. It was much, much bigger than just mobile money. I honestly couldn't keep up with how much innovation I was dis-

---

1   *Disrupting Africa: The Rise and Rise of African Innovation*, by Nnamdi Oranye. ISBN 9780620703154.

covering. When I released the book I was almost disappointed that it couldn't include a range of new innovations that I had found, but I realised that it would simply never get released if I kept trying to add to it.

What's more is I began to connect the dots on how everything can work together and that's when it hit me that we were on the cusp of something exciting and new. As more innovations came out of the woodwork, I started seeing a future where we could literally leapfrog traditional infrastructure. On my radio slot on Power FM, an interview with the BBC and Carte Blanche, several articles at CNBC, Destiny Man magazine and other places, I highlighted how we can (and should) create new ecosystems by simply connecting the dots in practical terms—by connecting innovations together. I continue to talk about that today and it's part of what the manifesto is all about. There are really impressive innovations out there, but no one knows about them, which is part of the problem. I only scratched the surface in my book. I soon realised I could write dozens of more books cataloguing what's going on, and it's become almost impossible to keep up.

It's important that we talk about our innovators and connect them to each other, to existing organisations, to those with the funding, and to the world. This has, therefore, become a major part of what Disrupting Africa is about—connecting innovators and business, key players, financiers, and anyone else involved in this process together. The end goal is to create a platform and work with partners who can promote African innovations.

2. CLASSIFY

This book hangs on this key element. In it, I will be identifying trends and looking at what we need to do about them. Silicon Valley is coming to Africa. The "Big Boys" like Google, Amazon, Facebook, and Uber have their eyes set on our continent. In many ways, they've been able to identify the problems better than we have, as they have (in general) been able to identify global issues and either find a way to fix these, or find a way to create a market where there simply wasn't one before.

How many people would have thought there was a market for Uber? Not even they really thought so at first, as explained by Travis Kalanick, co-founder of Uber in a 2016 TED Talk video. He says they didn't have grand ambitions for it. They just wanted to push a button and get a ride. "But," he says, "it just turned out that lots of people wanted to push a button and get a ride."

We have to classify the trends and see them coming. This is key for me because the more innovators we speak to in the "Connect" principle, the more we can classify and identify trends, and then we can promote and touch on these trends. These trends are often outside of the innovators themselves — they are cultural, historical, and regulatory trends. They are often outside of Africa, as in the case of Silicon Valley coming here. We must identify and know about them and then form a game plan to take advantage of them or regulate them correctly without stifling creativity.

As I began thinking more about this process, I realised that we need to also discuss the human element. Innovation has people behind it. It doesn't just happen out of thin air. Technology is driven by people. There are psychological and philosophical as well as technological trends we have to consider. This led me to think deeply about the African innovator—who they actually *are*. What makes them tick? What are the trends we see in their characters, personalities, upbringing, thinking, philosophies, and general thoughts about our continent? What is actually their *story*? So, as we examine trends technologically, I'm also going to examine these trends so that entrepreneurs and innovators can get to grips with how they ought to think in a way that makes us take on Silicon Valley ourselves. Hence the title, *Taking on Silicon Valley*.

3. CREATE

After connecting with innovators, seeing the future, classifying trends, and examining who the African innovator is, it's time to create something out of what emerges. What provides an incentive for action here is the first two cogs of the Manifesto. For example, we know that the "Big Boys" of Silicon Valley have their eyes on our continent and so we must find ways to work with that, take advantage of that, or counter-act that where appropriate. We must create something out of it. We must work together on projects that see the future and shape it in the right direction. Hence we have to think deeply about how we think, how we see the future, and learn from those who are already doing things.

The point is to show that we have to identify the trends of where innovators are struggling and attend to those. A brief history of Silicon Valley actually gives us a clue as to how to do this, and as you will see we'll discuss that next.

Underpinning all of this is a bold vision statement: **to leave a legacy of innovation for the generations to come.** As I mentioned earlier, if we don't shape and decorate our own home someone else is going to come and do it for us. History shows us that we have to take responsibility for the future and we must do that now, we can't just let it happen to us. We've been there. I don't want to go back there. I'm sure you don't too. We can discuss the nuances and I definitely don't blame the previous generations for all the hurt we've had to experience—I know there are socio-political reasons for why we ended up where we were, and a lot of it was out of our control. But despite this, I also feel the weight of responsibility to build the right thing in the right way for the future generations of our continent. Who will build if we don't? In 30, 40 years we need to be able to look back at a very different continent and be able to pinpoint those moments and those places where we fostered the right kind of change, where we triggered a shift in a positive direction, when we took down the giants that were rising against us in the land. That legacy is what I want to leave and I'm on a mission to invite others to join me. In the end, I'm not writing books and speaking at conferences and trying to do something for the sake of having another book in my name, but because the next generation deserves all my effort to build something for them that they can take even further.

If you have the same mind and passion, we're friends already. Let's talk and let's partner. Share your story with me. Have a look at my website or get hold of me through social media. Share stories on #KNOWYOURCHANGE. I don't just want to write books but I want to interact with those who have the same heart, same vision, and same purpose. Perhaps we can help each other achieve it.

PART I

"In today's world, paradoxically, it is the boldest action that is often the safest. Remaining where you are in a world that is changing so rapidly is in fact the most dangerous of all places to be in."

– Hakeem Belo-Osagie

CHAPTER ONE

———————×———————

SILICON VALLEY RISES

1939, Palo Alto, California, U.S.A.

A garage.

It's the tail-end of the Great Depression, with international affairs going awry and war looming. T.V.'s are not common household items, and people in the newspaper are still identified by their home address-es. If you had to glance at the classified section in the local newspaper you would find ads for "the removal of dead livestock," "Winchester Hi Quality Chicks: hatching every Thursday", or even "an analysis of whether your soil is sweet or sour." Phone numbers are still only four digits.

Palo Alto is a beautiful little town, which got its name from a tall coast redwood tree named El Palo Alto, which can still be seen there today. Palo means 'tree' in Spanish and alto means 'tall'. So hence, 'tall tree'. It was originally established by a railroad tycoon, Leland Stanford Sr. in 1885, when he also founded Stanford University—in honour of his son, Leland Stanford Jr, who died tragically of typhoid fever at the age of 15.

Stanford wasn't an instant success in the same way it is today, and spent many years in financial struggle after its founder died. Things went from bad to worse in the massive 1906 San Francisco earthquake, which did significant damage to Stanford, and devastated eighty percent of San Francisco — it had the highest death toll of any natural disaster in California's history. Stanford rebuilt, but it would only be many years later that this university would become a world-renown leader in innovation and technology.

Professor Frederick Terman is the man who really started it all, who had the vision. One might even want to consider him to be Stanford's second founder. He would be known as a very serious and detailed man who was passionate about what he wanted to accomplish, dressing in suits and wearing old-fashioned shoes and always driving a second-hand car. Two bright students of his, David Packard and William Hewlett, are thinking of starting an electronics business, but they don't really know how to get started.

"I did a number of little things then to help get their business started," Terman told Stanford in 1985. "A new idea in electronics (the so-called 'resistance-tuned oscillator') turned up. I told Bill, 'It looks to me as if you could use this to make an instrument. It would be a lot simpler and cheaper than anything on the market. But you'll have to solve a couple of problems to make it function.' Bill came up with an absolutely perfect solution. He designed and built an audio oscillator, a device that generates signals of varying frequencies. To remove serious instability, Hewlett took advantage of the nonlinear resistance-temperature characteristic of a small light bulb. The addition of one standard and inexpensive component turned a balky laboratory curiosity into a reliable, marketable instrument.[2]"

This is the kind of thing Terman would do. He wouldn't just have his students innovate and dream and come up with new things, but he would discover ways in which what they invented could actually be marketed and used in existing industries. Packard, in 1939, had already graduated and was working for General Electric. But he gave that up for a lower salary, moved back to Palo Alto, and rented the lower floor of a duplex with his wife. Behind the house was a small garage. This would be the garage that would later inspire millions of entrepreneurs and geeks for decades, even up to today, and be dubbed "the Birthplace of Silicon Valley." Today, it's a historical landmark, and you can go see it. They needed to call their new-found company something, so they thought

---

2   *Fred Terman, the Father of Silicon Valley.* By Carolyn E. Tajnai. Available at http://forum.stanford.edu/carolyn/terman

they would just use their names. But they couldn't decide whose name should appear first. Therefore, they turned to a coin, flipped it, and it favoured Hewlett. Their company was therefore called Hewlett-Packard. No doubt you've heard of them.

They received an initial investment of $538 (about $9,263 in 2016) and Terman managed to raise further money for them to help them with a salary. Their first product was a device for bowling alleys that would indicate automatically if the bowl was a foul. It was very clever, but no one really saw any value in it, and so was ultimately a market failure. They then decided to turn to the oscillator, which Terman also saw value in. So they invented an audio frequency oscillator which caught the attention of Walt Disney Studios, who wanted to use it for the soundtrack for its upcoming movie featuring Mickey Mouse, Fantasia. World War II, surprisingly, was great for the business too. They initially marketed through mail orders and, during the second world war, grew their company significantly by building radar, nautical, aviation, radio and sonar devices. Hewlett-Packard, or HP as it is known today, eventually became the world's biggest producer of measurement and electronic devices — a major producer of calculators, personal computers, laptops, printers, and other items. It was not just the technological innovation that led to the company's great success, but also the innovative ways in which Hewlett and Packard ran it. "What I'm most proud of is the fact that we really create a way to work with employees, let them share in the profits, and still keep control of it," Hewlett would frequently say.[3]

HP was the first of many, many more examples to come. The area soon became a thriving hub of innovation. But Terman and his team had an even bigger vision — to build an industrial park and tie the emerging industries, existing industries, and university together. This took the area during the 50's from an innovative hub to a thriving centre of startup businesses, forming what many first called the Valley of Heart's Delight and became known as Silicon Valley in the 70's. More than two thousand electronics and information technology companies exist there today. Terman would always call it their 'secret weapon'. "When we set out to create a community of technical scholars in Silicon Valley, there wasn't

3   *William Hewlett & David Packard: Maverick Managers.* Published at Entrepreneur Magazine, October 2008. Available at https://www.entrepreneur.com/article/197644

much here and the rest of the world looked awfully big," he said once. "Now a lot of the rest of the world is here.[4]" He is right. And today, Silicon Valley is in the rest of the world — in your pocket or on your desk or at your bedside right now, probably.

But what does all this have to do with Africa, you might ask? The answer, as far as I'm concerned, is everything. What I've highlighted above is the standard, stock story. But there is more to it. It's worth probing exactly *why* Terman encouraged these two men to do what they did, what opportunities came their way, how they took hold of these, and what was all bubbling under the surface at the time. I mean, it was the Great Depression and war was on its way, arguably the kind of time when risk-taking is not highly encouraged. Terman himself would tell stories of how they had literally nothing to work with. "An accident that burned out a few vacuum tubes or damaged a meter would produce a crisis in the laboratory budget for a month," he once said. "The pre-war electronics laboratory was in an attic under the eaves, over the electrical machinery laboratory. The roof of the attic leaked, and at times these leaks became quite bad. There was no money to repair the roofs, so they built big wooden trays and lined them with tar paper and tar. As the trays filled, we walked around them. Our morale didn't suffer. One winter Bill Hewlett added a homey touch by stocking the trays with goldfish.[5]" Terman and his colleagues were working upstream, against what was arguably a prevalent culture of safety, not risk. Yet they forged ahead and took a risk with a brand new sort of business and with emerging technology that was quite frankly unprecedented.

Over the years it only got better. Stanford produced advancement in research and saw dozens, then hundreds of companies, and now thousands form through what it was doing. It set the culture and pace for what has made Silicon Valley so highly innovative and productive, to the point that today the term "Silicon Valley" no longer just refers to the place but has become a synonym for anything hi-tech, innovative, enterprising, and disruptive. Thousands of inventions, Nobel prizes, strong

---

4   *Fred Terman, the Father of Silicon Valley.* By Carolyn E. Tajnai. Available at http:// forum.stanford.edu/carolyn/terman

5   Ibid

academia, and an entrepreneurial spirit now characterise Stanford and the Silicon Valley it has effectively built.

It seems to me Frederick Terman *saw* something of the future. Risks were opportunities. And he encouraged his bright minds to see it that way. Where we are right now in Africa, we need to somehow see what he saw, but *for us*. Obviously, our context is different, but we have to start somewhere, just like they did at the end of the 30's. We have to experiment, innovate, test, and play. Timothy J. Sturgeon, writing in the book by Kenney Martin on how Silicon Valley came to be, highlights that "perhaps the strongest thread that runs through the Valley's past and present is the drive to 'play' with novel technology, which, when bolstered by an advanced engineering degree and channelled by astute management, has done much to create the industrial powerhouse we see in the Valley today." We need to have this kind of thinking — there is a real sense in which we, in Africa, need to take assimilate some of this philosophy. Did all of that happen by accident? Of course not. Did that sort of thinking emerge on its own? Of course not. Under Terman's leadership, Stanford embarked on building "steeples of excellence" — networks of science and engineering researchers, a "community of technical scholars," who would entice the brightest and best students to the university. Terman fostered close relationships with students and technologies and industries emerging at the time. He encouraged his students to form companies of their own and personally invested in them, with money and time and emotional input. Today some of those students, in addition to Hewlett and Packard, include the founders of Litton Industries (a large defense contractor) and Varian Associates (a high-tech company specialising in electromagnetic equipment). After the war, as dean of the School of Engineering, he got the University to lease portions of its land to hi-tech firms, encouraging companies such as General Electric (and the aforementioned companies) to move in to the Stanford Industrial Park, which is the bulk of Silicon Valley. What he did, essentially, is he brought like-minded, like-hearted people *together*. He believed in them, invested in them, and saw that the future was theirs.

In an article, his son Lewis Terman highlights three core elements of his father's strategy. "There is the government money, there's the university, and the industry. He wanted a tight tie together between industry and the university with the government money supporting education of the students who would then go into the industry. That was the model he was working on that he thought had really great opportunities to do great things." Terman's vision was undoubtedly to create a true technological hub that involved human elements like community, study, and a pioneering spirit.

Of course, it's the Internet that has really made Silicon Valley a prominent player on the world stage today. But that would never have come about without the foundations that were set. Google started at Stanford when founders Larry Page and Sergey Brin developed their algorithm in the 90's. (Yahoo also emerged from Stanford, from alumni Jerry Yang and David Filo). At the time of writing this book, Silicon Valley is just two decades from turning a hundred years old. It has firmly entrenched itself not only into American culture, but into the culture of the world, and it continues to do so in overt and subtle ways. Today its presence is felt when you wake up, go to sleep, and walk around — all there in your pocket in that little device called your smartphone. And the idea of that itself comes from a philosophy, not just an idea but a way of *thinking*, that developed within Silicon Valley.

Sometime in the 80's its core philosophy became the 'personal'. It started with the personal computer. Adverts from Microsoft in the 80's can be found on the Internet, with Bill Gates quotes as saying, "A computer on every desk, and in every home, running Microsoft software." This was a new idea in those days — especially the idea of bringing the computer into the home. "I think it's fair to say that personal computers have become the most empowering tool we've ever created," Gates would say in the following years. "They're tools of communication, they're tools of creativity, and they can be shaped by their user." These days, the smartphone is the new version of that — and in fact, it seems Steve Jobs took Bill Gates' vision and realised it needed to go beyond a computer on a desk, but a computer in your pocket. All of this innovation, of course, means that today Silicon Valley holds a huge and prominent position in how economics, politics, and business is discussed and executed, even if it's not yet clear exactly what it will all mean. Its influence on our world is unprecedented. Its influence on Africa is felt in ways we probably would never have imagined, especially when it comes to the mobile phone and the incredibly huge way that simple invention is allowing us to leapfrog traditional infrastructure. Africa's mobile penetration is growing exponentially, and everyone knows that if we can solve the Internet connectivity issue, Africa will present the biggest market in the world next to China.

There is a 'dark side' to all this, however. Silicon Valley is not just about innovation and business and technology but is also starting to become a synonymous term for negative elements like "big business", corporate takeover, hostile takeovers, monopolising industries, and a new kind of technological colonialism. In Silicon Valley's own era of Facebook and Google and Amazon, it's easy to see why some people have started becoming almost afraid of the way things are developing, especially when we look at how much of our own world is run by these giants, and when we see how these companies are cannibalising so much of what's happening out there. Further to this, it gets even darker, with WikiLeaks recently releasing details of CIA code that showed just a little bit of the extent of its hacking capabilities and efforts — from hacking smart TV's and gaming devices and phones and listening in on your conversations; being able to read your messages before they're encrypted; and even taking control of smart cars to drive into a wall and assassinate an enemy. Technology has, indeed, become both the blessing and the curse the sci-fi writers always envisaged it would, and as we explore what some of Silicon Valley's brightest innovators are doing, you will find what those sci-fi writers dreamed is actually not far off.

Recently, I touched down at Jomo Kenyatta airport in Nairobi and instantly connected to Wi-Fi at the airport. I remember the days when you would first head off to a stationary shop to buy a map, would need to perhaps find a telephone to call the taxi company; or to call the company you've come to see and ask them where their lift was, and you would perhaps call the hotel you booked to confirm your booking. You'd have to find their number somewhere in a folder with a stack of other paperwork, and you would head next to the foreign exchange to cash in your traveller's cheques. What a slow world that was — although we would complain about how fast-paced life was!

Once on Wi-Fi, however, I first opened up Google maps to confirm the location of the hotel and its distance. I used Google Maps' travel feature to give me an idea on the location of my hotel. Satisfied with what I saw, I opened the app and called an Uber (yes, 'uber' has become a noun). Of course, I didn't need to worry about drawing any money — Uber is linked to my credit card, and my credit card works internationally anyway, so paying for my hotel won't be an issue as well. Google Maps helped me just to get a bearing of where my meetings would be, and I went through a few emails to confirm my itinerary.

The phone beeps. "Your Uber ride is 2 minutes away." Great, I've got my bags, I'm off to the exit. "Your Uber ride is 1 minute away." I track my ride's every movement through the app. I get out the exit and stand on the sidewalk for a few seconds, looking for the car that matches the description on the app. Ah, there it is. "Your Uber ride is here!" Great, I get in, greet the driver, confirm his name, and sit in the back feeling relaxed. There are a ton of innovators I'm off to meet, and I start to think about how each of them can create a difference on our continent. Lately, I've been thinking a lot about how our innovators can take on Silicon Valley—how we would be able to create our own technology giants here that could compete or partner with Silicon Valley in ways that are beneficial to us. I think of some of the industries Silicon Valley has disrupted on our very continent, and I think of what we need to do to ensure it all works for our benefit.

I freeze. Something in the back of my mind just sparked. My conscience, perhaps, or a sudden realisation. I look at my phone, I see the Uber ride moving on the map, showing me how far I am from my destination.

"I just did it!" I blurt out loud. "It was me!"

My Uber driver looks at me in his rearview mirror.

"Um. Sorry. Excuse me, sir?"

"Uh," I reply, frowning. "Um. Never mind."

I realise what it is I just did. In the space of five minutes, I have just disrupted several massive African industries. I was part of the disruption. I was the one who opened these apps and used them and loaded my credit card in them. I was the one who ultimately sent this revenue to Uber in California. Uber drivers themselves in Kenya aren't paid very much — and there have been several issues with how it is slashing prices in the third world, making drivers get paid even less. How would this all have worked if Uber wasn't here, I wonder?

I worry about the taxi guy who's probably out of a job because I ordered an Uber. What about his family? What will he do now? I think of how I'm creating demand for this service and being such a typical consumer. I think about the touristy conversations I may have had with a taxi driver because I used to take note of the landmarks and my surroundings, so I could get to grips with how to get around town. Now I don't even think about that anymore, as I know I can just rely on my phone and my maps there and whatever the Uber app tells me. I think about the printers and the cartographers involved in making maps in the old days. The entire process which I've just circumvented with my phone. That makes me think about the tourism industry. What about the tourist guides? The myriad of people who would connect you with a strange, new city?

Is what I've done a good thing? A bad thing? What do we do? And why didn't I rather try and find an African alternative to use? I look at my phone in my hands and I think about the telecommunications companies in South Africa where I've just come from. I think about the thousands of jobs that might be affected because I don't use international roaming capabilities anymore. I just use my data and Wi-Fi wherever I go—WhatsApp calls, messaging, email, everything I need. All giving California an advantage.

My mind won't stop ticking as I analyse the pros and cons of disruption. I think of Henry Ford and his T-Model cars and how it disrupted the horse and carriage industry – relegating it to a sporting activity we maybe now watch at the Olympics, if perhaps we're bored. I wonder if some our prominent industries would become relegated to "sporting activities". I think about which one of these could be. I rationalise that at a macro level, disruption is good for our growth as a continent, and I start a mental checklist of the positives and negatives. I remember articles I've read, ones that I've written, conversations I've had, the innovators I'm about to see, and then I'm covered by a deep sense of responsibility.

Because I realise I need to do something. It would be a travesty if our kids and the next generation only learn about Silicon Valley disruptors. I can see it now: lessons at school on Mark Zuckerberg, Larry Page, Brian Chesky, Travis Kalanick and …? What? No African innovators?

There has to be an "and". This is critical. There just has to be an "and". We need to be learning about these disruptors and our disruptors. It cannot be any other way. This book is about helping our innovators become that "and".

"There has to be an 'and'", I say out loud.

My Uber driver looks at me in his rearview mirror again.

"Excuse me?" he says.

"Oh, uh, never mind. Again." I reply.

"Er. So, er, where you from?" he asks.

In a way, I'm grateful for the interruption. It gives me some space to come down to earth, to engage with the real people involved. In between our chit-chat, I know that this book has to be written and has to be distributed across Africa. Because Silicon Valley has its eyes on us. The Big Boys of Google, Facebook, Uber, Amazon, and others are all looking for fresh opportunity on fresh cyber-soil, and we're in the target zone. They're here already, and they're here to stay. There are many positive to these winds of change blowing through our continent, and many of them are working to create positive change, such as better connectivity and the likes. But there are also many negatives as whole industries are upended. More than anything I believe we need to be ready for this because if we are not we are going to run into some serious trouble — and I was only just briefly skimming the surface of it in my wandering, worrying thoughts at the back of an Uber.

"Silicon Valley is a mindset, not a location."

— **Reid Hoffman**

CHAPTER TWO

THE TIPPING POINT

There comes a time when you have to choose a different path. These moments arrive unexpectedly, and usually, you don't realise the importance of the moment until many years later. I believe we are in one of those critical moments as a continent. We are on the verge of either going one way or another. But the trouble is, we can't afford to only realise this years later, because then it may be too late. We have so much going for us as a continent, and yet we have so many challenges at the same time, I wonder if we truly understand the power of our decisions right now — how our decisions will affect our future generations. Oliver Tambo once said, "A country, a movement, a person that does not value its youth and children, does not deserve its future." We would do well to remember this. We need to value our youth in such a way that we build for them and bring them into the process. They are our current and future innovators.

I was about twenty-three years old when that day arrived—when I was to choose a different path, but in many ways, I missed the significance of the moment. I was in the car with a friend who was also my roommate at the time, and we were driving to go see some friends. My window was open, it was a wonderful summer's day, we had both just completed our engineering degrees, and I was feeling relaxed and confident about my future.

"So, finally we're done with our degrees, huh?" I asked him. "Feels great."

"Yeah," he answered.

"So where do you think you're going to apply for a job first?"

He turned to look at me briefly while still keeping his eyes on the road. "I don't think..." he said slowly, "Well, what I'm trying to say is I don't think I'll be an engineer for very long."

"Aren't you enjoying it?" I asked. It struck me as odd as it seemed that doing engineering was a foregone conclusion. He studied it, so why wouldn't he do it? Was something else up?

"Nah, I do enjoy it," he said. "But I won't do it for very long."

"Why?" I asked, looking at him intently. "What will you do instead?"

"I'm going to have my own business. In fact, I'm going to run a few businesses."

"What? But you've just finished your degree. You can get yourself a good job. Why a business? What would the point of that be? It's such a risk!"

"Nnamdi, it is a risk. That's kind of the point."

I didn't quite know what to think of this. It seemed new, strange, and unnecessary to me. In my world, you studied, you got a job in your field, and that was that. You worked the nine to five and you enjoyed your hobbies on weekends. This was the middle-class dream, and I was to enjoy the privilege of living it. That was the plan. I never considered there could be another plan — growing up, that's the way I was taught it works. You became an employee. You studied hard, got a good job, raised your family, and retired after a solid career in a company.

"What about your parents?" I asked.

"They're cool with it. My dad has a few businesses."

"Is that why you're doing this?"

"Partly. I just don't think I could do one thing forever."

"Hmmm," I said. It seemed really foreign to me. Something about this conversation shifted my own personal view. It was the first time I saw that entrepreneurship was a viable alternative: that the nine to five wasn't some sort of natural law and wasn't the only way to live. There is nothing wrong with the nine to five and all that, of course, but the point is that I realised it's simply not all that there is. Pretty much everyone in my circle was in the space where we thought that was what you did, but this was something else. I simply never realised you could choose to be an entrepreneur and make some sort of career of it.

You might say this was a simple conversation, and perhaps it perplexes you that this was a big deal for me, but for a man growing up and trying to figure it all out, it lit a fire. I am sure if I ask my friend about it, he would probably never remember it. But for me, it was defining and silently, within myself, I began to choose a different path. Perhaps it was this, or perhaps it was something else, but I just remember having a deep restlessness in my soul from about my mid-twenties. It's taken me awhile, actually, to capture what it is and I'm probably still trying to figure it out.

I started on my journey in quantifying this restlessness and fire inside me when I was in Australia a few years later. I had bought my business and had done quite a bit of travelling back to Africa prior to that. Unfortunately, my business wasn't very profitable after two years, and I wasn't sure what that really meant in terms of entrepreneurship and if I was made for it, so I got a job with a division of Ford Motor Company instead. There I was tasked with growing my division and creating a positive turnover for the company in the automotive space. I remember walking through the building with the CEO at the time, during my interview, when she was discussing with me their plans and strategy and what the company would expect from me. I noticed that of the four floors we had explored, one of them was quite empty. I never said anything about it. She was the one who brought that up.

"Your job," she said to me, "Will be to fill this floor."

I nodded and pretended to be excited. "Sure," I said. "Sounds great." In reality, my mind was racing and analysing what on earth that would mean. How could I do it? Where would I find the right people? What if I brought on liabilities rather than assets to the company? It all sounded rather daunting to me.

I worked at it. Hard. Eighteen months later I filled that floor. One day I was sitting in my office, which had a large glass window overlooking my floor space, and I sat back and remembered the day it was empty. I mused over this a bit, remembering my conversation with the CEO.

"I guess I did it," I said to myself. "There it is. It's full!"

It was the first time I actually remembered my brief and realised I actually completed it. It's a great feeling when that happens. But something inside was bugging me — there was some voice at the back of my head telling me that this meant more than just filling a floor here in Australia. Prior to this role, I was travelling back and forth from various African countries and spent many hours in thought over the unemployment I encountered there. Then I looked at the faces of those working on the floor and proudly said to myself, "I've just created lots of jobs. Everyone on this floor would not have a job if not for me."

However, something was still bugging me. There was still some voice at the back of my head trying to tell me something. I got up. Then it hit me. Sure, filling this floor was something to be proud of, but there was something more to it than just me and what I did. I don't know where it came from but there it was, a little voice saying to me: *Why can't you do the same thing back home?*

This time, I didn't miss the significance of the moment. If I could just create twenty jobs back home in Africa, I realised, twenty more people would be able to feed their families, take care of their kids, build a future for themselves, and potentially even hire others. My contribution goes beyond just filling a floor, I realised, it *actually* contributes to the economy. It *actually* creates a snowball effect. It *actually* creates a future.

So I quit and moved to South Africa. And in doing so, I began to peel back the layers that for too long covered me. I started to see how I had bought into something that simply wasn't me. As each layer peeled off, I discovered my authentic, African self, and became it. This existential experience, if you could call it that, made me see my true identity, and I saw I wasn't the only African going through such an experience. In fact, something of my story began to merge with Africa's story today, and that started to uncover even more of my identity and, paradoxically, also uncover Africa's identity to me. I started to see the beauty and potential of our amazing continent, and our incredible people. And not only my identity as an African was being forged, but also my identity as an entrepreneur — as someone who could make a change if they just worked hard to do so. Africa entered my heart. And what formed wasn't just a flowing passion for Africa based on a philosophy or some idealistic notion, or unrealistic optimism, or because I was with the right friends or read some inspiring piece of journalism somewhere, although I appreciate those. It wasn't just because the Africa Rising train took me on board and I blindly went with it. It was far deeper and far more significant than that. I began to dream of an Africa grounded in technology and working with analysis and facts—an Africa which would forge new ways of doing things. And I began to see the beauty of Africans working collectively to achieve a single dream. "Look to Africa," said Marcus Garvey, "for there a king will be crowned."

Here's the truth of it. When I was young and envisioned my future, I thought of myself as an engineer or doctor or something along those lines. I envisioned myself living the American Dream somewhere. But all that was formulated by what *others* said I should be. It took me a long time to realise that I have to have my own view of what I should be, and it was around twenty-five I started figuring that out. Now years later, I am so very thankful for this process. And I believe this personal journey correlates with much of the tension we see in Africa and us as Africans. Of course, I'm not trying to minimise our history and immense challenge and our multiple identities through the small filter of my own personal life, but the fact is that the rest of the world is very much telling us what and who we *should* be. We've seen it do this again and again and again. Some of history's greatest African thinkers had keen insight into this process, and when we think we've shaken it off one side, it comes creeping back in another. In many ways, it's coming to us through Silicon Valley's approach to technology and innovation and entrepreneurship. We can learn from it, but we cannot *become* it. We have to find another way to deal with it. It also comes in the form of the development narrative — of how a nation or a continent should develop. We are told we must industrialise and manufacture, which is true but is not the full story. There's more to it than that, and later in this book, I will challenge these ways of thinking and present some new ideas we need to consider.

We need to shake this off. In my own life, I find it hard to shake it off. There are still voices trying to tell me who I should be, even while I'm forging a new path. I should listen to them only to learn, but not to succumb. I have to keep telling myself that I'm achieving things based on who I think I must be; based on the purpose I believe I ought to fulfil. When I buy into that concept, that I have my own purpose, I make an impact, and I love it and I love what I do and I enjoy it even when it's tough. Likewise, I believe that if Africa would buy into this concept to become her authentic self and fulfil her own purpose in history, everything will change.

My third personal inflection point along these lines happened during the months after I released my first book, *Disrupting Africa,* early 2016. I was just going to publish the book on Amazon's Kindle platform and let the chips fall as they may. But that wasn't meant to be. It just took off beyond what I imagined. The media got hold of it, loved it, and I ended up being featured on BBC and Carte Blanche, and publishers like CNBC and Mail & Guardian and others asked me to write for them on innovation. I was also on the radio station Power FM at the time with a weekly radio slot, and that also just kind of happened without me even doing much. I realised, in hindsight, that it all must have touched a nerve, and that what I was writing about *was* actually as important for our continent as it was personally for me. This was more than just an interest, something I always thought but never could quite quantify. Entrepreneurs and innovators were reading the stories I covered in the book and actually started to do things differently. It really did what I secretly hoped but was too embarrassed to actually voice — inspire and encourage and bring change. Just like African innovation, it actually changed lives. One day, through a conversation, I realised that I was also part of the change I was saying others were doing. I am part of changing the narrative and owning it — as is every innovator who is making a change. In thirty years' time, the kind of impact I want to have is not that I was still documenting people, but participated. You are also part of the change. I cannot stress this enough. I hope that when you finish this book you won't be just informed on what's going on, but you will be inspired to make the change we need to make.

When I was in High School in Nigeria and reading the beautiful and moving *Things Fall Apart* by Chinua Achebe, I wondered whether he knew, when writing it in the 50's, that it would have the kind of impact has today. I wondered if he knew he would become the father of modern African writing. I wondered if he knew the kinds of impressions it would leave on young readers such as myself, and how it would help us truly start understanding the clash of cultures in Africa and the rich heritage of our people. I doubt he really saw how far it would reach, although I bet he knew that what he was doing was significant. Looking back at his career, he once said as much.

"I'm a practised writer now," he said. "But when I began, I had no idea what this was going to be. I just knew that there was something inside me that wanted me to tell who I was, and that would have come out even if I didn't want it."

It's been the same sort of process for me, and I think anyone who wants to make a difference has the same sort of epiphanies. We know what we are doing is significant because every little thing means something, but we don't know how far reaching it will go. Not knowing the total of how what we will do will affect the future is no reason not to do it. I want to write books and catalogue innovation that future generations in thirty years' time can read and understand our histories, and see how come it is that their views of innovation are not clouded by Silicon Valley. I dream of hearing in thirty years' time of how we not only innovated in an African way but actually succeeded and thrived and created a whole new world. I have a role to play in the innovation landscape, and so do you. Whether you are on the technical side, entrepreneurial side, or on the writing and connecting side of this, you have an important role to play. We must all actively participate in this play and not just look at it from an arms lengths point of view.

I hope this book will, therefore, be a tipping point for you. Beyond this, I dream of seeing a tipping point for Africa collectively. We're in a position where we have to change as our current collective ways of doing things will not work for us going into the future. On the one hand, we have many young Africans going through the same sort of journey I've been on, looking to make an impact and be Africa Rising, be the African Change, the disruptors. On the other hand, we've got international conglomerates, Silicon Valley and the likes, with their eye on Africa and looking to come and disrupt. Sometimes to our benefit and sometimes to their own benefit. It's great that they're coming, but we need to ask: are we ready for them? And why should we not just take them on? We've been here before. This time, we have to take our future into our own hands. It's not so much that we should be putting up our borders and telling Silicon Valley thanks, but no thanks. It's rather that we need to challenge our thinking, our philosophy around technology, our ideas about our own borders between each other in Africa, and we need to rise up as leaders with a fresh vision for our continent.

A lot of this is already happening, as I look at all the innovations and innovators I've worked with in the last few years. But I will highlight in this book what I think we should be doing and how I think we should be thinking. I emphatically believe we should be competing with Silicon Valley where we can, and partnering with them where we can, always looking to how we can make sure we as Africans benefit from our disruptions and those coming from overseas. While the title of this book might sound adversarial, the intent is more a collaborative one. Our Silicon Valley friends are here to stay and I'm a big fan of their work. I can't imagine life without WhatsApp, Google or Uber. But we need to be playing with them in the sandpit, not just letting them take over while we sit on the side eating our oranges.

In fact, I'm not even sure many of us are even aware that there's a sandpit to play in. Sometimes I look at where our governments spend their time and what they are busy with. In many ways, they can often be fifteen years behind what's really going on in the world today—and while we focus on bringing traditional infrastructure to our nations, for example, Silicon Valley is busy disrupting those industries under our noses. Of course, there are many types of traditional infrastructure we should be developing, but we should never think that all that is going to suddenly make us able to compete with the likes of Silicon Valley. There is indeed a sandpit and there are many ways you and others can get in. We need to know that there's disruption happening on our continent – just not in the way we envisaged it—and we need to harness that disruption.

"Without change there is no innovation, creativity, or incentive for improvement. Those who initiate change will have a better opportunity to manage the change that is inevitable."

— **William Pollard**

CHAPTER THREE

IS THE AFRICA RISING NARRATIVE DEAD?

At a TEDx talk in London in 2014, Tanzanian Billionaire and founder of the Infotech Investment Group, Ali Mufuruki, came out with a guns-blazing statement: "Africa is not rising."

> "I think that there is quite a number of profound flaws to the Africa rising narrative. The first one being, we are coined not by an African, but a well-meaning Western journalist. Somebody who's standing outside, looking in. And comparing the state of the continent today to what it was fifteen years ago. Obviously, it's better today than what it was fifteen years ago. And we have embraced that narrative without questioning it, and I think that's why we are where we are."

I remember watching this and thinking to myself that Mufuruki might be gunning down the wrong enemy. In my own work in the field, I've found he is in line with what many others are saying. These days, there are many journalists and media representatives who look a bit sheepish when we speak of "Africa Rising". I've been told its old news, that it's just been a dream, and if I want to be relevant today I better find a different narrative or some other way to spin things It's become almost popular to disparage this much-beloved narrative.

I finally got the opportunity to meet Mufuruki on a panel at a conference in Durban, South Africa. I finally got to understand what he meant.

Mufuruki's reasons for saying what he said at TEDx was that we need to be realistic. From there, he went on to highlight several industries and challenges where he says there has not only been stagnation but regression. They were mostly the usual suspects – electricity, technology, education, amongst others. We all know this, and I don't think we should keep quiet about it. But there's far more than this going on. I've found the more time I spend there, the more my optimism increases. My optimism is based on realism — on what I actually see and experience happening with African people and entrepreneurs. I've taken a look at all these usual suspects and I've spent a great deal of time investigating what's going on with our innovators, and in my book, *Disrupting Africa*, I highlighted how innovation is morphing each of them and allowing us to dream up new technologies that leapfrog traditional infrastructure. I still believe that. Since starting my journey of cataloguing innovations, it's only gotten better. And this is why we must foster our innovators.

My parents' generation came out of the colonial era. Most of them either experienced the tail end of colonialism or the start of independence and revolution. In my own experience, I've found the common theme with most of my parents' generation was that you must get a good education. Most of them fought for that and some of them were able to actually experience what education is like or were able to make it into a professional career. Education was something you aspired to, a sure sign of success. Whether you were in Nigeria, South Africa or Kenya, the trend was the same. There was also a tie-in to the type of leadership my parents' generation had as well. Most of the leaders that came out of that era really promoted education and professionalism and epitomised it themselves. Think of Kwame Nkrumah, Nnamdi Azikiwe of Nigeria, Nelson Mandela, and even Robert Mugabe. These were professionally educated leaders that inspired the educated spirit and showcased that education is the key to strong, rational, independent leadership.

But there is more to this story. If you fast forward twenty to thirty years later, to where we are today, it's not far off (even if it's controversial) to say the leadership of that time effectively failed the education cycle. I've just found that too many of those from that generation have all of a sudden found they have no pension. What do they do now? And this is not just an African thing — this is one of the reasons why there is so much political turmoil in the world, as the system from previous years has failed a generation, and a new generation does not want to find themselves in a similar position.

I believe that one of the factors that has led to this is around how we viewed leadership, and therefore how we viewed entrepreneurship. It was a big deal for me to think of entrepreneurship as an actual career choice, as I related in the previous chapter. Being an 'entrepreneur' in Africa about thirty years ago meant that you sold tomatoes or oranges on the side of the road because you were unable to get a job anywhere else due to a lack of education. Obviously, this meant you didn't have the brightest future and governments should do something about it. You never aspired to be an entrepreneur, you aspired to get a good education and get a good job.

The next generation after my parents, which I belong to, obviously, have realised that this set up has not really worked. We still view education as important, of course. I certainly do. I think it's critical. For many, the set up has worked, but it hasn't delivered on all its promises. I can't see myself working for the next thirty years and finding out I have no pension, and I'm sure you're much the same. Moreso, education hasn't always meant you are able to get a job in Africa and contribute to Africa. In fact, it's often meant the exact opposite. Which has created a real problem for us with the diaspora, who have often found they need to come back to the continent but yet there is no work.

This problem, however, has created an interesting situation that we can (and ought) to take advantage of. According to Ndubuisi Ekekwe, founder of the non-profit African Institution of Technology, the Great Recession brought many African intellectuals with unique skill sets back home, because job opportunities ran out overseas. However, faced with the reality that job opportunities for their skill set in Africa were a dime a dozen, they began to use their skills to create markets, find solutions, form companies, and be entrepreneurs.

"The collapse of the commodity boom has pushed countries and their citizens to invent other ways to survive because benefits like unbridled imports are no longer sustainable. Now many things are coming together which will help transform some African economies by the sheer power of their entrepreneurs. The cloud, open source software, cheap computing resources, and ideas from local technology hubs are redesigning Africa. Even if the commodity boom returns, these structures will remain because they are homegrown and well-designed. In fact, it shows promise for a golden era of entrepreneurship anchored by local innovation.[6]"

This is exciting. It shows the positive side of why Mufuruki and many others are going negative on the African Rising narrative, saying we need to have a "reality check" in light of the downturn in China's economy which marked an end to the commodity price super-cycle that was driving a great deal of the economic growth of our continent. In a Sunday Times opinion piece, Jabulani Sikhakhane continues in the same mood: "Narratives about sub-Saharan Africa's economic growth have swung, during the past four decades, between two extremes: pessimism and exuberance. After much exuberance about Africa's strong growth over the past two decades, albeit driven by a few countries, the tide is turning back to despair."

However, the positive effect of this is we see African intellectuals with specific skill sets returning to our continent and being forced to take up entrepreneurship and innovate. This is why my work in researching, cataloguing, and writing about innovation, as well as connecting innovators together, has made me think differently to the two extremes Sikhakhane highlights above. I agree emphatically that Africa Rising isn't going to happen just because we talk about it or think positively about our continent. I understand the general sentiment. We want to be realistic. It's okay to dream, but we need to also just face the facts. But I believe we can justify the narrative and go beyond just talking about it, but to actually quantifying it today (and not to some distant future) by looking at our innovation. We need to look at the right things in the right places and in

---

6   *Why African Entrepreneurship is Booming*, by Ndubuisi Ekekwe. Published at Harvard Business Review, July 2016. Available at https://hbr.org/2016/07/why-african-entrepreneurship-is-booming

the right way. We need to be putting on the right set of spectacles to really see what's going on.

The system of 'study and get a job' has shown itself to be unsustainable for the long run, and arguably the Great Recession itself showed this to be the case. Many people living in what we call "developed nations" have felt this problem themselves, and many find themselves out of work because they are actually overqualified. There is such a thing as too much education, or rather, a purposeless education. You have to be educated to be going somewhere, not just to have a degree. What is the solution for overqualified people? Probably entrepreneurship. The trouble is, in the Western world, not only are they without employment, they have a massive student loan to service as well! Which makes taking a risk with entrepreneurship even more difficult to do, even perhaps out of reach. In our context, however, it might be different—and many of those who are innovating in the education space here in Africa have seen this and have been working at creating a new solution for us. There is a new wave of entrepreneurs coming out of the woodwork and looking at opportunities, grasping them, and exploding into success. Some of these I will highlight later in this book because how they think is important to think about. And this has certainly created a change of culture. We grew up with our parents instilling in us that you have to be a professional, and we never looked at entrepreneurs as the rock stars like they are today. We always equated entrepreneurship to someone struggling to get by or that they have not really done well in school. But now that's all flipped 180 degrees. Entrepreneurship has come to be seen as a pathway to success and a test for true leadership. Sure, we have to be careful with how we romanticise it. This isn't an easy path to take, I can assure you. But I want to encourage you to not be like me and only think of it as a viable alternative when you're well into your working career. Hopefully, you're in your mid-twenties and younger. That's not to say that you can't make the dive when you're older, only that you have a lot more risks to take.

We have gotten to a stage from an innovation point of view where we understand the basics, but we need a clear roadmap from here to fifty years from now to see what our legacy will look like. As opposed to just focusing on the challenges we have had or the opportunities we did not have, we must appreciate where we have come from and what we have done really well. One of the ways in which we need to do this, I believe, is to challenge the 'developing world' narrative head-on, and thus take our Africa Rising narrative seriously. We have to challenge present-day thinking around concepts such as "development" and a "developed nation". To apply Mufuruki's thoughts about Africa Rising to these terms, I say that we have "embraced" this "narrative" about how a nation should develop "without questioning it." And "that's why we are where we are." To be frank, I think he's right about some of our mistakes, but we now need to aim at the right target.

AFRICAN INNOVATION IS AFRICAN

With that, let's look at all this from a different angle. In mid-2016, I read an opinion article at CNBC by David Levin, entitled *Why Africa is missing among the Worlds Top Innovators*. The article seemed to be loosely based on the Bloomberg Innovation Index's "Fifty Most Innovative Economies" in the world. As the author rightly points out, Africa hardly featured on the list at the time. "How can this possibly be?" Levin asks. He continues:

> "How can there be no contribution from sub-Saharan Africa which contains two of the three largest economies on the continent as measured by GDP? From the standpoint of innovation – and by extension – contribution to the greater global good, Africa wasn't even on the map (pardon the pun). Of course, theories abound with respect to what plagues Africa – and there are plenty to choose from. I know what you're thinking. Poverty, corruption, electricity, food security, African strongmen, water, sanitation, land, terrorism, etc. And you're all correct. Unfortunately, these rationalisations all contribute to the distasteful reality that Africa is an emerging market that has, well... never quite emerged. It's stuck in the mud.[7]"

---

7   *Why Africa is Missing Among the World's Top Innovators*, by David S. Levin. Published at CNBC Africa, July 2016. Available at http://www.cnbcafrica.com/news/2016/07/07/why-africa-is-missing-among-the-worlds-top-innovators/

Levin shares my frustration and trumpets the opinion that the best way through is via education. I agree, although in some circles this answer has become a bit of a cliché, and I've already highlighted the limits of education above. The issue then, as far as I'm concerned, isn't whether or not education is the missing key but rather *how* we do education that matters. The history of Silicon Valley is a case in point. Education really happens when we put people and ideas together and create a community, which creates an ecosystem. Teaching goes far beyond academics but involves the full experience and exposure to industry and smart people. This goes beyond innovation hubs and the like.

I must admit Levin's article bothered me quite a bit, and for more than just his comments on education. I spent a few days trying to figure it out and then it hit me. I had just published my book filled with credible African innovators and could fill up another book based on new innovators I was coming across, and realised that Bloomberg's assessment is simply incorrect. When you look at what's happening on the ground, to deduce that Africans (beyond Morocco and Tunisia) do not innovate, you find a very different story emerging. The lack of visibility of African innovators and their inventions does not mean they do not exist. But there were other problems I had with the general sentiment of the article. I argue that Africa faintly featuring on the global map of innovation has less to do with whether Africans are innovating and more to do with the faulty preconceptions about the people of the continent and, quite frankly, a poor understanding of what innovation and its purpose actually is. Have you actually ever tried finding a definition for innovation? You get very vague answers. Google's dictionary simply says it is "the action or process of innovating." It further qualifies this by saying it refers to "a new method, idea, product, etc." That doesn't really say much. So how do we measure something as vague as innovation? The reason why innovation is difficult to define is because it requires *context* — it requires an antithesis of sorts, or a problem, an opposite.

Finally, my disgruntlement was also a culmination of being irked by another narrative of African countries classified as "developing". This idea paints the picture of a continent that is slowly tracking its way from a "developing" to a "developed" status. Perhaps it strikes you as odd that

I would take issue with this, but follow my train of thought for a bit. The definition of a developed country (according to Wikipedia) is "a sovereign state that has a highly developed economy and advanced technological infrastructure relative to other less industrialised nations". The word "industrialised" jumps out quite vividly for me. For most people, I imagine it invokes imagery of factories, production and manufacturing on a large scale. Fair enough. This is important and I don't discount it. However, what is implied is that the future of African countries – the path we must travel – is defined by the past of other nations. It presupposes that in order to transform, Africa must copy and paste the trajectory that other continents undertook. This view of development insinuates that there is only one way to a bright future, one way to progress, and that to transition from "developing" to "developed", Africa must follow this path and emulate the industrialisation trends of other continents that have been fortunate enough to be classified as "emerged".

I beg to differ. Allow me to add a little more to the thought process here before I show why. Let's turn our attention to the Bloomberg Innovation Index, as I mentioned above, which takes a similar tack. Every year it attempts to measure the top 50 most innovative countries in the world. In 2016 it scored South Korea at the top, with the U.S. coming in at eighth. Only two African countries made the list, both in the bottom ten. In 2017, South Korea still came tops, with Sweden climbing to second and Finland making it into the top five. Russia went down fourteen spots to No. 26, while the U.S. jumped down one spot further to ninth place. China still held its title as the strongest ranked emerging market. According to Bloomberg in 2016, this makes South Korea 'the leader in the world of ideas'. I know they are amazing, but does this mean that they come up with all the good ideas? If that's the case, why have they not solved so many of the problems we face as the world? I answer: *because they aren't looking to solve our problems, but theirs.* Perhaps Magnus Henrekson, quoted in a Bloomberg article discussing the 2017 index, scratches on the surface when he says, "In the [Nordic] culture, people are super individualistic — this means that people have ideas and are very interested in pursuing them in this way in order to become wealthy. The incentives are there and the tax system favours them.[8]" In other words: their focus is for themselves, and I don't think that's a bad thing, it's just that we need to be aware of it.

Let me go further. What definition does Bloomberg use for innovation? How is it working this out? Firstly, it defines innovation as "the creation of products and services that make life better".[9] This is also very vague as it is, and it implies that the actual environment — in other words, what's happening on a grassroots level, is not taken much into account. So I went to look at the methodology. Bloomberg looks at how much money is invested in research and development, manufacturing and patent activity, and other metrics. These are all very difficult to measure across borders, because patent laws, for example, are different everywhere. The bottom line, however, is that when one looks at the details an interesting pattern emerges: *the ideology of industrialisation still drives the metrics by which success in development is measured.* I realise that we obviously aren't going to find a perfect system to measure everything, and I submit the Bloomberg Innovation Index is incredibly helpful (and challenging). But I still am led to ask an obvious question: is it *really* innovation if it's measured by the old story of *industrialisation* and if this is measured by those who have already gone through that story?

Perhaps it also strikes you as strange to hear me say that industrialisation is the old story. I realise I'm simplifying things a bit to try and make a point. I also realise I'm going against the grain in a big way. But after connecting with African innovators, entrepreneurs and paradigm-shifters from across the continent over the past four years, it's clear to me that Africans want a new story, not an old one. We're living in the 21st century, which calls for a new path to development. The old story is not going to cut it in this world's future, and Silicon Valley knows that, so why don't we?

---

8   *These are the World's Most Innovative Economies*, by Michelle Jamrisko and Wei Lu. Published at Bloomberg Markets, January 2017. Available at https://www.bloomberg.com/news/articles/2017-01-17/sweden-gains-south-korea-reigns-as-world-s-most-innovative-economies

9   See Three Views (and Methodologies) on Global Innovation, by Kevin Stahler and Jan Zilinsky. Published by Peterson Institute for International Economics and available at https://piie.com/blogs/north-korea-witness-transformation/three-views-and-methodologies-global-innovation. This article provides a great overview of the challenges faced by these sorts of innovation indexes, and the different methodologies involved.

I am not saying we ought to throw out everything and start again, rejecting the industrialisation narrative because we want to arrogantly claim some sort of self-identity independent of everyone else. In fact, I'm saying the exact opposite. We are where we are, but what are we going to do about it? We need to take what we learn from others and use wisdom to apply what we learn to our continent, rather than try and just copy in some form or another. We cannot, to quote Mufuruki again (but use his statements differently) accept the industrialisation narrative "without questioning it." It seems odd to me that the Africa Rising narrative is held up to such scrutiny while we give the industrialisation narrative a free pass. Perhaps you say it's because it's already shown to work. I say, sure, it's worked there, but it's not working *here*—because we have different challenges to face. Perhaps you say it's because we have had all these problems in the past: colonisation, oppression, Apartheid, etc. I'm saying that *yes we have*. And note, *they didn't*. They had other issues to face, and these were not the same as ours. And even so, many instances of their success was done on the back of Africa and our people, and we are not going to make our success on the back of some other nation or people. So, therefore, we cannot expect to just emulate and see things work. The industrial revolution and subsequent development didn't happen in a vacuum, it happened in an entire context and history and pre-industrialised period which set the groundwork and foundation for it to work from.

This is all why Africa needs to be defined by what is uniquely African. And I firmly believe we can see the Africa Rising narrative becoming a reality when we look at African innovation. Nobody understands African challenges the way Africans do—they experience them every day. They are best placed to find innovative solutions to their problems, and they do. Innovation is about changing people's lives in *their* world. It should not be limited by what people in a different context think is valuable.

HERE ARE A FEW EXAMPLES TO ILLUSTRATE

In 2016, Dr Valentin Agon from Benin finally completed formulating his Api-Palu solution, which presents a new, cheaper, and more effective way to test for malaria, using a simple plant extract. Dr Eddy Agbo, from Nigeria, is also an African innovator taking on the same challenge. He invented a new 25-minute test for malaria that costs approximately $2.

Until now, the only way to test for the disease has been through blood samples, the results of which can take days to receive. According to the World Health Organisation (WHO), there were 214 million cases of malaria in 2015 worldwide. It goes without saying then that these two innovations are revolutionary for the continent. These change lives. But if both these innovators allowed themselves to be defined by the so-called 'tried and tested' methods, which work in other contexts but aren't working in ours, how many lives would they save?

Malaria is one of Africa's biggest challenges. Two Africans have found innovative solutions. When we look at the innovations coming out of the 2016 Innovation Prize for Africa (IPA), we cannot help but be positive. But it is interesting, and disheartening, to note that these kinds of innovations do not fit the definition of what the Bloomberg Innovation Index and other references define as innovative.

Ntuthuko Shezi, a South African innovator, is another example of an African approach to finding solutions to African problems. His app, Livestock Wealth, is a uniquely African innovation in the investment space. The majority of South Africans may not understand what shares, unit trusts and bonds are, for various reasons. But they do understand cows, which in many African cultures are considered an investment. Shezi's starting point for his innovation was a simple question: what if there was a way to own a cow and have it taken care of without having to house it? The concept appeals to many African urbanites. And that's what Livestock Wealth does – through the app, users can put money into a traditional African "asset class" (in other words, cattle) as an investment. One buys a cow for about R10,500 (about $800) and pays Livestock Wealth R295 (about $23) a month to take care of it. Another R99 (about $8) buys insurance for the cow. The cow's offspring is sold to abattoirs and the owner gets a dividend from that sale. Once the cow turns eight years old, a replacement can be acquired at no extra cost. The owner can even visit the cow, or see it through a 'virtual kraal'.

I can understand why someone in the U.K. or North America or Japan may not relate to this sort of innovation, but that doesn't mean that it isn't innovative. It is solving a local problem for local people. Sure, innovations like Uber or Airbnb are changing entire industries, and they are disrupting Africa, too—we will devote considerable time to unpacking that in this book. However, much more is happening on the ground, where it matters, than too many people realise.

Ugandan-born Ashish J. Thakkar – CEO of the Mara Group, a highly successful global conglomerate, once heard a young African girl say, "Don't blend in – blend out." In other words, be a unique individual. This wisdom, I believe, is for the Africa continent as a whole. No longer do Africans want to blend in with the old story. On the contrary, we want to blend *out*, to forge a new way, and to innovate according to our realities. Thakkar is a fascinating case study in this direction. Like him, I ask in my own way: is there some sort of natural law that means development and progress can only follow one path? Of course not. Through collective creativity, Africans can find a unique path. The old ways of thinking are simply proving not to work for us, who have a different context and a different history to deal with. We must use them where appropriate, adjust as needed, but also pioneer something of our own. I've seen this happen. If we put our innovations together, something exciting emerges: a new eco-system that creates a very exciting future that can leapfrog tradition infrastructure.

To illustrate my point when I speak to people regarding this, I ask the question, "What would be considered more innovative for Africa: A high-speed train into rural locations in Africa or a solar grid that kicks in when the national grid is offline?" Almost everyone says the latter because that's the most innovative solution for Africans. Then I proceed to tell them that this already exists in Rwanda. Their eyes always light up!

Yes, Africa is rising, and on its own terms. Perhaps redefining development is just what it needs. African innovation is tangibly changing lives, even without garnering the visibility it deserves, because it does not seem to fit into the pre-determined, acceptable metrics for what development and innovation are. I have no doubt that consistency, creativity and support will get us there.

I also have no doubt that if we do not innovate, Silicon Valley will do it for us. And so, now we turn to seeing just how Silicon Valley is coming to us, and how we need to approach this technological invasion to make it fit in with Africa Rising.

"The entire world is now a rival to Silicon Valley. No country, state, region, nor city has a lock on innovation in technology anymore."

— **Fred Wilson**

——————————✕——————————

THE BIG BOYS ARE COMING TO TOWN

When Mark Zuckerberg from Facebook visited Nigeria and Kenya in 2016, it was a pretty big deal. "The future of the world," he said, would be built on the African continent. "There's this energy here, you feel it as soon as you get off the plane. The world needs to see that. Here is Lagos, and across the continent, things are really shifting. Things are moving from a resource-based economy and its shifting to entrepreneurial, knowledge-based economy. It's not only shaping the country but the whole continent."[10]

This last point of his is an important one — and it's one of the major reasons why we, as Africans, need to reconsider where we are putting our energy. It shows that Silicon Valley understands the old narrative is not going to make the future and that the world is on a new narrative now, so why shouldn't we as well? Africa Rising fits in under these comments much more clearly than the old industrialisation narrative, so we ought to sit up and take notice.

But Zuckerberg wasn't here just for good vibes and high fives, he was here to see how Facebook could further its commercial interests on our

---

10   Toby Shapshak, *Africa Will Build the Future* Says Zuckerberg, Visits Kenya on First African Trip. Published by Forbes, September 2016. Available at https://www.forbes.com/sites/tobyshapshak/2016/09/01/africa-will-build-the-future-says-zuckerberg-visits-kenya-on-first-african-trip/#43d07a1c70b2

continent. Therefore, we have to ask, what is his plan? And how to do we work with him to the benefit of Africa?

Without question, Silicon Valley's "big five" — Facebook, Google, Amazon, Apple, and Uber, have consistently and creatively expanded and innovated on their product offerings, creating new services and channels most of us didn't even know we needed. They have practically invented markets where there were none and disrupted industries of all kinds all over the world. And without question, these companies (bar Apple, perhaps) have their eyes on Africa.

What's unique about Facebook, Google, Amazon and Uber in particular, and other companies like them, is they generally have a good understanding of context. They look at local needs and find ways in which their offerings can cover these needs, as opposed to just importing a model from home base. So what happens when these "big boys"—Facebook, Google, Amazon and Uber — come to town? We have to be asking this.

Since the U.N. released its "World Population Prospects" report in 2015, there has been a lot of talk about the incredible projected population growth of Africa. More than half of the global population growth between now and 2050, says the report, is expected to occur in Africa.

"Africa has the highest rate of population growth among major areas, growing at a pace of 2.55 per cent annually in 2010-2015. Consequently, of the additional 2.4 billion people projected to be added to the global population between 2015 and 2050, 1.3 billion will be added in Africa."

Even if there is a reduction in fertility levels in the near future, rapid population growth in Africa is still expected and the numbers would still be more-or-less the same. According to all the research I've seen, by about 2030 and beyond, Africa will have the largest working population in the world. In fact, 40 percent of the working population globally will be based in or from Africa. As the International Money Fund (IMF) further qualifies in its report: "The rising share of sub-Saharan Africa's working-age population is increasing the continent's productive potential at a time when most advanced economies face ageing populations and a declining share of their working-age populations."

At the time of writing, this is only about 15 years away. Even if you look at the numbers more conservatively, we're still only about 20 or so years away from this. And the fact of the matter is that all this is a huge opportunity. As stated by Omar Mohammed in Quartz Africa, "The increase in population, which will also be accompanied by lower mortality rates, presents the continent with an enormous opportunity, similar to the one experienced by East Asia in the second half of the twentieth century." This large working population would make Africa an amazing asset to the globe.

But while this is an opportunity, it will become a serious problem if we don't plan ahead, and it will become a problem not just for us, but also for the world. If we do not create sufficient jobs for this growing working population, we will hit severe economic and social issues. According to the IMF's projections, we need to be creating an average of 18 million jobs a year until 2035. We need to maintain our current levels of services while "increasing the per capita investment in health, education, and infrastructure in order to reap the full benefit of its growing working-age population," the fund says. To take advantage of this opportunity and to counter-act the possible issues, we have to focus on the key industries that will prepare this gigantic workforce positively. If this workforce is not prepared, Africa will become a liability to the globe and certainly not an asset.

Obviously, many of the industries we need to focus on are outside my expertise and the scope of this book. But as I've stated, our challenge is that while we realise there is an aspect of industrialisation that needs to happen, we must realise there is a huge call for innovation. We cannot, as far as I'm concerned, rely solely on traditional infrastructure. We really cannot rely on that story. We have to look to our innovations and emerging technologies to get around or, even better, leapfrog traditional infrastructure and create something new. We have to think of new ecosystems and we have to put our innovations together and put our innovators themselves together, and then tie them into industry. I will showcase the huge importance of this in the next few chapters as we see how Silicon Valley has grasped this concept and has been creating new ecosystems for quite a while.

Technology is already our biggest driver on the continent. According to World Bank projections, out of the 20 fastest-growing economies in the world, eleven are in Africa. We are largely moving away from labour-intensive economies to telecommunications, banking and retail taking a central space. Many people agree that investment in Africa's technology is where it must happen. I agree, but I also say we need to tread carefully. As I will show, these 'traditional' spaces of telecommunications, retail and even banking are under fire from Silicon Valley. Think of how WhatsApp has challenged telecommunications. At the time of writing this book, it has already made its first foray into the digital payments space in India, as it continues to explore ways in which it can generate revenue. And when thinking of WhatsApp, it's always important to remember who owns it: Facebook.

Let's turn our eye to America itself, the birthplace of Silicon Valley, to see how Silicon Valley's disruption is working even there. Without a doubt, disruption into these traditional sorts of spaces has caused major problems with America's traditional workforce. You can read that all over the newspapers and articles of today. Immigration issues aside, many political commentators have noted that Donald Trump's rise to power was off the back of speaking to the American traditional workforce who feel they have been largely left behind in the "New Economy" or the "Green Jobs" driven by the likes of Silicon Valley. "America First" speaks to these groups of people and stirs up memories of the days when roads were being built and factories were producing. Whole cities like Detroit fell when the recession came around, which affected manufacturing and production significantly, in addition to most of the manufacturing being outsourced to China and other places. Trump's image harkens back to the good old days before computers, when oil would always be king and good business didn't involve microchips and data, but things you could hold in your hands. While it's true that so much of manufacturing is in the hands of China and Mexico, and U.S. based companies have been outsourcing their manufacturing to other countries for decades now (which is what Trump is claiming to fight against), it's also true that there is a big change in developed nations with what industries are key and what skills are needed. (I wonder sometimes if we in Africa are therefore investing in the wrong things — or at least, not investing enough in the right things.) These changes revolve around the likes of Silicon Valley.

In California-Berkeley economist, Enrico Moretti's book, "The New Geography of Jobs", he speaks of "two Americas". The first is healthy, is growing, and is rich; the other is being left behind as each year goes by. I wonder to myself what Africa is looking like when it comes to this. Someone ought to write the book. Race or religion is not the core polarising problem in the U.S., but rather which industry you support. Cities that are home to innovative industries are wealthier, safer, and healthier; while cities and towns centred around traditional industries are declining—and in some cases, very quickly.

While I don't want to take this book down the line of a political commentary, the fact is that the Silicon Valley disruptors which are causing this shift in America—a shift that is now beginning to be felt even in the political sphere, as the centres of economies change—have their eye on Africa. As I asked before, does it make sense then that we should try to 'industrialise' along the traditional developed nation lines when, while we're doing that, Silicon Valley is disrupting it all under our nose? Might we not be short-circuited before, in many cases, we even get going?

WHAT IF SILICON VALLEY WERE A COUNTRY?

The best way I can illustrate the massive disruption we can expect is by thinking of these "big boys" as a country. California, where Silicon Valley resides, has a bigger economy than most nations of the world — in fact, the World Bank in 2016 rated it as the sixth biggest economy on the globe.[11] That's one State in all of America. And within this State resides states of their own, if you will – countries, nations that cross borders, generate revenue in almost every border of the world, and connect people across geographic regions in new, unthinkable ways. These are the countries of Silicon Valley, and the big five of them are undoubtedly Facebook, Google, Apple, Uber and Amazon.

If you were to think of Facebook as a country, it would be the most

---

11   Associated Press, *California's economy is bigger than all but five nations, World Bank data says.* Available at http://www.mercurynews.com/2016/07/05/californias-economy-is-bigger-than-all-but-five-nations-world-bank-data-says/ (July 2016)

populous on earth, with 1.86 billion people logging onto the network each month.[12] We could think of that as 1.86 billion living, active users—effectively, Facebook's citizens. That's more than China's entire population (about 1.4 billion). It's more than India's (about 1.3 billion). Facebook's users are more than the U.S. population itself, which comes in at about 0.3 billion, where the company comes from. As we shall see in the next chapter, Facebook's biggest problem is there will eventually not be enough people in the world who will actually log on and use it. It's still banned in China, but who knows for how much longer? To get Africans on board, Facebook is, therefore, finding ways to help us get online. More on that in the next chapter. Its plan is clearly to get everyone on the planet logged on and connected—and at 1.39 billion users logging on every month (according to 2017 statistics), it doesn't seem as if it is just dreaming. If you consider Facebook's earnings of USD $8.81 billion (Q4 2016), and you compare this to country GDP's, you see it's richer than many of the countries of the world!

Google isn't far behind. If it were a country, it would probably be the third biggest in the world. In 2016, it reported that it has now more than one billion active users on Gmail.[13] YouTube, Maps, Google Play, and Chrome also have more than one billion active users. And this doesn't account for active users on the Google search engine or users of its other products. In the same year, it reported it had reached 3.3 trillion searches in a year.[14] There are more than 1.6 billion Android devices in the market (2017). Alphabet, the holding company of Google, reported USD $21.33 billion in revenue in 2016; 24.8 billion in the first quarter of 2017.[15] It outstrips even more nations than Facebook if you had to compare GDP with Google's revenue. In fact, only just over 60 countries in the world beat it—while the rest trail behind. In 2015, Investopedia started putting it into perspective:

---

12   Timothy Stenovec, *Facebook Is Now Bigger Than The Largest Country On Earth*. Published by Huffington Post, January 2015. Available at http://www.huffingtonpost.co.za/entry/facebook-biggest-country_n_6565428

13   Frederic Lardinois, *Gmail Now Has More Than 1B Monthly Active Users*. Published at Tech Crunch, February 2016. Available at https://techcrunch.com/2016/02/01/gmail-now-has-more-than-1b-monthly-active-users/

14   See Google Annual Search Statistics – http://www.statisticbrain.com/google-searches/

15   See http://listings.findthecompany.com/l/8520977/Google-Inc-in-Mountain-View-CA

"What is more shocking is the number of countries at the bottom of the list that do not even put a dent in Google's total income for 2014. In fact, Google's revenue for the year outstripped the poorest 33 countries combined. With only 184 countries reporting GDP figures for 2014, this means Google's wealth exceeds roughly 18% of the global GDP. This can partly be attributed to the fact that many countries report GDP figures well below $1 billion. The tiny nation of Tuvalu reported a GDP of only $40 million for 2014. It takes a lot of Tuvalus to add up to Google's $66 billion.[16]"

Where does WhatsApp sit in all this? The messaging app boasted of 1.2 billion active users a month in January 2017. If you consider that WhatsApp is owned by Facebook, you can begin to see just how much Facebook would dominate if it were a country. And then, let's not forget Instagram with 600 million users at the end of 2016—which is also owned by Facebook.

These are nations within all of our nations. Realising this stark fact puts things in an interesting perspective. It's a good thought exercise to think beyond the statistics and consider the philosophy behind this, consider what it means to have nations of this size within your own nation, linked to your next door neighbours and across the world. When you think of these innovations as countries you can see the type of service they provide, and the way they provide their service is totally different to how we normally do things in an African context. The regulatory framework is different. The approach to technology is different. The way they view themselves, and their citizens, is different. What this means is if we were to try compete with the likes of Uber, for example, we can't compete in the way we usually do with other countries: with borders and regulation and security and so on. We have to start to think of things like VISA-less borders and we have to come to grips with what our response to that sort of thing is — what our regulatory framework will actually be. This regulatory framework has

---

16   Investopedia, *Google's Revenue Beats The GDP Of Several Major Countries*. Published June, 2015. Available at http://www.investopedia.com/articles/investing/061115/googles-revenue-beats-gdp-several-major-countries.asp. Of course, companies like Walmart and others still outstrip Google in terms of multinationals.

to be totally new; it can't just incorporate a 'business-as-usual' approach.

As we will uncover in the next few chapters, the sheer connected nature of these Silicon Valley companies — the way in which they truly want to connect us — speaks volumes into this and is truly globalism gone next level. And if we are looking at the economies of these companies and thinking of ourselves as African nations in comparison to them, we must realise that we cannot see technology innovations as 'startups'. We have to think of them as much more than that. We have to think of our own innovations, and innovators, in bigger, more forward-thinking ways. And, as I've argued elsewhere and will argue in more detail in this book, our innovators need to think Pan-African from the start. We only tend to think of our innovations as 'tech', yet they are considerably more than just that. We have to actually consider them as countries all of their own. We have to think in similar ways to how Silicon Valley is thinking. We have to start to incorporate a totally different view of things.

Acha Leke, director at McKinsey and Company and a member of the World Economic Forum (WEF) Global Agenda on Africa, represents, in my opinion, one way in which we need to be thinking about this. He puts some language on the thought, so to speak. He is actively campaigning for visa-less borders in Africa, for the African Union passport (which has just launched for diplomats at the time of writing) and believes this will accelerate socio-economic growth; boosting tourism revenue and increasing intra-African trade. As he said at Oxford in 2015, "We are the second fastest growing continent in the world, and Africa offers the second highest return on investment of any region in the world.[17]" What this means is that if we can make our borders more open, we can make it so much easier for businesses to expand across Africa and get even more investment with effectively less hassle, and that to benefit us all. We will create a more integrated market, make it more efficient for business, open up opportunities, which all will promote greater stability and investment. For me, this kind of forward movement is incredibly helpful for our innovators. They will receive better funding and be able to expand more effectively, helping to contribute to creating a new ecosystem for Africa.

---

17   Acha Leke at the 2016 Oxford Business Forum Africa. See the video at https://www.youtube.com/watch?v=nIX4ii7dWek

Silicon Valley does not think within borders. It's the kind of *connected* thinking that Silicon Valley innovators are employing that creates a better *working together* and the kind of prosperity these Silicon Valley companies enjoy. As will now see, the aim of the Silicon Valley "big boys" is to create a new ecosystem for the world. We need to be creating a new ecosystem for us as Africans through our own innovations, and working with these Silicon Valley innovations, our way. If we don't, these Silicon Valley "big boys" will cannibalise not only our potential markets but our existing ways as well. Along with the tremendous positive they can bring to help connect us, they can also bring significant negative in the forms of where the revenue generated will all be going, and several other problems. In the next few chapters I'll go through each of the "big boys"—Facebook, Google, Amazon, and Uber — and discuss what they are up to and both the positives and negatives of their disruption in Africa, in hopes that we as Africans will begin to take up the challenge put before us.

"When I wrote 'The World Is Flat,' I said the world is flat. Yeah, we're all connected. Facebook didn't exist; Twitter was a sound; the cloud was in the sky; 4G was a parking place; LinkedIn was a prison; applications were what you sent to college; and Skype, for most people, was a typo."

— **Thomas Friedman**

CHAPTER FIVE

———————×———————

FACEBOOK'S EYES ON AFRICA

" **T**o friend" has now become a verb. It's what you do on Facebook. The social media giant has single-handedly changed the way we speak, interact with each other, and process information. It's also responsible for creating a whole new sector. Think about what a 'community manager' was about fifteen years ago. Think of how it has transformed marketing. Think of how we often speak of doing something "offline" as opposed to "online". Think of what Facebook means for politics, the news, and how we process the world. Facebook has literally changed everything. As its CEO and founder, Mark Zuckerberg states, "Facebook was not originally created to be a company. It was built to accomplish a social mission—to make the world more open and connected."

It has certainly done this. Not only is there more freedom of information through Facebook from a knowledge point of view, but revolutions have begun through it, or at least been spurned on. For example, the Euromaidan protests in Ukraine in 2013—2014 owed a lot to Facebook where they could get unbiased news. In fact, up to 49 percent of those who protested learned about the protest first through Facebook.[18]

According to some studies, time on Facebook even improves your heart rate, can help you get a job, help you get a degree, and has helped to

---

18   Olga Onuch, *Social networks and social media in Ukrainian "Euromaidan" protests.* Published at the Washington Post, January 2014. Available at https://www.washingtonpost. com/news/monkey-cage/wp/2014/01/02/social-networks-and-social-media-in-ukrainian-euromaidan-protests-2/

raise stock prices for businesses with solid Facebook campaigns. Another study has even shown that a ten-minute break on Facebook makes employees happier and more productive.[19] It keeps us connected and allows for families to keep in touch across the world — something that was previously only realistic through the phone or the postal service. Now literally, grandparents can see how the grandkids are growing up almost every day. Kristy Campbell, Juniper Networks communications director, puts it like this: "I lived in California and my grandmother lived in upper Michigan, and I had felt really badly about losing touch until she got a laptop and signed up for Facebook. Our world opened up to her. She attended my daughter's graduation and prom via Facebook, and when she suddenly passed away, I was left with a digital record of our interactions that I will never take down. I really don't remember life before Facebook."[20]

On a continent like Africa, this ability to easily connect has many, many advantages — most notably with the diaspora. But the challenge, of course, is our Internet connectivity, a challenge Facebook itself wants to address. In 2015, while no one was looking, Facebook quietly partnered with Eutelsat, a communications satellite operator (which is also partnered with DStv) to, as a press release put it, "get more Africans online". It is part of Zuckerberg's vision, as stated in an October 2015 Facebook post, to "connect the entire world" because "connectivity changes lives and communities." Or as a press release stated, it will "accelerate data connectivity for the many users deprived of the economic and social benefits of the Internet." It all kind of slipped under the radar and everyone just went back to business as usual.

While it was all happening under the radar, and I think this is because Facebook doesn't want to give too much of its game plan away, I saw it though, and I've been watching it with guarded fascination. I did have the CEO of Eutelsat on my radio show at the time of the announcement, and I must admit was thoroughly fascinated by the partnership. Facebook has looked at Africa's Internet connectivity problems and is hinting at leveraging Eutelsat's

19   Chad Brooks, *7 Unexpected Ways Facebook Is Good for You*. Published at Business News Daily, May 2012. Available at http://www.businessnewsdaily.com/2534-facebook-benefits. html

20   Brett Molina, *How Facebook Changed Our Lives*. Published at USA Today, February 2014. Available at https://www.usatoday.com/story/tech/2014/02/02/facebook-turns-10-cultural-impact/5063979/

framework to do something about it. But Facebook is a for-profit company, and you can bet this isn't a purely altruistic venture, as much as I will openly admit it has tremendous benefits for us. Zuckerberg has something up his sleeve and it can potentially change everything about Africa's telecommunications industry—for the bad if we're not ready; for the good if we are.

Facebook's Free Basics app (See internet.org) gives you a clue in what this behemoth of a technology disruptor is thinking. Free Basics allows users to explore useful online services and websites—such as the news, health information, education, local information, weather etc.—at no (or very little) cost. With the Eutelsat deal, the idea is that consumers in Africa will get free access to the Internet through Facebook's platform. And it sounds like a great idea, right? But obviously, it can be used for a kind of censorship. Facebook can limit your access to certain sites, or make you pay for other sites that don't fit into its service. For example, you can get WhatsApp (owned by Facebook) for free, but you might need to pay to use any Google services through their platform. You could perhaps be able to browse the news sites they've partnered with, but other news sites might be more difficult to find and could require additional payment. This is all quite relevant today when you consider how much Facebook has come under fire for spreading or allowing the spread of, fake news. While Facebook has been adamant that it sees the danger of fake news and wants to do everything it can to tackle the problem, it's clear that it has become a go-to source for news by masses of people. Meaning, that if it can control the news, there can be a potential issue with the freedom of information.

Gbenga Sesan heads up Paradigm Initiative Nigeria, an organisation that helps young people in poverty still get online. As far as he is concerned, Facebook's service is problematic. "Even if people are hungry, we shouldn't be giving them half a loaf," he told the Guardian.[21] He was referring to the fact that Internet.org does not provide full Internet access, but yet gives the impression to users that it does. Think about that for a moment—users are willing to see Facebook's Internet as full Internet,

---

21   Maeve Shearlaw, *Facebook Lures Africa with Free Internet—But What is the Hidden Cost?* Published at The Guardian, August 2016. Available at https://www.theguardian.com/world/2016/aug/01/facebook-free-basics-internet-africa-mark-zuckerberg

meaning that many users would quite blindly accept that whatever information they find through the service is all there actually is. That's why in India, Free Basics was actually banned because of support for net neutrality, the principle that Internet service providers and governments regulating the Internet should treat all data on the Internet the same, not discriminate or charge differentially by user, content, website, platform, application, type of attached equipment, or mode of communication.[22]

Of course, if Facebook had to put control measures like this in place with its Free Basics service (or something like it)—measures to drive profitability—we can't claim it's unfair, given that Facebook is a for-profit company. But what happens if they manage a monopoly on Internet coverage on the continent? That is something we have to prepare for ahead of time. We can't have a 'wait and see' approach here. Facebook itself has shown us that everyone having a 'wait and see' approach is precisely what has helped the company to propel itself in the way it has. We simply cannot wait until that sort of thing happens. Gustav Praekelt, who has helped Facebook provide educational and health information through Free Basics via his foundation, is on the money when he says that everyone else is moving too slowly, that in a perfect world access to information would be a human right, but "there's a vacuum and Facebook are plugging it".[23] Exactly. And there is a second side to this as well, and this requires for us to take a macro view of things. Facebook could potentially cannibalise our existing telecommunications industries. And it's this I don't think we're prepared for at all.

Let me talk you through it, otherwise you can miss it. Facebook owns WhatsApp. Did you notice when WhatsApp very subtly added video calling to its service? I bet that you, like me, didn't know it was working on that. When it was released there was no hype—press releases, press conferences, talks about the future and how WhatsApp is going to change everything, and so on. What we saw was a lot of publications talking about it the next morning when journalists woke up to find a

---

22   Wikipedia's definition—see https://en.wikipedia.org/wiki/Net_neutrality

23   Maeve Shearlaw, *Facebook Lures Africa with Free Internet—But What is the Hidden Cost?* Published at The Guardian, August 2016. Available at https://www.theguardian.com/world/2016/aug/01/facebook-free-basics-internet-africa-mark-zuckerberg

strange new button on their WhatsApp. It already had voice-to-voice for a while, another feature it added with a bit more build up but nothing we generally see from a big Silicon Valley leader. By now, it's become patently evident in Africa that voice revenues are declining while data usage is going up. In February 2017, it was reported that voice had "slipped to below 50 percent of the core service revenue for the first time ever" in Vodacom's previous quarter.[24] And while this stat is applicable to South Africa, and voice is still king in other African nations that Vodacom operates in, there is very little reason to think the trend won't match what we see happening worldwide. Now think about this: what if Facebook offered you free Internet access, and you know that with it comes WhatsApp, allowing you to make not only free voice-to-voice calls but also free video calls? What service are you going to use the most? Which service will begin to look a bit archaic in your mind? I'll give you a clue. In the middle of 2016, WhatsApp boasted of 100 million voice calls made *daily* on its service.[25] (It also reported 42 billion messages sent daily.)[26] Remember, it has more than 1.2 billion users as of 2017!

Our telecommunications industry would be disrupted in an instant and would collapse very quickly. From a consumer point of view, all of this makes perfect sense. Of course, we'll all go to where it's cheaper and more convenient, and Silicon Valley knows that. We can talk about supporting local companies as much as we want, but we'll still gravitate towards where we can get the same service (or a service we never had before) for basically nothing. But from a macro point of view, we have to ask different questions, and we have to ask them now before it's too late. There is a lot of investment into data because we all know that's where things are headed. But now imagine if this sort of revenue is no longer moving in the economy because a Silicon Valley disruptor now owns both voice

24   Hilton Tarrant, *Data to Finally Overtake Voice on Vodacom.* Published by Moneyweb, February 2017. Available at https://www.moneyweb.co.za/news/companies-and-deals/data-to-finally-overtake-voice-on-vodacom/

25   Statista – *Number of monthly active WhatsApp users worldwide from April 2013 to January 2017* (in millions. See https://www.statista.com/statistics/260819/number-of-monthly-active-WhatsApp-users/

26   DMR, *65 Amazing WhatsApp Statistics* (June 2017), available at http://expandedramblings.com/index.php/WhatsApp-statistics/

and data revenue. Revenue that is actually rightfully ours. Obviously, this would be a massive blow. Our telecommunications companies would not be able to sustain their workforce, resulting in massive job losses and skill sets that become redundant. Then also there is the supply chain that services these industries. Engineers, salespeople, call centre agents… the line is a long one. And this is just the tip of the iceberg. Think about how much investment we would have put into traditional infrastructure that could potentially become redundant, even perhaps overnight. Sure, new industries will arise, as they should, and new skills will be needed—but the question is are our telecommunications providers ready enough to handle this kind of change? Are we as a continent ready for it? Have we prepared enough? Have we put any thought into it at all? Because this change can come quickly—history is showing us that it does—and for us, it could come *too* quickly.

Maybe this sounds a bit far-fetched for you, but you can't negate the cultural change and perception change in Africa around the Internet and even Facebook's involvement. For example, Facebook is incredibly popular in Nigeria. In 2015, Geopoll did a survey in Nigeria which stated that up to 65 percent of those who participated in it agreed with this statement: "Facebook is the Internet".[27] In further research, it appears many people are confused about the fact that Facebook is actually part of what we call "the Internet". The three most popular Internet-based services or apps in Nigeria are Facebook, Instagram and WhatsApp. Guess who owns all three of these? Facebook.

Furthermore, it seems that Facebook wants to move into the remittance and financial space, whether it be via WhatsApp or the Facebook platform itself. In 2016, it proposed the ability for users to transfer money to each other using the same channels already set up to purchase online games on the platform. The proposal is only for the European Union for now, but it's obvious that Facebook would have a bigger plan. Given Facebook's success on the continent, and how few people have bank accounts, and the success of mobile money on the continent already, can

---

27   Leo Mirani, *Millions of Facebook users have no idea they're using the internet*. Published by Quartz, February 2015. Available at http://qz.com/333313/milliions-of-facebook-users-have-no-idea-theyre-using-the-internet/

you imagine what would happen if Facebook moves into this space?[28]

What is also important to consider is where the revenue goes if Facebook goes ahead with everything I have just been describing. I can guarantee you it's not going to stay in Africa. So from a macro level, we need to put ourselves in a position where we embrace the change and innovation that Facebook is initiating, because change will happen, but we insist that it must comply to certain kinds of regulation or implementation—for example, revenues must stay here, or they must create a certain amount of employment, and they must be part of fostering a new eco-system with its infrastructure, and not just provide a viable consumer-oriented product and take all the revenue home. Instead of fighting this change, telecommunications providers might want to embrace it and use it as a catalyst to put the right frameworks in place. In fact, that does seem to be what some of them are doing — MTN, Cell C, Airtel, Tigo and others have already partnered with Facebook's Free Basics service in various parts of Africa[29] — but I'm not sure that this is being done for the same reasons I am outlining. I say this simply because, in all of the press releases and information, the way it is being advertised indicates such to me. I wonder if they're seeing where this can go. I understand that as they focus on their bread and butter, it's difficult to see the disruptor's coming through. But the fact remains that they have to see it as they are poised to be the one collective force that can instigate the right kind of change, how much change should come, and make sure it benefits our economies. They've got to work with regulators, government, and the likes to make sure this will be a positive change.

Large corporates need to find ways to embrace change and channel it in a beneficial way for our continent and to ensure it's sustainable for everyone involved. The change is coming, it's inevitable, and when it comes, are we ready? We better be, because otherwise, I think we're going to find ourselves in a fair spot of trouble.

---

28   *Western Union and Moneygram Are No Friends of Africa*, published by Critique Echo Newspaper, May 2016. Available at http://www.critiqueecho.com/western-union-and-moneygram-are-no-friends-of-africa/

29   See the full list at https://info.internet.org/en/story/where-weve-launched/

"If it isn't on Google, it doesn't exist."

— **Jimmy Wales**

—————————×—————————

CHAPTER SIX

GOOGLE'S CONNECTED WORLD

Google always seems to surprise, disrupting industries most of us never thought it even had its eyes on and creating new industries we didn't think were possible. The scale of its innovations, and what it is working on right now, truly boggles the mind. It seems crazy that one technology company could be involved in so much.

Google's founders, Sergey Brin and Larry Page, studied at Stanford. The first version of their Google search engine, dubbed "BackRub", was on the Stanford servers, and it became so popular that it caused Stanford's computing infrastructure to experience problems, requiring additional servers. From August 1996, this version of Google was made available to the Internet, while still on the University website. By mid-1998, they realised they were onto something: "Pretty soon," says Page, "we had 10,000 searches a day. And we figured, maybe this is really real."[30] As is typical of Silicon Valley stories, Google was to be another company initially operating out of a garage. David Vise and Mark Malseed, writing *The Google Story* in 2005, noted that "not since Gutenberg... has any new invention empowered individuals, and transformed access to information, as profoundly as Google."

---

30   See http://www.notablebiographies.com/news/Ow-Sh/Page-Larry-and-Brin-Sergey. html

In August 2015, Google formed "Alphabet", a holding company for its incredibly successful Internet business and its other ventures which are not going to turn much of a profit anytime soon — such as trying to create immortality (yes, that's right, Google wants to help us reach immortality). This was done to make the operational side of the business much cleaner, and increase accountability. I'm sure it'll certainly help its internal processes as well! Besides its super-sci-fi ventures, the company will also include other ventures like Nest, it's connected home solution.

Nest is a bit different to the other 'connected home' or 'smart home' solutions out there — the idea that your fridge should be able to order your milk when it detects stocks are low. What separates it, I think, from those solutions is it wants to help *connect* smart devices, not make you buy into one system. Nest itself supplies Wi-Fi enabled thermostats, smoke detectors, or security cameras. The thermostats are also 'self-learning'—they learn what you like, when people are home, when the family is sleeping, and over time it regulates the temperature based on what it has learned. Using your phone's location, it knows when you're at home and when you're not. It then conserves energy, turning down your geyser or turning down the lights. And, the Nest Cam means you can check out your home via your phone while you're out and switch the lights off and on. It also now works with Google Home, a smart speaker that you can instruct to do certain things (tell you the weather, play music, and the like). Google Home is much the same as what other innovators are doing, such as Amazon's Echo. However, Nest will eventually fit into Google's Android @home project, which does order milk for you when your fridge runs out. Light bulbs, coffee pots, and other household items are all being developed in ways to help connect them together. I imagine the idea is to monitor your lifestyle, get the kettle going during what is tea time for your family, make sure the coffee is hot when you wake up, and all the sort of thing we all joked about when we were kids.

Much of this seems far away for most Africans, where we are still figuring out how to supply energy to the masses. But I want to emphasise how Google connects the dots — it connects its products together, it connects its products to others, and it creates *ecosystems*. The idea of the smart house is a perfect example of how we need to think of creating eco-systems with our innovations. A case in point for our energy problems, actually, is Google's buying into renewable energy, particularly the startup Makani Power. Makani is developing high-altitude wind turbines that can generate power. Moreso, Google's own ideas for providing the whole world with Internet seem far-fetched and yet are actually showing to work. As part of this, it is developing balloons that can be stationed high above rural areas and provide wireless signal. We think this sounds crazy, but that's what they thought when it was suggested that we should lay telephone wire across all of our oceans. Furthermore, like Facebook, Google is also investing in Space X low-orbit satellites and drones, to all bring connectivity to the world.

Google's wearable computing is another example of Google's philosophy to connect things, and how we need to be thinking the same way. It, along with many others, has been developing smartwatches to help you keep track of your health and activity. It's been developing Google Glass, a wearable screen that provides notifications and the like without you having to pull your phone out. More than that, it is diving into the realm of 'augmented reality'. Already you can walk around certain cities and pull up your phone, and wherever your camera is pointing, it provides you details of what it is you're seeing. For example, reviews of the restaurant you're facing, details of their food, etc. All of this is about finding ways to provide you with the information Google has been collecting for decades. Google even has a stake in Adimab, a company that creates small sensors that are ingested to collect information about the body and help doctors develop antibodies to disease. Project Jacquard is also another interesting one. It is essentially Google developing smart clothes, by inserting "gesture-sensing fabric" into your clothes. In other words, when you swipe left or right, it swipes on your phone or another device, and recognises you doing things to access certain kinds of technology.

For some of us in Africa, this sounds like something we shouldn't expect to see in a long while. But, as of 2017, you can buy it, for about $350. In collaboration with Levi's, you can purchase the 'Commuter Trucker Jacket' which has gesture-sensing fabric in its left sleeve. Touching the sleeve in the same way you would your phone carries out instructions on your phone — changing to the next song, and so on. In other words, if you're cycling, you can carry on listening to music without having to stop and take your phone out or even push buttons on your smart watch — and without the frustrations that would come with voice activation as a loud and enormous truck passes by. The original prototype also allowed for you to place pins on your map on your phone as you went along. Developers can already develop for it; gesture-sensing fabric is being made available to all clothes manufacturers; and you can machine wash it, too.

For several years now, Google has been working hard at its driverless car program, which it has now dubbed "Waymo". This involves more than just developing the technology, but also working with lawmakers to allow testing to happen on public roads, and (no doubt) in the future, working with legislation in terms of how it will all be managed. Can you imagine if driverless cars became the future, but the kind of lawsuits Google would face if something went wrong? This may be why it has partnered with Lyft, another innovator in the transportation space. According to investment firm Morgan Stanley, Alphabet's driverless business could be sitting on a USD $70 billion goldmine.[31]It's no wonder Google isn't the only company working on 'autonomous cars'—Uber, BMW, Ford and Volvo in the UK are all reportedly testing their own models. But Google has certainly been the front-runner. And it's getting better it at. It is expecting to release self-driving cars to the public sometime from 2017 to 2020. This will come to be a new and very efficient mode of public transport, one that, as CEO of Waymo John Krafcik says, "Will be to let people use our vehicles to do everyday things like run errands, commute to work, or get safely home after a night on the town.[32]"

LET'S GET A BIT MORE DOWN TO EARTH, SHALL WE?

I want you to notice how all of this can *connect*. If you've got smart cars, smart homes, smart phones, and smart clothing, all connected to each other everywhere thanks to the internet being available even from

---

31   Alan Ohnsman, *Morgan Stanley Sees A $70 Billion Self-Driving Startup In Alphabet's Waymo*. Published at Forbes, May 2017. Available at https://www.forbes.com/sites/alanohnsman/2017/05/23/morgan-stanley-sees-a-70-billion-self-driving-startup-in-alphabets-waymo/#678264b755b8

32   See Wikipedia at https://en.wikipedia.org/wiki/Waymo#Commercialization

the sky, you can pretty much see how it all creates a new ecosystem—how the world will be a truly connected one; and how the Internet may even disappear as something we 'do' or 'use' to something that is practically invisible; just a part of everyday reality. Gone are the days when you used to 'connect' to the Internet. Even more so, with all the information Google collects in this process, it can begin to sell you things. And there is the point of how it could potentially cannibalise almost everything.

On the 26th of May, 2011, Google launched Google Wallet. Google Wallet allows you to send and receive money via the app or email or someone's phone number. It's another version of the digital payments space, where you can effectively have money stored up in a digital space without the need for a bank account. This sort of idea, as I note throughout this book, is really taking off in Africa. But think about what it means for Google to enter this industry — think about what Google could do in the financial services industry. What it can do goes way beyond what M-PESA in Kenya or other mobile money products can do. What it can do goes way beyond what our current banks can even do.

Google already owns the kind of information on individuals that banks dream of – a search history, an understanding of our interests, where we do our shopping, how we spend our money, what it seems we're planning on purchasing next, our Christmas lists, where we might want to go on holiday, if we're having a baby soon, and even who our friends might be. Discovering what Google knows about you — or is at least happy to tell you it knows about you — is a very interesting experience.[33]Don't forget, with all the above-mentioned projects, Google is making a foray into the health industry through its Wear products and into the home industry with its own development of the 'connected home' concept. Soon they will be collecting more data than just your search history, but they will come to know if you're sick or not sleeping well, or how much time you spend at home. And they already know where you frequent through your maps history.

---

33   See this article at Business Insider: http://www.businessinsider.com/everything-google-knows-about-you-2016-5/#its-not-easy-to-find-your-web-and-app-activity-page-you-must-be-logged-in-to-google-to-see-it-once-logged-in-go-to-httpshistorygooglecomhistory-and-click-on-all-time-1 that provides you details of how to access and see what Google is looking at.

Further to this, Google also probably already knows which businesses are the most popular in Africa (or, at least in those countries with high Internet penetration), which shopping malls are frequented the most, where people of a certain demographic gravitate towards, how masses spend their money. Plus, it probably already knows what banks are the best in Africa, which ones are used the most by customers, and so on — it could easily guess which bank yours is, and so it could for masses of others. With all this data in the hands of Google, what stops them from competing in the financial services and insurance space? They already own information about you that your bank wishes it could own! And Google acquired that all by just providing you other services that you already enjoy using! Plus, Google is investing heavily in healthcare. A third of its investments from its venture capital fund, GV (previously Google Ventures) was in the healthcare space in 2015.[34] You bet that health insurance is somewhere in the mix, especially when you think of America's own troubles with universal health care!

Even if Google decided it didn't want to compete without an existing client-base in financial services, what stops them from buying the best bank in Africa, or even an Insurance company? It wouldn't be a cheap acquisition, but for Google, it wouldn't be a problem either. If they wanted to enter the financial or insurance space through an organisation with existing infrastructure and a client base, a bank acquisition could be a good idea. Google's ability to make the user never think about the payment, similar to Uber, Amazon and iTunes – a secret of successful Internet outfits – is imperative. For banks to evolve they almost need to disappear. Who really wants to go into a branch these days? So put this all together and imagine a scenario with me.

You're checking out the Internet for a pram and other goodies for the new baby. Google notices you're doing that a lot lately, so it obviously guesses you (or someone in your family) is going to have a baby soon. You're wondering to yourself about health insurance. Then when you go to your email, you find Google offers you a new deal on family health

---

34   *Google Bets on Health: 'The Most You can Lose Is All Your Money.'* Published at Bloomberg. Available at https://www.bloomberg.com/news/articles/2016-02-12/google-ventures-seeks-to-make-name-as-farsighted-health-investor

insurance. Moreso, it offers you financing for a new home (which you're going to need since your flat is no longer big enough) using its already very effective, innovative experience-centric models and its ability to target advertising so effectively.

None of this is an impossibility. If Google can create gesture-sensing fabric, it definitely could do this. And it would literally change the way our financial industry looks overnight. Think about it: if Google offered you a credit card right now, why wouldn't you sign up? What if Google just used your Internet search and all it knows about you to measure up who you are, your financial capacity and socio-economic status, and then offered you 'tailor-made' (well, automatically generated) loans based on what it knows? Or insurance? And you could sign up by just a few taps on your phone?

In 2015, Accenture discovered that 67 percent of consumers would be interested in receiving insurance offers via their mobile device. Plus, they prefer a digital interaction in practically every situation. Then, about 80 percent of the consumers it surveyed would happily switch to a service that is more personalised.[35] The fact is that with everything going digital, organisations in fields such as banking or logistics or insurance are more and more realising that they have to basically become software companies, offering new apps and solutions for clients in addition to products — apps and software that basically accentuates or serves that product along with the customer — and also finding ways to collect information of its users so that it can use this information to create better products. Google, however, is way ahead of the curve on all these fronts and could very easily slip into pretty much any space it wants to.

The big question is when Google decides to just add a little bit more to its existing Google Wallet service — something I bet they're going to do sooner rather than later — are we ready for what it might mean? Is our financial services industry thinking like Google and working on products that make payments seamless, that speak to us where we're at, and don't feel intrusive? Have you ever noticed Google never cold-calls you or makes you feel as if they're trying to sell you something?

---

35   See *Accenture Digital's Digital Transformation Survey*, available at https://www.accenture.com/us-en/insight-cmo-digital-transformation-summary

Google's entire ecosystem of the future is something we in Africa ought to be thinking carefully about. It sounds great in principle, but again — as with Facebook — where will all the revenue go? I love technology and I support it, and I don't think we need to be telling Google not to get involved here. I just believe we need to be controlling the narrative, otherwise, we could be in deep trouble. Furthermore, I believe we need to be thinking like Google — we need to be discussing how we can use our innovations to create a new kind of ecosystem.

Up to now, I've covered how the Silicon Valley giants Facebook and Google can have an impact on who we are. Next up, we need to look at Amazon and Uber—two Silicon Valley giants who will impact industries I don't think we're considering. We tend to think Uber only impacts the taxi industry, but there's more to it than that. We tend to think Amazon only impacts retail, but as we'll see next, it can already impact other industries I bet you haven't thought they ever would. Or could.

"I think frugality drives innovation, just like other constraints do. One of the only ways to get out of a tight box is to invent your way out."

— **Jeff Bezos**

CHAPTER SEVEN

————————×————————

AMAZON OWNING EVERYTHING

A mazon's disruption in the retail and logistics space is unprecedented and in need of no introduction. When Jeff Bezos, its founder, started it about thirty years ago in (you guessed it) a garage, it was a typical case of being in the right place at the right time, and having open eyes to see what was transpiring at the time.

Bezos was working on Wall Street and noticed how well the Internet was growing. "The wake-up call was finding this startling statistic that web usage in the spring of 1994 was growing at 2,300 percent a year," he says. "You know, things just don't grow that fast. It's highly unusual, and that started me thinking, "What kind of business plan might make sense in the context of that growth?[36]"

He began to think of the top twenty products he could potentially sell on the Internet, and books seemed to make the most business sense, as they were low cost and had universal demand. Within thirty days of launching, he was bringing in $20,000 a week in sales. By 1997, the company went public at $18 a share. In 1998, it acquired three companies — and by 2017 had acquired about 63 in total. In this time it has disrupted many industries and created new markets. But, at the time of writing this book, it is set on disrupting two industries that seem to have surprised everyone and will have an effect on Africa.

---

36   See *Fundable's Amazon Startup Story*, available at https://www.fundable.com/learn/startup-stories/amazon

The first is the pharmaceutical industry. I have the great privilege of being invited to conferences and think-tanks all over the world, and towards the latter end of 2016, I started noticing Amazon making certain moves that made me reiterate that it will be moving into this space. I was met with some scepticism. After returning from the Forum on Public-Private Partnerships for Global Health and Safety in Washington D.C. in May 2017 where I raised the point again, I opened up my news sources the day after landing back in South Africa to find CNBC just confirmed what I suspected all along. It had made note of a seemingly uninterested point by Amazon that Amazon will be hiring a general manager to pave its path for entering into the pharmaceutical space.[37] The report revealed that, apparently, entering into this space had been in Amazon's discussions for a number of years. I felt vindicated.

It makes perfect sense. To be honest, we really shouldn't be surprised when companies like Amazon are making a move into unexpected spaces. Silicon Valley wants to own everything, and Amazon certainly has a track record of being relentless at that sort of thinking. One of the reasons why Silicon Valley has gone this way, in my opinion, is it has assimilated a vision of *connecting* everything—the previous chapter being a case in point. Since its early days as just a bunch of professors and students at Stanford with a vision, this was the original thinking – they found ways to connect their innovations to existing industries. They're doing the same. That's what made the original "outfit in a garage", HP, so successful. And today they continue to do the same.

Here's why Amazon moving into this space makes a lot of sense. It has been relentless in trying to solve the 'last mile of logistics' problem. With drone technology, it can literally deliver to pretty much anywhere in the world. Why wouldn't it look to deliver pharmaceuticals as well? It has already been in this market in some ways, selling equipment and medical supplies, and interestingly offering cloud services to the biotech and pharma industry.[38]

---

37   Christina Farr, *Amazon is hiring people to break into the multibillion-dollar pharmacy market*. Published at CNBC, May 2017. Available at http://www.cnbc.com/2017/05/16/amazon-selling-drugs-pharamaceuticals.html

38   See https://aws.amazon.com/health/biotech-pharma/

An example of Amazon's vision comes from rural Africa, actually. Here we have an obvious challenge with the "last mile" problem — the movement of goods from the supply depot to the consumer's home, or wherever the consumer may be. Amazon's models for solving this, including its use of drone technology, open up questions we seem to be ignoring and solutions we're not exploring. Perhaps most of us just don't know what is actually happening on the ground. Or perhaps it's because Amazon is in the retail space that we don't connect the dots as to how what it is doing is disrupting so many aspects of so many other industries, and disrupting many of our regulations. Those who live in the cities can literally buy almost anything from Amazon, including certain kinds of medication, and have it delivered to their home, regardless of local regulations.

It wasn't long ago that drone technology seemed to just be a sci-fi dream. But now it's already happening. And it's actually already happening in Africa. For some time, UNICEF has been piloting a drone project in Malawi to deliver medical supplies and also pick up blood samples. The drone speaks to a phone held by health workers in a village, who can send the drone off to the right location with a swipe of the screen. To find them, it uses their phone's GPS signal. The drones are designed to carry up to 1kg of goods. Tanzania and Ghana, I have on good report, are also piloting drone projects that will carry off birth registration forms from villages to the nearest Home Affairs.

In speaking to Christopher Fabian, an 'adopted African' and is the brainchild behind this innovative Venture Capital concept at UNICEF, I was hugely impressed by his vision and optimism about the continent. Even more impressive is that he has managed to implement such a model for a humanitarian organisation that provides developmental assistance to children and mothers. This interests me because if UNICEF is doing this, surely private equity should be taking notice. In fact, UNICEF seems to be changing its approach and is, according to Fabian, looking to partner with businesses to get involved. They want this commercialised because there is an understanding that this sort of approach will create much more innovation, freedom, investment, and opportunity. So if UNICEF can do this, why can't we do it? Everything we need is already there – it's not like we need to reinvent any new technology. Why can't any of our home-grown companies just tweak things to work for us?

This is something we really should explore because Amazon clearly has the same idea in mind. If we don't move on it, Amazon will. While it is true that distribution of medicine comes with legitimate red tape and regulations that would all be new for Amazon, I am sure they will find a way. I can already imagine legitimate systems that would work—say, an app a doctor or health worker can download via a medical aid such as Discovery Health in South Africa. Instead of writing you a prescription, the doctor just accesses the app, taps on the medicine he is prescribing, and the transaction goes through your health insurance at the same time as an order goes to Amazon. No need to go to a pharmacy. No need to ask the doctor to write another prescription if you lose the original—or need more medicine (he can obviously create a recurring prescription, or could put a future prescription on standby, or just create another prescription if you need it, and run it all through the app). Or, if you don't have health insurance, he could put the prescription through to Amazon who asks for your Amazon account details, and then send you a confirmation you just have to tap to buy it. Whatever the case, your medicine could be on your doorstep by the time you get home. Or, it could just get to wherever *you* are. So if you're away on a business trip or at a holiday home, or live out in a rural village, Amazon will find you and deliver to you your medicine.

Think about how such a simple system could work – using existing technology. It's only the legalities standing in the way. Steve Kraus, a health tech investor with Bessemer Venture Partners, and expert in the field is confident that Amazon could break open the pharmaceutical space. In his view, reports CNBC, every major technology company should have a play in health care, an estimated $3 trillion sector.[39] The news of Amazon's foray into this industry saw pharmacy stocks in other companies drop by the next day, but as Kraus says, it's not just pharma-

---

39   Christina Farr, *Amazon could 'break open' the pharmacy space, says health tech investor.* Published at CNBC, May 2017. Available at http://www.cnbc.com/2017/05/17/amazon-could-break-open-the-pharmacy-space-steve-kraus-bessemer.html

ceuticals who should be worried. "Look at what Amazon has done to malls," he says. In the future, he adds, Amazon could work directly with manufacturers, become a distributor, negotiate discounts, and have such big buying power that most of us will just rather buy there as it will be so much cheaper. "In Amazon style," Kraus said to CNBC, "it will want to own the consumer's mind and wallet."

And, once again, this is how our innovators ought to be thinking—to own the consumer's mind and wallet. We might not be able to compete with Amazon head-on, and in fact, if it brings this sort of solution to Africa it will benefit us greatly. Having said that, however, we need to make sure we have the right framework in place so that Amazon's role on our continent in pharmaceuticals sees us benefit economically as well as from a health point of view. Otherwise, it is just monopolising. UNICEF's example shows we can do it, we just need to invest.

AMAZON AND THE FINANCIAL INDUSTRY

Further to this, I believe Amazon has the key to disrupting the remittance industry – and at first I thought maybe they don't know it, but the company has been making several moves into the financial services industry. In July 2016, the company announced that it had partnered with Wells Fargo, to offer student loans at a better interest rate to select shoppers. In February 2017, it was rumoured that Amazon is wanting to buy Capital One, a U.S. bank holding company that specialises in credit cards. In speaking about this, Neil O' Brien, a former director of digital banking at Santander Bank, says that owning more of the card payments value chain provides Amazon opportunity for cost reduction and more extended data analytics about consumer behaviour, but this could also make it turn into a merchant's bank.

"Amazon is already a merchant, payment processor and a credit card issuer. With the acquisition of Capital One, Amazon would also become the acquirer – i.e. the merchant's bank. It could offer this service to all of the merchants participating in its ecosystem.[40]"

---

40   Tanya Andreasyan, *Amazon looking to buy Capital One?* Published at Banking Technology, February 2017. Available at http://www.bankingtech.com/735552/amazon-looking-to-buy-capital-one/

When it comes to Africa, Amazon's access to a bank specialising in credit cards could mean it is positioned to open up the remittance space in new ways.

Many Africans know the huge challenge of sending money back home. Have you ever tried to do it? You've got to go to the retail branch of a Money Transfer Operator (MTO), for instance, fill out all sorts of forms, show your identification, get a special code, get that to those you are wanting to send the money to, or get your bank to help you, and so on. While the mobile money space is certainly making huge headway in this space, it is also beginning to encounter significant roadblocks in the form of regulation.

In August of 2016, in a sudden move, the Central Bank of Nigeria (CBN) changed its International Money Transfer Operators (IMTOs) policy. The change was so drastic that the licences of all money transfer services, save three, had been revoked. The three remaining are old players in the scene relatively speaking – Western Union, Moneygram, and Ria. The decision was made in the interests of curbing the growing unlicensed money transmitters operating in the country, and also – in the words of a press release – to ensure that no "attempt aimed at undermining the country's foreign exchange regime" is condoned.

I'm interested in this from an innovation point of view, and from the point of view of the many people who were using newer, more innovative money transfer solutions. Several startups like WorldRemit, MFS Africa, Transferwise, or Azimo found solutions for these people where money transfers can be almost seamless, and a lot cheaper. Many of the solutions make use of Digital Payment Services (DPS) where money can be sent using mobile phone apps and SMS services, in partnership with retailers and service providers. Overall, the issue is a rather simple one. The African diaspora is huge, and many Nigerians need easy and cheap solutions that will help them get money to loved ones in their home country. It's got to be an easy transaction without a lot of friction. There's a good reason why Nigerians are sending money home – they didn't just wake up in the morning and decide it's a good day to send money. There are obligations, needs, and family commitments. After all, most of them are somewhere else in the world because they found they could get a decent job that could help with their responsibilities at home.

Ismail Ahmed, WorldRemit founder and CEO, was pretty vocal about CBN's decision, and things got political quickly. "This reverses the progress made by the country when the Nigeria Central Bank banned Western Union's exclusivity agreements that had created a near-monopolistic position in the international money transfer market. Western Union controlled 78 percent of the market share when CBN outlawed exclusivity agreements with local banks[41]," he said. CBN's response was one over licensing, stating that only the three providers listed above were actually licensed. However, at the end of August, WorldRemit announced that CBN had given it a letter of approval.[42]

Often in Africa, we focus our regulatory framework in the wrong direction, as we don't have the bigger African picture in mind. The original CBN announcement had its pros and its cons. The pros were obvious – better control, more safety, and so on. There obviously needs to be adequate and effective regulation. It's good that CBN consolidated the numerous avenues to send money into the country – with only select partners to work with, managing fraud and laundering is much, much easier and effective. That's a plus.

The cons, however, were much more complicated. There are still questions about the original three providers that needed to be answered. All three have been around for a long time, but with that also often comes antiquated systems and unnecessary costs in the retail network in today's technological landscape. Do these partners have the capability, or the plans, to provide seamless transactions for users at a low cost? In order to get at the big fish involved in laundering and fraud, the common person is being cut off from valuable services that are really changing lives. I've had the luxury of working with all three and realise they recognise and have digital capabilities, but I would argue that they still have a

41   Press release from Worldremit – *WorldRemit calls for urgent restoration of money transfers to Nigeria.* See https://www.worldremit.com/en/news/worldremit-calls-for-urgent-restoration-of-money-transfers-to-nigeria

42   Chris Tredger, *WorldRemit commends Nigeria's turnaround on remittance.* Published at Web Africa, August 2016. Available at http://www.itwebafrica.com/e-commerce/700-nigeria/236716-worldremit-commends-nigerias-turnaround-on-remittance

big cash focus. Perhaps some of this is in the mind of the customer, but it goes without saying that there doesn't seem to be a quick move towards innovating in this area by those companies that have been around for a while.

According to statistics from the World Bank, ten of the most expensive cross-border remittance corridors are all in Africa.[43] South Africa remains the most expensive. Why is that? It may be simply because the service is so needed, and certain companies are genuinely taking advantage. Can you imagine sending money over to your loved ones and finding that the fees cost more than the actual money you're sending? By the way, I saw this in the rates schedule for a Money Transfer Operator. On the flip side, startups such as WorldRemit reduce costs by five percent, which is in line with international standards. Given that only 34 percent of adults are recorded as having a bank account in sub-Saharan Africa, while a growing percentage (12 percent in 2016) have mobile money accounts through a service like M-PESA, it makes sense to not just allow these startups to function but to foster them and create an environment where innovation such as this is encouraged. Business-as-usual is not good enough.

The beauty of DPS, as you can see, is the ability to circumvent so much of the antiquated systems and just get the job done. You can pay someone directly to their cell phone, with digital money they can actually use. Or if they need the cash, they can draw it from hundreds of agents around the country. DPS also allows you to pay for goods and services, and then send a coupon or code via SMS to someone else, who then simply pick up those goods and services from the relevant retailer or service provider.

I love the example of Tanzania. In 2008, less than one percent of Tanzanian adults had access to mobile financial services, but by 2013 this shot up to 90 percent. These services are effectively offering a huge amount of people the security and benefits of bank accounts (these days, even interest is being paid out) – it's making it easy for people to invest into the financial system. It's just that the financial system is looking very different! Perhaps in contrast to CBN, The Bank of Tanzania (BOT) has

---

43   Nadir Khamissa, *How to fix Africa's remittance industry.* Published at CNBC Africa, July 2016. Available at http://www.cnbcafrica.com/news/2016/07/04/mobile-money-transfers/

taken a "test and learn" approach, inviting the private sector to partner with them in opening up solutions and freeing up financial services to the common person. "We have learned that new technologies that augur well with the Central Bank's objective need to be nurtured and monitored closely to ensure they do not cause any financial instability or reputational risk that may affect the country's payment systems. This approach has made digital payment services in Tanzania a success story," says Prof Benno Ndulu, Governor of BOT.

DO WE HAVE TO SEND ACTUAL MONEY?

Here's the real issue, though, and it's where I'm going with this. We're all assuming that you have to send *money*. But this isn't right. When I send money to my folks in Botswana, it's because I want them to use it for something. Maybe I'm helping them pay the rent or buy their groceries, maybe I'm buying them a gift or a book. Maybe I want it to go to textbooks for my younger sister. This is what remittance hasn't figured out. However, Amazon has.

There's no doubt that this company has disrupted the way we purchase online, and the way we think of buying today. Every African with a phone or computer and internet coverage has access to Amazon. What is brilliant about Amazon is that whilst it has a consistent global approach, it does make local and relevant content available, especially to those countries it has offices in. Think about this: if I want to give this book to someone in Gambia, I don't need to send them money to go to a bookstore and try find it. I don't even need to buy a book from my stock and send it to them. All I actually need to do is hop onto Amazon and buy it there and put their address in. Amazon will ship it to them themselves and can even track it on the way.

In my opinion, remittance itself has to disappear from the customer's experience. Amazon has shown us the value of the 'one-click payment' service. Amazon is also a good example of how borders are closing – I can order almost anything from Amazon from almost anywhere, and have it delivered to just about anywhere. The costs will change, but the borders don't mean much. This is the sort of thing that needs to start happening in the money transfers space. For example, instead of sending money home to Nigeria, why can't I be allowed to pay for groceries and medical supplies from select partners, and then those goods are delivered to my loved one's door? That kind of thinking is what needs to enter the money transfer space, and in the case of many startups, it has.

This kind of thinking can work for anything and everything, really. Amazon began to move into the grocery space just last year, with their first store expected to open in Seattle this year. Think about what it would mean if you could order groceries on Amazon and have it delivered anywhere in the world. And it's not like they can't do it. Amazon has, in effect, figured out how to conduct remittance without having the onerous regulatory requirements. It's actually very clever how they have done it. They have delegated all the regulatory requirements like Know-You-Customer (KYC) and Anti-Money-Laundering (AML) rules to the banks, who must report to the Reserve banks on who is buying what where, while they themselves just focus on providing a good service.

They've removed the friction in remittance. To buy on Amazon is a simple one-click process. I don't need any supporting docs, FICA requirements, ID, whatever. I know I can click and it'll be delivered. In theory, if an individual can buy textbooks for his/her nephew in another country via an online or digital portal and the book is delivered to the home, that presents a whole new channel for the remittance market.

Some players have realised this and have created businesses to provide this sort of remittance. However, I don't believe we're thinking hard enough about the sort of disruption the likes of Amazon can cause here. When the big boys come to town, what do we do? See, innovators can provide solutions, but on their own, they simply cannot compete with Silicon Valley. Those who can compete, in my opinion, are actually the existing players. Western Union, as an example, is not an African-based corporation, but they've been around so long on our continent that we can consider them pseudo-African. Their presence gives them a huge advantage and huge experience with how Africa works. The pan-African banks are also well suited for this. Nothing stops them, technologically speaking, from sending money from one Bank account to another across borders and even extend that to the purchase of goods and services. They already have KYC regulations and have everything required to do it.

But yet these sorts of players aren't quite there. They have to either re-invent themselves or, in my view, partner with innovators. They need to think like innovators. The reality is, if the present players don't, it's inevitable that Silicon Valley will simply take things over. Again, consider how Amazon could simply sweep the current remittance players from under the carpet – simply through their already-built innovations, established name brand, and frictionless user experience. Wouldn't you use them if they started playing in this space in this way?

When they come – and they will – will we be ready for them? Whilst the likes of Google or Amazon or Facebook may never get into the financial industry in a way that seems to directly compete with the banks, the point is that it will disrupt at least at some level. More than that, my thesis is that our local industries and innovators need to think like them. We need to be asking ourselves: how would Google disrupt the finance industry? And then we go and do that. How would Amazon disrupt the logistics industry? Well, let's go and do that. I don't mean to say we should box ourselves by these innovators' models, but I do believe we have to look at what makes them so successful and use that information as a means of getting our own thinking and innovating going.

"As an entrepreneur, I try to push the limits. Pedal to the metal"

— **Travis Kalanick**

CHAPTER EIGHT

UBER WILL DISRUPT MANUFACTURING

"This morning I want to talk about the future of human-driven transportation; about how we can cut congestion, pollution and parking by getting more people into fewer cars; and how we can do it with the technology that's in our pockets. And yes, I'm talking about smartphones, not self-driving cars."

These were the words said by Travis Kalanick when he opened up a TED talk in February 2016, which was a fascinating talk about Uber's new car pooling strategy and how it wants to change the transport industry. "The beginning of Uber in 2010 was — well, we just wanted to push a button and get a ride," he continues later in the talk. "We didn't have any grand ambitions. But it just turned out that lots of people wanted to push a button and get a ride."

Most people think of Uber as disrupting the taxi industry, but I don't think this always the case. In fact, I think what Uber will disrupt — or is disrupting — goes beyond just that. Note Kalanick's words — "more people into fewer cars." That shows you exactly what is due to be disrupted: manufacturing.

The question is, are we ready for this in Africa?

Here's why this is the case. Who are the users of Uber? I'm one occasionally, especially when I travel, but I don't use it all that much because

I already have a car of my own. Theoretically speaking, on the road, with my car, I'm not competing with taxis. Hold that thought for a bit. When I'm off to the office in the morning, I hop in my car and I drive—I don't have to call anyone, stand outside, or wait. My car is clean (well, generally!) and I know it's pretty consistent. Every day I'm going to be using the same car. I don't wake up in the morning and wonder if my car is going to make me late or if I'm going to have a driver that doesn't know the streets and the shortcuts on the way to my work.

But a taxi is generally a shotgun approach. You keep your fingers crossed, hoping that you're going to have a pleasurable ride this time. This is one of the reasons why Uber competes with your car, not the taxi. It emulates a similar experience to using your car — the driver asks you what music you want, he makes sure it's quiet when you take a call and will keep the conversation on the down-low when you're not in the mood for any talk. He doesn't even need to ask you for directions, he just follows the shortest route as instructed by his GPS.

Taxi drivers often think that since Uber is in the market it means fewer people are using taxis. No. It just means more people are using fewer cars. And this is why ultimately Uber will disrupt the manufacturing industry and not the taxi industry.

Travis Kalanick, co-founder of Uber, hit on this last year February in a TED talk about Uber's plan to get more people into fewer cars. He starts off by speaking about a service in Los Angeles in 1914 called the "jitney". It was actually a very similar idea to Uber. People were basically hiring out their cars as a lifting service for a 'jitney' (slang for a nickel). The idea became so popular that by 1915 there were 150,000 jitney rides per day in Los Angeles. Uber only hit 157,000 rides per day in L.A. last year. Think about that for a second.

So what happened to is   t? The existing transportation industry got in a huff and started shutting it down through getting certain regulations put in place. By 1919, the whole thing was no more.

Uber still likes this idea, however. So here's where it's going next. Kalanick explains that what the company began noticing since its inception and large-scale usage is that there was a lot of duplicate rides. "We saw a lot of people pushing the same button at the same time going essentially to the same place. And so we started thinking about, well, how do we take those two trips and turn them into one. Because if we did, that ride would be a lot cheaper — up to 50 percent cheaper — and of course for the city you've got a lot more people and a lot fewer cars."

In other words, Uber started noticing that you and I stay in the same area and leave around the same time for work, which is also in the same area. So what if we carpooled? Hence Uber launched its UberPOOL service, which connects you and I together on the same ride. The result? Since launching the service in Los Angeles late 2015, Uber has created 100,000 new carpools every week and taken 7.9 million miles off the roads, the result being 1.4 thousand metric tonnes of CO_2 out of the air. They didn't expect that their small idea would result in less pollution. Watch what happened in China: 15 million uberPOOL trips per month, which amounted to 500,000 per day. Despite this, however, Uber eventually had to pull out of China for several other reasons..

And here's the clincher: more people carpooling with Uber means fewer cars on the road. Fewer cars on the road mean fewer cars are being sold. Fewer cars sold means fewer cars are being manufactured. See who is most affected by this?

When you think about it, cars are very resource-heavy products. They need parking space, idle half the time, create pollution, create noise, and so on. Carpooling or using the original Uber service means fewer cars, less traffic, more productivity or more rest (as we get to work in less time) as more people use the service. If this is a viable alternative to using my own car, especially if the costs are halved via carpooling, wouldn't you use it? Of course, you would. It's not like in Africa that they're usually much choice when it comes to public transportation or alternatives to having your own car.

So we see as this becomes more viable to the masses, it's manufacturing—not the taxi industry—which suffers the most. The problem with this, however, is manufacturing is one of the big pillars of the African economy (certainly the South African economy). Even China and America will face the same problem. Trump's "America first" policy is all about boosting (or in many cases, rebooting) the car manufacturing industry in America. One of his main constituencies has been those towns and States where car manufacturing was a booming industry — middle-class towns that have collapsed under the "new economy" and Silicon Valley innovations. Even the financing side of things will be affected by this.

So the big question, again, is are we ready for Uber here? In my view, manufacturing (broadly) on our continent has to do three things:

(1) It must realise this is happening or is about to happen. This needs to be taken seriously.

(2) It must find a way to partner with Uber — not just focus on manufacturing cars but also get those cars to Uber drivers, provide training, and create a new service industry.

Then, (3) manufacturing, along with financing, need to create the right kinds of protection and regulation. Uber has been quite open to the fact that it sees a need for regulation — it just speaks of having the right kind. Rather than work against the innovation, an innovation that clearly has other positives for us all (less pollution, congestion etc.), there needs to be a new way forward.

In my view, now is the time for Africa to find ways to work with the disruptors coming in—before the carpet is swept completely under our feet. Uber will even come in those spaces where we are already innovating. EmptyTrips, operating out of Johannesburg, is one such innovation focusing on the freight side of things, where you are able to match and connect spare capacity on vehicles to those requiring goods transported. In 2017, Uber entered the freight space through its system.

So we need to have open eyes and ears to what's going on and support our own innovators in the various spaces, otherwise, even our innovative industries could be usurped.

"Success doesn't necessarily come from breakthrough innovation but from flawless execution. A great strategy alone won't win a game or a battle; the win comes from basic blocking and tackling."

— **Naveen Jain**

CHAPTER NINE

———————×———————

THE DARK SIDE TO INNOVATION

When the digital camera was released, most people never dreamed that it would single-handedly destroy one of the most lucrative businesses in photography — the film roll. Author Ankush Chopra explains the conundrum well:

> "If photography companies embraced digital technology, they would cut their own profits. If they avoided it, and the digital technology succeeded, they would have been driven out of business."

Interestingly, it was the company that owned a monopoly in photography, Kodak itself, that actually invented it. In 1975, a relatively new and young employee (he was 24), Steven Sasson, invented the entire process that allows for digital photography to take place. He had been given the task to see if there was any way the company could make use of a new invention, the charged coupled device (CCD). This is a device for the movement of electrical charge, usually from within the device to an area where the charge can be manipulated, for example, conversion into a digital value.[44] So he concocted a frankenstein of a device that could take pictures and imprint them on a digital cassette, allowing for them to be viewed on a T.V. screen.

---

44   See Wikipedia – https://en.wikipedia.org/wiki/Charge-coupled_device

"It was a photographic system to demonstrate the idea of an all-electronic camera that didn't use film and didn't use paper, and no consumables at all in the capturing and display of still photographic images," he told the New York Times in 2015.[45] Obviously, Kodak owned most of that process—the film, the consumables, the paper, and pretty much everything involved in photography. When he showed his invention to executives and those in marketing, he told them how the quality could improve, and even predicted that pictures could be sent via a telephone line. It was not well received.

"Print has been with us for over 100 years," he was told. "No one is complaining about prints, they are very inexpensive, and so why would anyone want to look at their picture on a television set?"

They allowed him to continue his work, however, and the first digital camera was patented in 1978. Sasson was under a non-disclosure agreement and was not allowed to speak about his invention to others. In 1989, he and Robert Hills, a colleague, invented the first digital single-lens reflex (SLR) camera, which functions like our digital cameras do today, with memory cards and image compression and everything we have come to know. Marketing at Kodak, however, was again not interested. They knew it had a market, they knew it would sell, but they also knew it could kill their lucrative film sales business. The camera, therefore, was never released. Kodak, however, did make money off of patents. And it filed for bankruptcy in 2012.

The digital camera cannibalised whole industries and did not come into the market with the blessing of professional photographers, either. It's still seen as something for the amateurs. Famous British war photographer, Don McCullin, calls it a "totally lying experience" and claims you cannot trust digital images.[46] But digital photography has certainly opened up a whole new world to hobbyists and enthusiasts, and most certainly made things more efficient for professional photographers, and has made our lives so much better and personal with the ability to take pictures using our phones.

---

45   James Estrin, *Kodak's First Digital Moment.* Published at the New York Times, August 2015. Available at https://lens.blogs.nytimes.com/2015/08/12/kodaks-first-digital-moment/

46   Mark Brown, *Digital images can't be trusted, says war photographer Don McCullin.* Published at The Guardian, November 2015. Available at https://www.theguardian.com/artanddesign/2015/nov/27/don-mccullin-war-photographer-digital-images

That little innovation also came with a lot of head scratching. "I remember Sony Ericsson in 2001 showed off a phone with a clip-on camera," says Jonathan Margolis, a technology writer for the Financial Times. "Along with everyone else, I thought 'why would you want a phone with a camera?'"[47]

The digital camera revolution was the end of Kodak's core business. After filing for bankruptcy, it sold off parts of its business and now focuses on digital printing. As Chopra says, "It is not the strongest of the species that survives, nor the most intelligent that survives. It is the one that is the most adaptable to change." While every technology company, business, advertising agency and those in the creative space seeks to "disrupt", it's important not to lose sight of the fact that disruption has many knock-on effects, and not all of them are positive – especially not in Africa where the stakes are particularly high.

This is the 'dark side' of innovation. As we have seen, Uber has changed the face of the taxi industry forever and is poised to disrupt manufacturing. Facebook has the potential of disrupting our telecommunications and practically swallowing it up whole. If Google wants to, it can very easily disrupt our banking sector and insurance industries. Amazon has its eye on one of the biggest industries in the world, the pharmaceutical business, and can very easily disrupt our remittance sector in ways we probably never thought of before, and is most certainly entering banking. All of these 'big boys' bring tremendous benefits: access to information and the Internet for all Africans, innovative health solutions, cheaper transport, and more. But they are also poised to benefit in such a way that other industries, and our economic growth, could be hindered.

Such is the nature of globalism—a hot topic right now, but for different reasons than in the 90's. Globalism has a tremendous plus side, but its negative sides need to be curbed and guided because right now many aspects of it is further accentuating the rich and poor divide. Moreso, Silicon Valley's transformative technology has truly saved lives — but who is benefiting economically? In America, not even all of America is benefiting. As a very scathing article by David Rotman in Technology

---

47   Tom de Castella, *Five ways the digital camera changed us.* Published in BBC News Magazine, February 2012. Available at http://www.bbc.com/news/magazine-16483509

Review put it:

> Given impressive advances in artificial intelligence, smart robots, and driverless cars, it's easy to become convinced that we are on the verge of a new technological age. But the troubling reality is that today's advances are having a far from impressive impact on overall economic growth. Facebook, Twitter, and other digital technologies undoubtedly bring great value to many people, but those benefits are not translating into a substantial economic boost. If you think Silicon Valley is going to fuel growing prosperity, you are likely to be disappointed — or you'd better be patient. While the high-tech industry creates impressive wealth for itself, much of the country is mired in a sluggish economy. It might be that driverless cars and other uses of advanced AI will eventually change that, but for now, these technologies are not radically transforming the economy.[48]

If America is feeling it, when California is one of its States, you can bet we will feel it.

Outside of the 'big boys' of Silicon Valley that we've mentioned, there are others, of course. AirBnB has reshaped holiday and business travel rentals. Tesla, while still in the car manufacturing business, is sure to disrupt other industries. Sure, it is creating new industries and supply chains, but at the same time, it is dismantling some of our older mainstays. The name of the game is disruption, and every business in every industry is hoping that they'll be the next to shake things up. But it's no secret that a service like Uber has made a lot of people unhappy (and poorer) as traditional taxi companies have lost fares, and many of those employees that did not defect to the Uber system have lost their jobs. The driverless car – the disruptive force we've all been waiting for – will have a massive impact on the automotive industry, public transport, insurance industry, manufacturing and more besides, as individual car ownership possibly becomes a thing of the past.

---

48   David Rotman, *Dear Silicon Valley: Forget Flying Cars, Give Us Economic Growth.* Published at Technology Review, June 2016. Available at https://www.technologyreview.com/s/601682/dear-silicon-valley-forget-flying-cars-give-us-economic-growth/

Another oft-cited example of positive disruption that also has a dark side is that of mobile money transfer in sub-Saharan Africa, utilising mobile networks to transfer virtual money from one individual to another using the smartphone—no bank account required. I touched on this in the previous chapters, especially when speaking of remittance payments, and in my last book, I covered this extensively. It is a prime example of how we can leapfrog traditional infrastructure through innovative means. Mobile money is huge in Africa as a whole, although it seems to consistently fail in South Africa. These days, it functions very much as a bank would — offering the ability to save through the platform or invest, or offering micro-insurance. It started out with MPesa in Kenya but has spread to other countries and operators. South Africa again re-attempted to re-launch MPesa, while Orange Money International links up Cote d'Ivoire, Mali and Senegal, and the partnership between MTN Mobile Money in Cote d'Ivoire and Airtel Money in Burkina Faso is the first case of operators from separate groups partnering for international transfers. This is a massive step forward for a continent upon which money transfer was charged at a higher percentage of the transfer than anywhere else in the world (Africa pays, on average, 12 percent per transfer, while the global average is 7.8 percent and the target set by the G8 is 5 percent). At the same time, it is estimated that Africans received USD $32 billion from relatives working elsewhere in 2013, and this was expected to increase to more than $40 billion by 2016. The percentage points of these fees are not insignificant to people already struggling for an income. And it has already been shown in East Africa that cash-theft crime has been reduced and rural economic activity stimulated.

All of this is brilliant and I'm a big supporter of mobile money, but there is a dark side to it, believe it or not. For one thing, because there is now an easy and cheap mechanism for the transfer of funds to rural villages in East Africa, city-living workers no longer have to make the journey to their family to bring the money to them, or they no longer need to ask a friend to deliver cash. Analysts have looked into the potential of this reduction in visitation frequency and found it has the very real potential to weaken social ties between migrants and their home communities. Technology has a way of bringing us together and yet at the same time keep us apart. Just look at all the studies going into smartphone usage and how it affects our health and family life. In one sense, it brings us together, in another, it disconnects us.

> Mobile devices like smartphones and tablets can be distracting from child-rearing, upending family routines and fueling stress in the home, a small, new study finds. Incoming communication from work, friends and the world at large is "contaminating" family mealtime, bedtime and playtime, said study lead author Dr. Jenny Radesky. She's an assistant professor of developmental behavioural paediatrics at the University of Michigan Medical School. Her comments stem from her team's study involving interviews with 35 parents and caregivers of young children in the Boston area. "This tension, this stress, of trying to balance newly emerging technologies with the established patterns and rituals of our lives is extremely common, and was expressed by almost all of our participants," Radesky said. "We have to toggle between what might be stress-inducing or highly cognitively demanding mobile content and responding to our kids' behaviour," she said. The result, said Radesky, is often a rise in parent-child tension and overall stress.[49]

None of this, by and large, was expected—and no one probably thought that easy remittance could lead to social breakdown, however small.

Over and above this, there has also been a natural necessity for traditional money transfer services to lower their fees in East Africa or risk going out of business. This, of course, affects agents and many others in the process who earn a living off the system.

Both of these consequences are worth considering for the broader impact that they will have on East African society and business respectively. They are clear indications of how no advance operates in a vacuum and the ripple effects of any new technology will be felt in far-reaching and unexpected corners of society and business.

---

49   See the forum conversation at Slashdot – https://science.slashdot.org/story/16/10/14/2225244/smartphones-are-contaminating-family-life-study-suggests

Another example that I was personally involved in has to do with the simple matter of parking. I show this because disruption often occurs on levels we don't expect. We literally don't think of how a simple convenience can cost people their jobs. One South African shopping centre in Johannesburg has over ten thousand instances of parking in a month. At an average cost of R10 per parking stay, this means that the parking operation nets the mall R20 million in a month. However, to help with the parking and flow of traffic, a solution was implemented where customers can pay for parking using QR code technology. QR code payments have already gained traction in the market by allowing people to pay for drinks in bars or goods at markets by downloading an app. Having downloaded the app and loaded their credit card on it, users can then pay directly to the vendor with the scannable QR code.

The same technology, applied to parking, provides extensive benefits. First of all, it frees the parking customer from having to queue to interact with a parking machine. After they have downloaded the scanning app, they can simply pay for parking on the go. If enough people adopt this technology, it significantly reduces the amount of cash that the parking operator has to deal with. This reduces the need for collection by cash-in-transit vans – a significant cost and risk reduction for the parking operator. So for every link in the parking operation chain, QR code payments are a massive win.

However, there are a number of people whose jobs are provided by the current parking system who won't have jobs when QR code payments become pervasive. The cash-in-transit drivers and security guards will certainly experience a reduction in need and collections. The security personnel who deal with faulty tickets and out-of-money machines will no longer have a function. And so it goes on.

This is the sad truth about disruption – while it's almost always beneficial for the end user and for the business behind it, there are often a number of people between these two points who lose their income along the way. This obviously can't hold progress back, but those responsible for disruptive technologies need to be cognizant of the whole value chain that they are disrupting. They need to be aware of it and take some responsibility for the knock-on effects of their actions. They just need to think a little bit more about how they can make a difference beyond the innovation itself. For example, in the case of the new parking solution, it's possible to take that security personnel and train them up as support staff, able to help customers with their downloads, transactions or any other form of troubleshooting. They could be equipped to help out in the event of a power failure or network stoppage, able to provide meaningful support and to prevent a bottleneck of departing customers. The added benefit to this upgrading of their skills to an entry level of IT support is that it would make them employable elsewhere. While we can't pretend that this will be a huge upward trajectory for all erstwhile security staff, if we do make their future the responsibility of the company delivering the disruptive solution, it's possible that a better outcome can be achieved for all the people in the value chain.

None of this is by any means a discouragement from aiming for disruption. Far from it. It is simply a caution that no game-changing journey should ever be embarked upon without due consideration for the "unknown unknowns". It's easy to say that these things are the cost of progress, but I believe that businesses should take responsibility for the societal and financial change that they bring about.

The Internet has given us free access to information, which is a plus for journalism, education, research, business, agriculture, and health workers. But yet it has its dark side to it—terrorism, child pornography, human trafficking, and much more besides. It is always this way with technology and innovation, and our task is to look far enough into the future to guide things on the right path. We can't just accept that innovation will have a dark side and think that will make it all go away. We have to do something about it, and prevention is always better than cure. Remember that when you set the ball rolling, you don't always know where it will end up, and you have to be sure you are agile enough and have made sufficient allowance to respond to what happens next and keep catching that ball.

This is the kind of thinking we have to employ when we collaborate with Silicon Valley innovations; when we innovate for ourselves; and when we decide to take on Silicon Valley. If African innovation has a conscience, we do so much better, and also win the hearts of the African people.

Silicon Valley has its eyes on Africa. But so does China. We need to, then, also examine the trends on that side of the world and be prepared for possible disruption. In doing so, I believe, we will find some further lessons that will help us piece the puzzle together of how we can do this— how we can take on Silicon Valley.

"Victorious warriors win first and then go to war, while defeated warriors go to war first and then seek to win."

— **Sun Tzu**

×

CHAPTER TEN

HOW "MADE IN CHINA" CHANGED

The year is 1980. China's youngest researcher in the Physics Institute of the Academy of Sciences, Chen Chunxian, is about to have an experience that will change his life.

On a government-sponsored trip to the U.S., Chunxian visits Silicon Valley. What he sees there he realises is the future - and a revelation hits him. He can do this back home. So writes Ling Zhijun:

"He noted that American scientists and engineers always wanted to realise their inventions in patented technology and to put the results of their knowledge into products. As a result, they sometimes succeeded in creating new industries worth billions of dollars."

And that inspired him. He also noticed, says Zhijun, that the density of talent in the Chinese town of Zhongguancun was "no lower than that in the San Francisco or the Boston area." To him, then, it seemed as if China had the perfect set up already, they just needed to guide it correctly. Much like with Stanford, Zhongguancun was close to the Chinese Academy of Sciences and is also today close to Peking University and Tsinghua University, which all participate in the rampant innovation going on there. Back in the 80's, Chunxian knew he could tap into the vast talent already there and connect it to industry.

Soon he set up a company, the first of what became known as a *min-yin* ("people administered enterprise" as opposed to a "state-owned" enterprise) in Zhongguancun. This was all quite revolutionary for China at the time, and he was seen to be something of a rebel for doing it. He started with seven young people and, you guessed it, in an old garage. He also resigned from his post at the Academy, which was unheard of and highly controversial. Ultimately, his business was a failure for himself, and when he died at 70 many years later, he died in a shabby apartment without healthcare. But his business inspired many, many others. It's clear that Chunxian saw the future. After his company was set up, many other companies began to spring up on the streets of Zhongguancun, and China's first Silicon Valley was born. The city transformed very quickly from a farmland to what we see today, a magnet for tech-savvy, young twenty to thirty-something crowds with some of the nation's biggest Internet players. It's lined with office buildings, incubators, and electronic malls. As from 1999, it has been called the "Zhongguancun Science & Technology Zone". In 2014, Zhongguancun produced 13,000 new startups, with revenue of 3.5 trillion yuan ($560 billion).

Can you imagine a city in Africa producing 13,000 new startups? I dream of that. Chunxian, much like his counterparts in the U.S., had a passion for innovation. By creating something of a community with the universities and Academy close by, including (today) a host of technical universities, we see things happen. By tying this all into industry, we see things happen. This is an important lesson for us when we consider how we can take on Silicon Valley, which I will summarise in a later chapter.

Today, a network of academic institutions creates close relationships with the organisations in Zhongguancun. Multinationals such as Google, Ericsson, Microsoft, and IBM are found within the same district. Much investment capital is concentrated around Zhongguancun, and there are tons of startup-themed cafes, incubators, hubs, and more. It's where Lenovo came from.

While we can pick up similarities with this story to Silicon Valley, the Chinese story is also different to the U.S. one. Zhongguancun is buzzing, yet a lot of China's innovation also comes from Shenzhen, a sprawling metropolis that links Hong Kong to China's mainland and has a population of 11.91 million (2016). Shenzhen has been dubbed in various corners as the "Silicon Valley of hardware" as most of the world's electronics are made there. It is another hugely successful story but also shows us that a nation's "Silicon Valley" does not need to be concentrated in one place—a fact I will explain the relevance of in more detail later.

The story of Shenzhen pretty much illustrates how none of this really happens by accident. It was only just under 40 years ago that Shenzhen was a small fishing village. However, when Deng Xiaoping became China's leader in 1979, he had other plans for it, obviously seeing the great geographic position it held linking Hong Kong and China's mainland together. He declared the city to be named a "special economic zone", one of the first of its kind. It was part of an economic reformation by the government of China. Special economic zones enjoy more flexible government measures and special economic policies, such as tax and business incentives, which attract foreign investment and technology. Foreign and domestic trade and investment can be conducted on the ground without the Chinese central government in Beijing getting involved.[50] It was basically the first step in liberalising China's economy. The result of this Chinese programme in Shenzhen was that this small fishing village grew into a city faster than any other in history. In the 80's and 90's, migrant workers flocked from all over China to work in Shenzhen's factories. The town exploded from 300,000 people to over 10 million in one generation.

Part of its phenomenal growth had to do with the invention of the smartphone. While Finnish multi-national Nokia was clearly dominating the market in the early 2000's, and selling smartphones at premium prices, Shenzhen had a different model in place. The rate and speed, of which the city could manufacture and distribute for the market, and the cheaper price of manufacturing and shipping, changed the game in an unprecedented way. It's why cell phones and smartphones are now so widely available to so many people, and why there are an estimated 24,000 different smartphone models today.[51] It went from something like 5,000 models to 24,000 plus models in just a few years! Samsung was

---

50   See Wikipedia – https://en.wikipedia.org/wiki/Special_economic_zones_of_China

51   Leo Mirani, *There are now more than 24,000 different Android devices*. Published at Quartz, August 2015. Available at https://qz.com/472767/there-are-now-more-than-24000-different-android-devices/

doing 56 models a year at one stage.

All of this has been paramount to Shenzhen's success. As Jim Demuth told WIRED, "People have realised that if you go to Shenzhen to prototype hardware you can do that at ten times the speed you can anywhere else." It's here in Shenzhen where you find Tencent and Huawei, amidst other Chinese giants, as well as the world's most dominant and innovative brands.

No longer satisfied with being just an electronics manufacturer — which is really what boosted it in the beginning—Shenzhen is now becoming a worldwide innovator hub. Under Xu Qin's leadership, the city's investments are shifting from manufacturing to research and development. But one of its major strengths over Silicon Valley, according to Sean Konieczny and many other commentators, is its "open source" philosophy.

"Evolved from its manufacturing background, the city has learned to share technology, creativity, and innovation all in the spirit of creating efficiency. The open-source model has proven to work wonders for a number of companies. Some argue that open-source is the reason why Shenzhen is beginning to lead the world in selective industries, with virtual reality as one of the best examples."[52]

Silicon Valley is arguably moving towards open source in certain spaces. But it just doesn't have what Shenzhen has right now, and its complicated patent agreements make things considerably more, well... complicated. That's not to say that its front-of-the-line innovators don't like open source. Elon Musk, as one example, is a clear contender for the model. Microsoft has also changed in recent years, having recently joined the Linux Foundation. Google dabbles in open source and supports it through a number of platforms, including its website opensource.google. com. "We know that our particular approach to open source might not be right for everyone," it stated in a press release when launching the site.

---

52   Sean Konieczny, *Here's why Shenzhen will replace Silicon Valley in 2017*. Published at Tech Node. Available at http://technode.com/2017/01/10/shenzhen-will-be-2017s-new-silicon-valley/

"There's more than one way to do open source."

But here's the clincher: Minal Hasan of the venture capital firm K2 Global (based in Silicon Valley) says China will adopt virtual reality quicker than the U.S. because of "how the country is structured, and how involved the government is." The point is that, based on several commentators and observers, Virtual Reality has the most potential as an emerging technology in the world today. Shenzhen leads in the field. So as Konieczny (quoted above) says, "Judging by the existing infrastructure inclination, Shenzhen will take ownership of the market and Silicon Valley will trail in a distant second."

Put this together and the city's long history of open source, and its continued community of shared ideas and skills and innovation, and its on-going successes, and many think the city will soon take over Silicon Valley as a global leader in technology and innovation—even as soon as 2019. This, along with the fact that the group of venture capitalists in Silicon Valley is quite exclusive, and in some ways closing rank, leads for the real 'buzz' to start happening elsewhere. Conversely, China's approach right now is almost the exact opposite to Silicon Valley, and Silicon Valley's own history shows that China's approach may be more successful.

Regardless of whether you believe Zhongguancun or Shenzhen is "China's Silicon Valley", the point is to show that China has been doing this for a while. We cannot emulate either the U.S. or China in creating our own Silicon Valley. Silicon Valley has been around for almost a hundred years, and China has been doing this for several decades already. It would be ridiculous to believe that we can just copy what's happened in the U.S. or China, implement it, and see the same results. It won't work. And more than just this, these disruptive industries are now here in Africa, so how could we possibly think that by emulating them we can compete?

In reality, I don't believe any of what we've seen in Silicon Valley or China can be *emulated*. Both have risen in a specific time and place and context, with distinct personalities, histories and thought processes. Both are significantly ahead of us economically, culturally, and socially. It takes decades for something like Silicon Valley to develop. There are many lessons we can draw from Silicon Valley's birth, but the trouble is we're not in any place to emulate it. I don't think any of this is necessarily a bad thing. What it means is there is an opportunity to think differently and create something unexpected and, therefore, highly competitive. When I say we must compete with Silicon Valley, and we must, I don't mean that we must be idealistic, and I certainly don't mean we must shut them out of our borders so that we can "do our own thing". Rather we need to take some of the core thinking behind the inception of these disruptors, look at what it all actually means for our time in our own context, and put these together and see what we find.

So what can we learn from China and Silicon Valley? With everything we have covered, I believe we can summarise it into a few important points:

1. We need relationships and communities.

We need to find ways to connect our innovators *together*. In my first book, I highlighted how so many of our current innovations could work together and have the potential to create new kinds of ecosystems that leapfrog our traditional infrastructure. This is the first step. The second step is to actually put them together.

2. We need to think Pan-African from the outset.

If you put innovators together and tell them that their job is to figure out how to leave a legacy of Pan-African innovation that can compete with Silicon Valley, I think we will have a very real tangible outcome. I myself have in mind something like a group of innovation fellows who are a team of the brightest minds in African innovation, who can begin to work this out. This is how I think we will start to facilitate change, at least from an innovation point of view.

3. We need to connect innovators with all parties.

Above and beyond we need to be prepared for Silicon Valley and then embrace the change. I am very intrigued by the level of thinking of disruption. I am trying to foster and align the level of thinking in all parties, from innovators, corporates, the regulatory environment, the public sector and everyone on the continent to raise their level of thinking.

4. We need to think open source.

Let me illustrate by looking at how China's 'open source' culture developed, and why this is so important to what we're dealing with right now. It's also important in understanding China's strategy for coming to Africa.

MADE IN CHINA

What do you think when you read the words "made in China" on a product? In the past, most of us thought that this meant it was a cheaply made, mass-produced product, and probably a knock-off of some or other well-known brand. This stigma is fast fading away, however, as Chinese innovation comes to the fore, and as the government, itself is on a quest to revamp its manufacturing sector. Its programme, launched in 2015, has been dubbed "Made in China 2025". At the time, Chinese Premier Li Keqiang said, "We will implement the 'Made in China 2025' strategy, seek innovation-driven development, apply smart technologies, strengthen foundations, pursue green development and redouble our efforts to upgrade China from a manufacturer of quantity to one of quality.[53]" It has a long way to go, but the strength of innovative companies like Huawei are surely helping.

The change in perception begins in China itself. In 2011, Nokia, Samsung and Apple together held the market share of up to 70 percent of the smartphone sales in the country. Only about five years later, eight of the top ten smartphone brands in the country are Chinese. Oppo, a Chinese hi-tech and media company, toppled Apple's growth in the country in 2016. According to McKinsey in 2016, 62 percent of Chinese consumers preferred Chinese brands in 2016, if the prices were equal.[54] This then extends out into the rest of the world. Huawei is now enjoying the second top spot in Europe and is rated the third best smartphone brand in the world.[55] This seems to be the beginning of a new trend. Why

---

53   Li Hui, Made in China 2025: *How Beijing is revamping its manufacturing sector*. Published at South China Morning Post, June 2015. Available at http://www.scmp.com/tech/innovation/article/1818381/made-china-2025-how-beijing-revamping-its-manufacturing-sector

54   Daniel Zipser, Yougang Chen, and Fang Gong, *Here comes the modern Chinese consumer*. Published by McKinsey, March 2016. Available at http://www.mckinsey.com/industries/retail/our-insights/here-comes-the-modern-chinese-consumer

55   Wade Shepard, *How 'Made In China' Became Cool*. Published at Forbes, May 2016. Available at https://www.forbes.com/sites/wadeshepard/2016/05/22/how-made-in-china-became-cool/#495b86e877a4

is this happening, though?

Interestingly, the answer lies in the very thing that created the "made in China" stigma—the Chinese phenomenon called *shanzhai* (Cantonese slang that means 'counterfeit', 'imitation goods', particularly electronics). A *shanzhai* factory refers to an ill-equipped, low-end factory, usually owned or run by a family. *Shanzhai* factories essentially operate under the radar, avoiding the red tape that comes with being an electronics manufacturer, as well as the taxes and regulations. This allows for cheaper manufacturing, of course, as they do not go through the licensing costs and cheat quite a bit. *Shanzhai* simply copy what's out there and sell it for cheaper.

This links to what has become known as "Shanzhaiism" which, in English, refers to a 'tinker'. They tinker with existing technology and create copies of it. And the amazing thing is that *shanzhai* phones, while carrying a stigma, still sell remarkably well—in 2010, the Financial Times reported that about 20 percent of the global phone market were *Shanzhai*[56]

At another very interesting article outlining this development, writer and tech media contributor Wade Shepard quotes David Li from the Shenzhen Open Innovation Lab, who says, "If you look at what happened to Motorola and Nokia, they didn't really get killed by Apple... they all got killed by *shanzhai*[57]" The idea of 'tinkering' has helped Chinese manufacturers to find ways of doing the same thing on a much cheaper budget, innovating on it, and releasing it to the market quickly. Essentially, the market is part of the testing process — something Apple could never, ever do. Further to this, when the European recession hit, many manufacturers in China who were contracted to create Western electronic products now found themselves losing these contracts as demand for these products dropped. So these manufacturers starting putting their own labels on what they were making already and tinkering with the design. The result was that they moved from original equipment manu-

---

56   See Wikipedia – https://en.wikipedia.org/wiki/Shanzhai#cite_note-mediatek-4.

57   Wade Shepard, *A Look Inside Shenzhen's High-Tech Empire*. Published at Forbes, July 2016. Available at https://www.forbes.com/sites/wadeshepard/2016/07/14/a-look-inside-shenzhens-high-tech-empire/3/#812d0193c61e.

facturers (OEM) to original design manufacturers (ODM) within twenty years, creating their own empires.[58]

But here's the other key part that speaks directly to our own situation: *shanzhai* collaborate. It's a network, an ecosystem. As explained by Andrew "bunnie" Huang, an American researcher and hacker who studied at MIT:

> The West has a "broadcast" view of IP and ownership: good ideas and innovation are credited to a clearly specified set of authors or inventors, and society pays them a royalty for their initiative and good works. China has a "network" view of IP and ownership: the far-sight necessary to create good ideas and innovations is attained by standing on the shoulders of others, and as such, there is a network of people who trade these ideas as favours among each other. In a system with such a loose attitude toward IP, sharing with the network is necessary as tomorrow it could be your friend standing on your shoulders, and you'll be looking to them for favours. This is unlike the West, where rule of law enables IP to be amassed over a long period of time, creating impenetrable monopoly positions. It's good for the guys on top, but tough for the upstarts.[59]

Whatever your own views on copyright and patent laws — a complicated subject, to be sure—it's worth noting the benefits of what the West would call an open source sort of model. As a special economic zone in China, Shenzhen seems to have cottoned-on to this aspect of what has made it a success thus far, and actively supports grassroots innovation through its media, creates workshops, provides low interest (or no interest) loans, and sponsors tech fairs. Innovators like David Li, who are on the ground, have also begun to set up support structures. Hax, for example, is an investor in crowdfunded hardware and helps to foster this sort of culture. The Shenzhen Open Innovation Lab, of which Li is a part,

---

58   Wade Shepard, *The Revolutionary Rise Of the Chinese Brand*. Published at Forbes, May 2016. Available at https://www.forbes.com/sites/wadeshepard/2016/05/23/why-chinas-manufacturers-started-building-their-own-brands/#31b577bd31b5

59   Andrew "bunnie" Huang, *From Gongkai to Open Source*. At the bunnie:studios blog. See http://www.bunniestudios.com/blog/?p=4297

is a collaborative network that invites innovators from across the world to come to Shenzhen and effectively 'make their things' there, by providing space, access to funding, and partnership.

In some cases, we are starting to see the benefit of this sort of thing, and are setting up similar structures at home. For example, Kigali Innovation City in Rwanda; or the African Leadership Group (ALG), which in my mind is doing an amazing job. I'll cover these and other projects in more detail later. For now, I'm building an argument to show just how necessary all this is in our own thinking, and I want to, therefore, look at three innovators from China that are rising and could have their eyes on Africa. As we look at these, it would be good to remember Shenzhen's approach to innovation, and keep the *shanzai* phenomenon at the back of your mind, is these are key in understanding three Chinese big boys: Tencent, Alibaba, and Huawei.

"Help young people. Help small guys. Because small guys will be big. Young people will have the seeds you bury in their minds, and when they grow up, they will change the world."

— Jack Ma

CHAPTER ELEVEN

---×---

CHINA'S BIG BOYS

Silicon Valley has its eyes on Africa. So does China. But the ways in which both of them are coming here from a tech and innovation perspective are decidedly different, and we can learn from both so we can collaborate with them effectively and, best of all, compete with them.

In the last chapter, we examined China's *shanzai* phenomenon, and what it means for open-sourcing our innovation: for bringing our innovations together. I want to briefly look at three "big boys" from China that play a part in Africa's development, or will play a part, and see what we can learn from them. These are Tencent, Alibaba, and Huawei.

TENCENT

Tencent, based in Shenzhen, is a Chinese investment holding company with subsidiaries in media, entertainment (including gaming), payment systems, mobile phone services, the Internet, and advertising. It is run by Ma Huateng (also known as Pony Ma), a somewhat elusive figure known for his secretive lifestyle and his maxim: "Ideas are not important in China – execution is."

Tencent's new headquarters in Shenzhen, still under construction at the time of writing, is a sight to behold, and are a case in point when we consider the future development of the Internet of Things — the interconnection of devices via the Internet in everyday objects, such as kettles and fridges and watches, which sums up pretty much all we've discussed thus far with Google and the likes and how it wants to connect everything. The headquarters, a USD $599 million project, includes a 50 story tower, connected by a sky bridge to a shorter skyscraper of 39 stories, "making them look like giant robots in a lover's embrace.[60]" The bridges have a 300-meter running track, pantries, conference rooms and auditoriums, and other common areas. Inside there will be hologram tour guides, conference rooms that automatically adjust the temperature depending on how many people are inside, and a system that alerts you on your device telling you the best parking spot when you arrive. Doors will open using facial recognition technology, and your work badge tracks you wherever you are in the building — meaning, you won't be able to sneak in a smoke break without anyone knowing. The heat generated off of the building's servers will be used to provide hot water for the pool, kitchens and bathrooms. The idea, reports Bloomberg, is that its own headquarters will be a giant testing lab for its own products.[61]

Towards the latter end of 2016, Tencent became China's most valuable company—which is unusual as it is not a state-owned enterprise.[62] Its biggest revenue comes from its mobile gaming and online advertising, both of which are linked to its messaging services, WeChat. WeChat also acts as a sort-of link for almost everything Tencent is involved in. It boasts almost a million monthly users and in addition to messaging, lets you book trips and holidays, order meals, make in-store payments, play games, transfer money, split bills, call a ride service, catch up on the news, get your laundry picked up, book a karaoke session, send instructions to an online concierge service, share your location, trade in bitcoin, pay your bills, manage a personal wealth fund, donate to charities, scan barcodes in shops and compare prices of that item online...

---

60   Robert Fenner and Lulu Yilun Chen, *China's Biggest Internet Company Wants to Use Its HQ as a Giant Testing Lab*. Published at Bloomberg, August 2016. Available at https://www.bloomberg.com/news/articles/2016-08-30/tencent-china-s-biggest-internet-company-wants-to-use-its-headquarters-as-a-testing-lab

61   ibid

62   Lulu Yilun Chen, *Tencent Now China's Top Company in Private Economy Triumph*. Published at Bloomberg, September 2016. Available at https://www.bloomberg.com/news/articles/2016-09-05/tencent-becomes-china-s-top-company-in-private-economy-triumph

and no doubt you've run out of breath reading that. Yet, there's even more it does. It partners with startups and innovators to bring its services to the public. Realistically, people in China just use WeChat all day.

Tencent also owns well-known gaming companies like Epic Games and Riot Games and is investing in movie-making and anime in a big way. In fact, many commentators believe its strategy is to become something like a Disney. While it's clear that WeChat is behind Facebook in terms of revenue, it's certainly ahead of Facebook in all the things you can do through it. I believe it moves faster in its development because it partners with startups and innovators in a way that Facebook doesn't always seem to. In other words, the general philosophy is somewhat more collaborative. This shows us the value of a collaborative approach when it comes to African innovation.

In the case of Tencent, it also does this through QQ Music, the only music streaming service that is claiming profitability (others continue to run at a loss). QQ Music doesn't just provide music streaming but also sells concert tickets, exclusive song downloads, books cabs to a concert, and so on. Of course, it helps that Tencent has a massive negotiating ability with record labels in terms of royalties, and it helps that QQ Music can be found on WeChat—meaning, you can bring the two experiences together.

WeChat has been active in South Africa for a few years and is ramping up its efforts in a bid to rival WhatsApp across Africa. It has a long way to go with six million registered South African users to date, while WhatsApp enjoys 14 million South African users, but it has a unique product and its strategy is certainly an interesting one. One of the ways in which it plans to do this is through a partnership with Naspers, Africa's largest media company. Naspers owns MultiChoice, SuperSport, DStv, Showmax, MWEB, Media24, OLX, PayU, Avito, and other brands you probably know. Naspers also has a 34 percent stake in Tencent and, with its serious media clout, is continually introducing WeChat to the market in diverse and subtle ways.

This sort of partnership should make us understand that Tencent certainly has its eye on Africa. As we have noted above, WeChat offers additional services through the platform, and it does so through partnership with innovators and startups. In Africa, therefore, it's looking towards what Africans need and providing such services through the platform, and encouraging local innovators to start and run those services. For example, you could pay for prepaid electricity or airtime through the platform, and conduct money transfers. It has extensive experience in providing services that people with a lower income need and use, unlike Silicon Valley which sometimes focuses on services that make sense in its Western, upmarket context. As Claire van der Heever writes in The Huffington Post:

> "WeChat's success at home will no doubt be difficult to replicate outside China, but much of its experience in a developing market with no revenue model can be applied to Africa, too. When Tencent launched its original instant messaging service QQ in 1998, just 0.2 percent of China's population were Internet users, according to World Bank data. Today, digital banking, investing and lending have gone mainstream in China, with millions of consumers skipping straight from cash to mobile finance. The African market shows similar potential."[63]

In line with this strategy, WeChat/Tencent recently launched a $3.5 million venture capital fund, which it will use to invest in companies that offer services through the app in Africa. Money For Jam (M4JAM) is one such service. This is a 'micro-jobbing platform' that allows employers to pay employees through the app. (In other words, it connects casual, part-time workers with employers needing quick access to staff with very little notice). In addition to payments, it allows for real-time instant messaging communication between the employee and employer, has a referral system ('refer to earn' incentivises jobbers to invite their friends) and provides data to businesses about employees, what's going on in the market, and other insights. More than that it opens up a platform for learning and even provides market research (it connects brands with its workforce, letting that workforce test out the brand and provide

---

63   Claire van den Heever, *Move Over Facebook: WeChat Is Set to Become the Only App African Internet Users Need.* Published at Huffington Post. Available at http://www.huffingtonpost.com/claire-van-den-heever/wechat-africa-facebook_b_9149794.html

feedback). It's a pretty smart app and sits in a line of similar apps that will, and are, disrupting the human resources space.

Obviously, as smartphones continue to become such a core part of African life—in a 2016 study, Deloitte claims that smartphones are not just 'a part' of life in Africa, but 'are our lives'[64] — Tencent wants a part of all that action. Most Africans have their 'first internet experience'[65] through the mobile phone, says Brett Loubser, head of WeChat Africa:

"They've missed the entire desktop, PC, laptop, whatever thing, and because of that, I think we're seeing innovation come out of Africa from a mobile perspective that is just leagues ahead of anywhere else on earth really."

Interestingly, Standard Bank has also partnered with WeChat. And in case you didn't know, Standard Bank is partly owned by China's ICBC bank. Standard Bank's addition to the service is it is providing a digital wallet through WeChat, and it uses WeChat for an Instant Messaging service that customers can use 24/7 to get hold of the bank. The partnership with Standard Bank also allows for WeChat to piggyback off of SnapScan—a QR code payment solution — which now integrates with WeChat Wallet payments.

In Ghana and Nigeria, where WeChat is expanding, it's also including start-ups such as an online shopping service (Traclist) and another job service, Jobberman. According again to Loubser, WeChat's aim is to localise and not just provide the same services that it does in China.

So what is the trend we see here? Interestingly, *partnership with existing African enterprise* — although arguably both Standard Bank and Naspers already *had* a stake in the Chinese market. Nevertheless, it doesn't seem as if straight-on cannibalising is what Tencent wants to do. This fits with what Foreign Minister Wang Yi said in 2015: "We want to replace the old practice of 'going it alone' and reject the old mentality of

---

64   See Deloitte's survey, *Game of Phones – Africa Mobile Consumer Survey* 2016, available at http://www.deloitteblog.co.za/game-of-phones-africa-mobile-consumer-survey-2016/
65   See Pew Research Center, *Cell Phones in Africa: Communication Lifeline*. Available at http://www.pewglobal.org/2015/04/15/cell-phones-in-africa-communication-lifeline/

'the winner takes all.'" It wants "partnership rather than alliance" he continued to reiterate. While his comments were mostly directed to the U.S.'s military strategy, it's interesting to note that China's open source model, illustrated in the *shanzai* model and encouraged in cities like Shenzhen, appears to mean that when its silicon valleys look at Africa, it sees things differently.

However, the converse is that this policy has often made it difficult to protect intellectual property—meaning, as China has done in the past, it copies what other innovators are doing, innovates on it, and then sells it. Whether this is a good thing or a bad thing will depend on your point of view, and it'll also take some time to see the long-term result.

ALIBABA

As of April 2016, Alibaba became the world's largest retailer, surpassing Walmart, and is one of the world's largest Internet companies. It ships upwards from 12 million packages a day — which, by the way, overshadows Amazon's 3 million packages a day. In 2014, Alibaba processed 278 million orders on its "Singles Day", a shopping holiday it created itself in China; while in that same year, Amazon processed 37 million orders on Cyber Monday, the American online shopping holiday that follows the traditional Black Friday day of sales.[66]

Alibaba controls about 80 percent of the Chinese market — and its customer base is much larger than Amazon when you compare China's population to the U.S. It generates more gross merchandise volume (GMV) than Amazon.com and eBay combined — and in 2015 its online sales and profits surpassed U.S. e-retailers combined. When it launched its IPO (initial public offering) in the U.S. in 2014, its IPO was priced at US $68, raising US$21.8 billion for the company and its investors. It was a record-breaking IPO and is considered the biggest in the world.

In addition to its retail services, which extend beyond Alibaba. com, it has an online payment processing division, which controls 51 percent of the Chinese market and is in 2,000 European locations.[67] Its

---

66   Catherine Clifford, *By the Numbers: Amazon vs. Alibaba (Infographic)*. Published at Entrepreneur Magazine, July 2015. Available at https://www.entrepreneur.com/article/248345

67   The Sovereign Investor, *Bigger Than Amazon?* Published at Value Walk, April 2017.

cloud division, Aliyun, has been very successful in recent years and is a big part of its phenomenal growth. It has also been investing in Youku Tudou (a YouTube-like company), Meizu, a smartphone manufacturer, and even shopping malls.[68] The latter is incredibly interesting. While the likes of Silicon Valley tend to focus on new technologies, Alibaba has been snapping up traditional kinds of businesses—an appliance and logistics company (Haier) and a film and TV studio (ChinaVision), as some examples. It also has a messaging app, Tango. Furthermore, it is looking towards playing more in the financial services space, especially as the Chinese government begins to de-regulate such industries. Given Amazon's foray into this space, it is sure that Jack Ma, Alibaba's founder, will be thinking the same.

Jack Ma himself is an upbeat, visionary character, and the Alibaba story a very interesting one. In fact, it correlates closely with Jeff Bezos, in that Ma saw the phenomenal potential of the Internet much before many others. He has never claimed to be a tech guy, saying that he sees "technology with the eyes of customers, normal people's eyes." This has been key to the success of Alibaba.

In 1995, Ma visited Seattle and a friend showed him the Internet. He was impressed. Of all things, he wanted to find out more about beer, so he searched for it on Yahoo and was almost shocked to find there was nothing about beer in China. Well, that gave him an idea. He got back home and borrowed $2000 to set up China Pages, China's first Internet company.

But unfortunately it was too early for China at the time, and the government couldn't really get on board. It would take four years of slogging and reworking the model until, in 1999, and with the help of friends, he launched Alibaba.com.

"I gathered eighteen people in my apartment and spoke to them for two hours about my vision," he told Inc.com.[69] "Everyone put their money on the table, and that got us $60,000 to start Alibaba. I wanted

Available at http://www.valuewalk.com/2017/04/amazon-vs-alibaba-stock/

68   Richard Macauley, *Alibaba vs. Amazon: How the world's two online shopping giants stack up*. Published at Quartz, November 2015. Available at https://qz.com/545687/alibaba-vs-amazon-how-the-worlds-two-online-shopping-giants-stack-up/

69   *How I Did It: Jack Ma, Alibaba.com*. As told to Rebecca Fannin. Published at Inc. Available at https://www.inc.com/magazine/20080101/how-i-did-it-jack-ma-alibaba.html

to have a global company, so I chose a global name. Alibaba is easy to spell, and people everywhere associate that with 'Open, Sesame,' the command that Ali Baba used to open doors to hidden treasures in One Thousand and One Nights."

Even though Ma says they had no money, technology, or even a plan, the time was right as the platform filled a serious void. He went on a tour to get businesses on board and also find investment. He found the latter in Goldman Sachs and Softbank. The first five years were hard work, but it finally started earning revenue.

The big challenge then was to take down eBay in the country, which at the time completely dominated the Chinese online market space. After launching a consumer-to-consumer site in the similar vein (Taobao), Alibaba was on its way to achieving its objective. Ma had the confidence that they knew the Chinese market better than eBay, and he was right. It was all part of Ma's philosophy that he regularly reiterates: "Global vision, local win."

I want to stay on this last point for a few beats because it's important. Who knows the African market better? America? China? Or Africa? Obviously, Africa. In Alibaba's case, it even came down to simple design aspects. Western people prefer clean interfaces, while the Chinese like emojis and a lot going on. Alibaba capitalised on this while eBay had just gone for the same design as it uses in the West. This simple element had most Chinese flock to Taobao when they launched it.

I wonder what Africans prefer? How much research has gone into that? A quick glance down any typical African street should give you a clue. Sometimes I think that because these other regions have the technology and the money, we think that makes them more able to speak to our market, and smarter with things like design. But that might not actually be the case. We see this in many industries, in fact. I've noticed that international writers tend to get more credit here than many of our local writers — even though these writers have never even been here. I've noticed this with innovators as well; we find that any innovator who comes to our shores because they see an opportunity tends to have to work less hard yet get more credit than a home-grown innovator. This kind of thinking must be challenged. And it's actually not like we don't have the technology. We do. And we have the innovators. What we don't perhaps have is the investment — but quite honestly, we do have the money to invest.

Jack Ma regularly speaks about small business and has a real passion for seeing small business grow. He sees the platforms he creates as tools businesses can use. Speaking to CNBC and New York Times columnist Andre Ross Sorkin at the World Economic Forum in early 2017, here's how he compares Alibaba to Amazon:

> "The difference between Amazon and us is Amazon is more like an empire — everything they control themselves, buy and sell. Our philosophy is that we want to be an ecosystem. Our philosophy is to empower others to sell, empower others to service, making sure the other people are more powerful than us. With our technology, our innovation, our partners — 10 million small business sellers — they can compete with Microsoft and IBM. Our philosophy is, using Internet technology we can make every company become Amazon.
>
> "To hire people to deliver for us, we need five million people, to deliver the things we sold. How can we hire five million people? The only way we can do it is to empower the service companies, the logistics companies. Make sure they are efficient. Making sure that they make the money. Making sure they can hire more people.
>
> "The world can never have one model. If the world has only one correct model, the world is too boring. The people who use the model should believe in the model. I believe in what I do.[70]"

Note carefully what he said above: "we want to be an ecosystem." This comes back to the point of collaboration and connecting. It is what we need to be thinking of as Africans.

It remains to be seen, under this sort of thinking, how disruption from China will come — although it's clear that it will. But besides that, there are lessons we can learn and apply here, and similar themes that keep coming up again and again.

---

70   Anita Balakrishnan, *Jack Ma explains the difference between Alibaba and Amazon: 'Amazon is more like an empire'*. Published at CNBC, January 2017. Available at http://www. cnbc.com/2017/01/18/jack-ma-difference-between-alibaba-and-amazon.html

HUAWEI

The days of *shanzhai* may be coming to a close as these manufacturers begin to become leading innovators in themselves. Eight of the world's top ten smartphone brands now come from China. Huawei is one of them. When Ren Zhengfei, an ex-military officer, formed the company in 1987, it sold telephone exchange equipment (PABX systems) from Hong Kong. Now it is a worldwide conglomerate and in many cases a worldwide phenomenon. Based in Shenzhen, it is quickly closing the gap in its sales when you compare it to Samsung and Apple. In the latter half of 2016, it managed to overtake Samsung as the world's most profitable Android device company, making it the second most profitable phone company in the world. It wants to hit Apple next.[71]

This may have been partly due to Samsung's complete crisis with the Note 7, which was even banned from plane flights, but it is also helped considerably by Huawei's increasing acceptance in the European market. Earlier in 2016, Huawei held an 8.3 percent market share[72] for smartphones — risen to such a prominent position in the phone space in just over five years. (By the way, in the same year, Chinese upstarts Vivo and Oppo also enjoyed huge success, while Apple and Samsung suffered a particularly bad year).

Huawei is an example of a company that has long moved on from being some sort of copycat brand to producing quality, innovative products that are challenging the perception of "made in China" itself. It has a strong core of Enterprise products for most industries. At the time of writing, the company also announced that it would begin to manufacture laptops. Europe has taken incredibly well to it, thanks to key partnerships like the one it established with Leica, a prominent German photography company.

---

71   Ben Sin, *Huawei Has Achieved Its Goal Of Overtaking Samsung (For Now), But Apple's Still Far Ahead*. Published at Forbes, November 2016. Available at https://www.forbes.com/sites/bensin/2016/11/25/huawei-has-achieved-its-goal-of-overtaking-samsung-for-now-but-apples-still-far-ahead/#5cd0228a5cd0

72   Wade Shepard, *China's Huawei 'Growing Up' To Become The World's No. 1 Smartphone Brand*. Published at Forbes, May 2016. Available at https://www.forbes.com/sites/wadeshepard/2016/05/25/chinas-huawei-growing-up-to-become-the-worlds-number-one-smartphone-brand/#329e71a13adf

And the perception of Huawei's devices in the African market is changing quickly, too.

In the background, away from most consumer eyes, Huawei has been earning respect as each year goes by. For example, in November 2016, Finnish telecommunications provider, Elisa, sent data through its network at a rate of 1.9 gigabits per second — a complete world first. This speed makes it possible for virtual reality to be streamed without so much as a glitch. Who was behind the test network? Huawei[73]. I suppose this is no surprise given that many of the patents and technologies for 5G—which is expected to roll out in 2020 — are owned by Huawei as well. 5G is expected to hit up to 10gbps, or if you believe the more enthusiastic reports, 30gbps. This kind of work in the background makes it no wonder that Robert Scoble, world-renowned futurist and technology blogger said, "The Chinese are coming and this is the company that is positioned the best to become the world mobile brand that most people around the world use and that everyone looks up to.[74]"

It's not just innovating when it comes to technology, however, but is trying something new with the way the company is managed itself. About 98.6 percent of the company is employee-owned, with only 1.4 percent owned by founder Ren Zhengfei himself.[75] It rotates CEO's every six months, under a democratic voting process that includes all of its 82,000 plus employees. These employees select 51 shareholder representatives and nine alternate representatives. These 60 representatives then select candidates for the standing committee. The selected candidates must then deliver a speech to the 60 shareholder representatives, who will then vote.[76]"

But why do this? Just in the name of trying something new? The reasons are very interesting. Zhengfei, firstly, believes that if a company

---

73   Scott Cendrowsi, *Is the World Big Enough for Huawei?* Published at FORTUNE. Available at http://fortune.com/huawei-china-smartphone/

74   Travis Wright, *How Chinese Company, Huawei, is Setting Itself Up to Take Over the Tech World.* Published at Inc. Available at https://www.inc.com/travis-wright/why-huawei-is-setting-itself-up-to-take-over-the-tech-world.html

75   ibid

76   David De Cremer and Tian Tao, *Leadership Innovation: Huawei's rotating CEO System.* Published at European Business Review, November 2015. Available at http://www.europeanbusinessreview.com/leadership-innovation-huaweis-rotating-ceo-system/

only has one CEO for a long time and that CEO passes away, the company is pretty clueless about its business direction—at least for awhile. He has a point. Look at Apple. It is clearly wavering with its visionary leader, Steve Jobs, no longer at the helm. Under Huawei's system, however, the vision and values of the company and the CEO exist somewhat separately. The CEO performs a function for a time, but overall the company does not exist to serve his vision, but rather a bigger vision.

This insight apparently comes from two stories from the animal kingdom. The first involves buffalos, who follow their chief buffalo anywhere and everywhere — but if he dies, the herd dies as well, as it lacks any form of direction. This, therefore, represents the traditional style of leadership involving one visionary leader who gives direction.

The second story involves how ducks fly in a "V" formation, with the leader of the group changing regularly, giving each space to rest. Given this idea of the vision and values being more important, in a way, than the CEO, Huawei plans in spans of decades—20 years at a time.[77] As reported in the Harvard Business Review:

> Ren Zhengfei is known for avoiding quick decisions and forcing himself to take time to reflect. His company reflects these traits. Again, he ties this in part back to their ownership structure: it keeps the decision-making power under company control – no outside investor will gain relative control over Huawei. As we've seen, they have much more freedom and less pressure from the market to consider their next steps to take.[78]

The vision and values are further entrenched through the Huawei University, where people are trained on how the company conducts business and how it values its customers, and through a value training camp for all new employees. One of its main values is what it calls "the power of

---

77   Travis Wright, *How Chinese Company, Huawei, is Setting Itself Up to Take Over the Tech World*. Published at Inc. Available at https://www.inc.com/travis-wright/why-huawei-is-setting-itself-up-to-take-over-the-tech-world.html

78   David de Cremer and Tian Tao, *Huawei's Culture is the Key to Its success*. Published at Harvard Business Review, June 2015. Available at https://hbr.org/2015/06/huaweis-culture-is-the-key-to-its-success

thinking." It continues to reiterate that the most valuable power to have is the power to think. Intellectual exchange, therefore, is formally encouraged. Ideas are communicated to every employee, and frequently — and feedback is highly encouraged.

Huawei has also been emphatic that electricity and the Internet are basic human rights, and are thus involved in much of our telecommunications infrastructure even in Africa—often in providing equipment in the background, as noted above. In fact, it seems Huawei's strategy is frequently to sit in the background, as illustrated in 2015 when it announced an operating system it has been developing that will work with Internet-connected objects; in effect, its strategy to get in on the Internet of Things game. When asked if Huawei would also look to manufacture products and connected devices, in addition to its phones, William Xu, global head of strategy and marketing, said "We want to provide the connections, not the devices.[79]"

However, after all this, it's difficult to understand or grasp how Huawei might be looking at Africa, and what its plans for our region might be. But we can learn some lessons from its innovative management style, and think about African culture in relation to it. As Africans, we've always been more about the community than the individual, and the philosophical concept of Ubuntu — that a person is not a person without the other — pervades. We needn't feel that this is a weak culture for fostering and brewing leaders. Indeed, our best leaders like Nelson Mandela have shown the strength of our cultural approach. In many ways, I think, we look at leadership styles in sharply individualistic cultures like Europe and America and wonder why it is we can't seem to generate leaders like Steve Jobs and Mark Zuckerberg and the likes. For some reason, we think that makes us second-rate — or it makes our leaders second-rate. But Apple, as mentioned above, is already flailing. And what will happen to Facebook when Zuckerberg moves on?

While individualism surely helps to generate strong leaders, there's always a question of sustainability — that too much rides on single leaders, and that community flounders and vision vanishes when those

---

79   *Hauwei Launches 'Internet of Things' Operating System*, published at Financial Times. Available at https://www.ft.com/content/240ef87e-fea8-11e4-8efb-00144feabdc0

leaders are taken out. I think we can do better if we look at the strengths of who we are and think about leadership and entrepreneurship in our context more seriously. I'm not saying we need to adopt Huawei's six-month CEO rotation programme, although it might be worth some organisation's doing that. I'm just trying to help us think a little through how we approach entrepreneurship here and consider if we aren't trying to import models from other cultures rather than leaning on the strength of our own.

For as I've shown, innovation boils down to *community* and the *sharing of ideas*. While I believe strongly in visionary leadership, it's obvious that vision does not occur in a vacuum — and that the more we connect, the better we can build.

PART II

"Whether you're a farmer, builder or engineer, the opportunities are equal: Just add a little innovation."

– Strive Masiyiwa

CHAPTER TWELVE

✕

AFRICAN INNOVATION LESSONS

Since 2006, I've had the immense privilege of travelling all over Africa and it's our innovation that continues to inspire and impress me. It's amazing to see how we are actually disrupting traditional views of innovation, leapfrogging traditional infrastructure, and forming new stories for the continent. We are starting to quantify Africa Rising — we're starting to make sense of it — and if we continue in this way, we can build an incredible future.

But I worry that we haven't left it too late, or, that all of our efforts will be sabotaged in a way with Silicon Valley coming in. The Africa Rising narrative is, as far as I'm concerned, an amazing movement, a feeling we have as Africans, a grass-roots understanding between us. But we have to see Africa rising on its own terms. We cannot just assume the traditional views of development are exactly how we should develop as nations, especially in today's highly technological world and context. African innovation is actually, truly and tangibly changing lives.

In the next few chapters, I want to highlight some of the touch points of innovation in Africa, which I believe provide valuable lessons in taking on Silicon Valley. I cannot be exhaustive, of course, and anyone who knows about African innovation may feel I am skimming over important and exciting examples, such as Kenya. In my previous book, however, I wrote a great deal about Kenya and its huge success as an innovator in

Africa, and much has been written about its "Silicon Savannah", as the country builds a multi-million dollar infrastructure that will foster its emerging tech startups. I do not want to repeat myself or what others have said here in this book, as the information on Kenya is extensive and easily available. Rather, I would like to make some new points around the topic of an African Silicon Valley and African innovation and draw out the important lessons that will help us form a workable strategy.

One of the reasons why we don't look at African innovation in the same way we look at Silicon Valley or China is because much of our innovation is happening in very disparate locations across Africa. While each has been successful in their own contexts, outside of their area of influence, the rest of us don't really know about them. Yet when you put them together, something exciting emerges and you begin to see how we can really put it together. Central to it all if this is the very real possibility for new eco-systems, new infrastructure, and a matured Africa. As I've highlighted in the previous chapters, eco-systems are key. It's what Google wants to do: create a new, connected eco-system. It's what Facebook wants to do. It's what Alibaba wants to do. In many ways, these innovators have all done it, but they want to do it all the more, and they want to continue to do it *here*. And nowhere is it illustrated better than in the realm of the "Internet of Things" and the rush of innovators all over the world to get in on that game.

INTEGRATING INNOVATIONS

To illustrate how our innovations can form new ecosystems, let's look at several innovations working together in a way that enhances people's lives. M-Kopa Solar essentially sells pay-as-you-go solar power—a solar panel with a prepaid meter. People who live in rural areas far away from traditional power infrastructure can pay a deposit for the solar panel and then pay as they use it every day, through micro-payments with the M-Pesa mobile phone payment system. The pay-as-you-go price for the solar system is less than what it costs to buy fuel for a kerosene lamp, which is what most people would use (and has potential health and safety dangers). Then, once the solar panel is paid for—which usually takes a year—users enjoy free electricity.

But M-Kopa is also developing interesting solar products that con-sumers can access once they have a proven track record in payments, in-cluding a LED Flat Screen solar TV (that has a two-year warranty) – and they're looking into developing solar ovens as well.

Now when you start thinking in the lines of integrating innovations – having them work off each other in an ecosystem – and start looking at other innovations, you begin to be amazed at how so much can change. In my last book, I wrote about Grandma Nojongile ("Gogo") who was blind and received surgery using the Vula App, developed by Dr William Mapham in South Africa, which helps health workers in rural areas detect cataracts and communicate with a specialist. Cataract surgery is a simple 20-minute routine, but rural people don't have access to it. Using the Vula App, however, the specialist can diagnose the problem and book Gogo in for appropriate surgery in a nearby city.

However, this all might be too expensive for her—even with her trips to the city cut to only one. Perhaps it would be helpful if she could have health insurance. MicroEnsure from Kenya, a sort-of pay-as-you-go in-surance, is able to fill such a gap. For most poor people, insurance is a risk and doesn't really make sense because if nothing goes wrong, the money seems wasted. However, most Africans see tremendous value in buying airtime, and they see the value in being able to transfer money to others through digital payments services. So, put it all together. If you could sign up with certain digital payments services partners, you can receive health insurance that increases and accumulates off the back of the amount of airtime you use. This is already what MicroEnsure does.

Now, on her way to the clinic (a one-time trip rather than several), Gogo calls family, friends and health practitioners. The more calls she makes the more free health cover she gets using MicroEnsure's insur-ance cover on the back of airtime spend. When she gets to the doctor for her op she's covered. The doctor prescribes medicine that she gets on the way home. She's got good reason to be concerned about counter-feit medicine, which is often ineffective or even deadly. But with Sproxil, the brainchild of Ghanaian, Ashifi Gogo, you simply SMS a unique code (for free) hidden on the packaging to a number and they SMS back and confirm whether it's genuine.

Then, when she gets home, her solar panel has been charging all day – providing her with electricity for lighting, heating, and a bit of T.V. for relaxation. And the question is, how much do you think this would all cost her? When I worked it out, just above 40 U.S. cents, depending on her electricity usage. The other services are free.

That showcases just five innovations currently out there that can work together. This isn't far-fetched. These innovations already exist and are enjoying success. The true strength of innovation is what it solves. Here Gogo has a brand new lease on life without having to move to a city (thereby even curbing our urban migration issues).

There are challenges to innovation, of course – budgets, thought patterns, and even the very definition of 'innovation' itself. Instead of all these innovations working in a vacuum, they need to come together. I see no reason for one of these innovations to try and do it all — rather, partnership is key. But for partnership to happen, there must be an environment where our innovators themselves are put together. There needs to be a culture of open-source, a culture of collaboration. And there needs to be a culture of active *support*. Any venture capital firm worth its salt ought to realise that we're on the cusp of something important here – all we need are innovators, investors, and entrepreneurs coming together to put it in workable ecosystems.

What we need, therefore, are eyes to *see* and the creativity to put our innovations together. What we need to do is create environments where we do this. What we need to do is see entrepreneurship and innovation differently. And what we need to do is know the new African story intimately.

THE RISE OF THE AFRICAN CONSUMER

When McKinsey released its "Rise of the African Consumer" report in 2012, it became the talk of the town. "By now, most investors and businesses know about the tremendous potential of Africa — the world's second-fastest-growing region, topped only by emerging Asia," stated the report summary. "But it may come as a surprise that Africa's growth is fuelled not by resources but rather by a rising consumer market.[80]"

---

80   McKinsey, *The Rise of the African Consumer* (2012). Available at http://www.mckinsey. com/industries/retail/our-insights/the-rise-of-the-african-consumer

Consumer-facing industries, according to McKinsey, were predicted to grow to USD $400 billion—becoming the single-largest business opportunity by 2020. Five categories of consumption were highlighted as the main players: apparel, financial services, groceries, the Internet, and telecommunications.

> "Several factors are shaping this new consuming class. Africa's population, the fastest growing and youngest in the world, is concentrated in urban areas. This new class of consumer has a smaller family, is better educated and higher earning, and is digitally savvy. Africans are exceptionally optimistic about their economic future: 84 percent say they will be better off in two years."

Africans being 'digitally savvy' is something I want to focus on. In addition to that, notice how most of these industries mentioned above are the exact industries our Silicon Valley big boys, and to a lesser degree our China big boys, have an eye on. Facebook and Google are definitely finding new ways to own telecommunications, and Huawei already has a big stake in the market as it currently stands. Microsoft, who we haven't covered in detail, has been investing in "white spaces" technology for Africa. This refers to using unused radio broadcasting frequencies to deliver Wi-Fi. It's a fascinating technology that can provide 4G speeds and be broadcast up to 10 kilometres. As reported by TechRepublic:

> "Google and Microsoft are already chasing the emerging White Space market in Africa, where only 16 percent of the population is online. Because the waves can travel up to 10 kilometers in radius, it is great for remote, off-the-grid villages. Google and Microsoft have also invested in White Space technology in developing countries. Google recently launched a program in 10 schools in Cape Town, South Africa. Microsoft's 4Afrika initiative is focusing on White Space technology throughout the continent, hoping to bring millions of people online, and has projects in place in Tanzania and South Africa.[81]"

---

81   Lyndsey Gilpin, *White Space, the next internet disruption: 10 things to know.* Published at TechRepublic, March 2014. Available at http://www.techrepublic.com/article/white-space-the-next-internet-disruption-10-things-to-know/

Google could come into the financial services industry easily, at least if my predictions are right. Moreso, Tencent already has the kind of technology and know-how to upset our industry on that front. Groceries, or at least retail, have Amazon and Alibaba knocking at the door. And, of course, the Internet is owned by pretty much all of them. The only industry that may be left alone, at least for now, is apparel. But let's not forget how Google's new gesture-sensing fabric could provide some unseen upsets or the beginning of some unexpected plan. This is all only some of what we know because—as I stated earlier—often the big boys surprise us with something they have been working on under the radar, and then before we realise it they have cannibalised whole industries.

Perhaps at this point, you may be wondering why I have not included Microsoft as part of the 'big boys' of Silicon Valley coming to town? The reason is that, by and large, Microsoft's strategy appears to line up with what I am advocating: partnership. Rather that coming to cannibalise, it seems Microsoft is wanting to find better ways of collaborating and partnering. For example, its White Space Innovation has launched commercially in partnership with local firms in Ghana, South Africa and Kenya. Its 4Afrika initiative has brought 500,000 SME's online, upskilled almost 800,000 Africans and helped 82 local start-ups to grow their own ventures.

Here's another example from Ethiopia. Microsoft 4Afrika supported the Tulane Health project, which helped 3,000 healthcare clinics in ten regions to digitally transform. With Windows devices, Tulane collects relevant health data and now stores over 150 million digital records. Using Power BI, Tulane then analyses this data and produces real-time insights, empowering the federal ministry to make data-driven decisions. As per Amrote Abdella, 4Afrika Regional Director, "For the average patient, this means more informed consultations, a more accountable government and overall better quality healthcare. In addition, 2,500 new Ethiopians have also been trained and upskilled as health information technologists, to run and maintain the system locally.[82]" Microsoft seems to have a solid understanding of how technology will transform Africa, and so it is investing and helping to incubate startups, transferring full ownership of

---

82   See https://www.microsoft.com/africa/4afrika/technology-gamechanger.aspx

hubs it sets up to local organisations.[83] A core part of the 4Afrika project is to actively promote Africentric technologies, and not just bring Silicon Valley technologies here.

THE RISE OF THE MOBILE PHONE

Our consumer story sits back to back with our mobile phone story — which is the principle driver behind much of the positive reporting and data. It's also what drives the idea that technology is where Africa's future lies, and where investors should be looking. And no doubt it's one of the main reasons our "big boys" are coming to town in the first place, and why they're spending so much effort to try and get us online.

In my book *Disrupting Africa: The Rise and Rise of African Innovation*, I went into considerable detail outlining the stats and reasons for the explosion of the mobile phone market in Africa. It truly is unprecedented. And the fact is, it still has a long way to go—meaning, it is a market full of potential. I don't want to repeat myself here and devote many more pages to it, but at this point, it would be a good idea to bring some of my previous points up to date, even though my previous book was published just over a year ago from this one (technology moves quickly!). Plus, I would like to look at this from a more consumer point of view.

Ovum, a market analyst firm, expects mobile broadband connections to rise 76 percent by 2020, from 147 million in 2014.[84] Africa has an 80 percent mobile penetration rate, compared to an 18 percent Internet penetration rate. In many cases, there are as many (or more) mobile phones than adults — subscriptions in Kenya grew from 330,000 in 2001 to 38 million in 2016, where the total population is 45 million. The big success story there and throughout many African nations is M-Pesa. M-Pesa is well known these days, but for those that don't know, it basically allows you to purchase items or send and receive money using your mobile phone, without the need for a bank account. Seven in ten adults

---

83 See https://www.microsoft.com/africa/4afrika/Microsoft-4Afrika-hands-IPHub-COMESA-World-IPDay.aspx

84 Murithi Mutiga and Zoe Flood, *Africa calling: mobile phone revolution to transform democracies*. Published at the Guardian, August 2016. Available at https://www.theguardian.com/world/2016/aug/08/africa-calling-mobile-phone-broadband-revolution-transform-democracies

use M-Pesa in Kenya, with 9 million transactions happening on the platform every day. It's a key driver for financial inclusion and is one of the innovations helping Africans to leapfrog traditional modes of infrastructure and industry.

Speaking about their own report highlighting the mobile trends in Africa, Frost & Sullivan's Joanita Roos says the introduction of affordable smartphones is changing the game — especially smartphones specifically designed for the African market. "This uptrend reflects the gradual change in consumer habits, as they gain their first Internet experience through a mobile device," she says. "For example, the large unbanked population and rural environment in the region is fuelling the use of mobile financial services. As a result, manufacturers are creating sustainable business models to leverage broadband in the mobile financial services market.[85]"

Deloitte's 2016 study entitled "A Game of Phones" goes a little deeper to show just how much mobile phones has become a part of our lives in Africa, coining a headline that reads, "Smartphones are not just part of our lives, they are our lives." It continues in the report:

> "The African market has seen significant growth in social media as well as local information and news services. Similar to global trends, consumer attachment to mobile devices is high across all markets surveyed. The ritual of checking the phone as one of the first and last things of the day appears to be collective across the markets. More than half of consumers across the region check their phones within 5 minutes after waking up and before going to bed."

Interestingly, Chinese mobile brands dominate the market in some areas. Infinix, Innjoo, Tecno, Samsung and Yezz are top brands for Nigeria's Jumia retailer. Infinix continues to be Jumia's top smartphone brand across all of its fifteen markets.[86] But this does not mean to say that

---

85   *Why Africa Mobile Phone Penetration Rising TO 79%* by 2020 is Good News, Published by AMGOO, April 2015. Available at http://www.amgoo.com/blog/why-africa-mobile-phone-penetration-rising-to-79-by-2020-is-good-news

86   *The Rise and Rise of Mobile in Africa*, published by IT-Online, April 2017. Available at https://it-online.co.za/2017/04/24/the-rise-and-rise-of-mobile-in-africa/

African consumers are not brand conscious. If a brand speaks to us in the right way, we can be extremely loyal. According to McKinsey's aforementioned report, about 35 percent of Sub-Saharan Africans are willing to try new products and services — meaning there is both opportunity here for innovators to get a new market and, if they do things right, to also keep them. Just like Apple did in America. In fact, Sub-Saharan Africans are more willing to support a local brand than North Africans. But, as would seem obvious, price is a key point — much like it is in China. As stated by Cobus Rossouw, Imperial Logistics chief business development officer:

> "One of the stories that's commonly touted by media and manufacturer alike is that Africans are not brand conscious. It is absolutely not true. They are conscious spenders who would rather hand over money for something that they trust, because they cannot afford to make a mistake. When you have a lot of disposable income, buying the wrong product or brand isn't that big a deal, but when you have only a small margin of cash, you buy something you know and that you believe in.[87]"

All of this shows how we are becoming more aware of brands and our needs are changing, as well as receptivity as Africans to technology and how technology is shaping us. Local innovation in technology is influencing just about all of our sectors, including energy, agriculture, entertainment, transport, finances, and more. We are fast becoming an app nation—M-Pesa being the biggest example, but certainly not the only one, as you will see in the forthcoming chapters. No matter from what angle you look at it, Africa is on the cusp of a technological revolution just like every other nation on earth. Professor Klaus Schwab, founder and chairman of the World Economic Forum, says this revolution will fundamentally alter the way we live, work, and relate to one another. "In its scale, scope, and complexity, the transformation will be unlike anything humankind has experienced before. We do not yet know just how

---

87   Tamsin Oxford, *The myth of the African consumer*. Published at Mail & Guardian, August 2015. Available at https://mg.co.za/article/2015-08-28-00-the-myth-of-the-african-consumer

it will unfold, but one thing is clear: the response to it must be integrated and comprehensive, involving all stakeholders of the global polity, from the public and private sectors to academia and civil society," he says.[88] It already is and has been fundamentally changing how we live, work, and relate to one another — and, as Africans, we need to be guiding this process. As Erik Brynjolfsson and Andrew McAfee, two world-renowned economists have stated, this technological revolution could yield greater inequality since it tends to disrupt labour markets immensely. But this also has positive impact by creating safer jobs.[89]

TAKING OUR SPOT AT THE TABLE

It's time we took our spot at the global table. We cannot afford to let the likes of Silicon Valley or China come in and disrupt our continent without us being a part of this disruption and guiding it, and ultimately taking them on. The Internet of Things disruption is coming to Africa, but we want to see it come in an African way. Consider the differences between these two scenarios, both relevant for Africans but one for up-market city individuals and the other for most of Africans today:

1. You're driving and it's raining. Mobile data and your maps app, along with sensors in the road, warn your car about the wet road and traffic ahead, and your car automatically slows down.
2. You get home and your car connects to WiFi. Your radio starts downloading the newly released album from your favourite group.
3. Your fridge noticed you were out of milk and has ordered for you. The delivery is waiting at your front door.
4. You have a relative with a pacemaker. It noticed they were having difficulties and automatically alerted the hospital which dispatched an ambulance. You've been receiving messages all day from their health insurance telling you about their progress.

---

88   Klaus Schwab, *The Fourth Industrial Revolution: what it means, how to respond.* Published at the World Economic Forum's website, January 2016. Available at https://www.weforum.org/agenda/2016/01/the-fourth-industrial-revolution-what-it-means-and-how-to-respond/
89   ibid

That's a first-world Internet of Things vision that Silicon Valley is working hard to achieve, and within it, many industries will be disrupted, perhaps even cannibalised. But now consider this scenario:

1. You live in a rural village. It's a far drive to see the doctor for a follow-up appointment. You're planning to go on Wednesday but what you don't know is stock at the closest pharmacy of your repeat prescription is depleted.

2. However, thanks to the Internet of Things, you receive an SMS informing you about stock but not to worry because your doctor has prescribed an alternative. And by the way, that will be delivered by drone to your front door tomorrow.

3. Behind the scenes the stock system at the pharmacy noticed stock levels and automatically ordered new stock, sending a message to the pharmacist and your doctor.

Your doctor thus prescribed the alternative and he alerted the system, which alerted the pharmacist. You were then alerted.

4. You then receive an SMS from the bus company, which automatically booked your tickets for your check-up trip to your doctor – you just need to confirm the transaction.

This is, actually, an entirely plausible scenario in today's context and with today's technology. It is innovation by Africans for Africans. Western definitions and measurement tools for progress are limited and ineffective in telling the real story of Africa, or, at best, just not entirely up to the task. If you assume innovation in Africa must look like innovation in Japan, then obviously you're going to draw faulty conclusions. Which is why, I believe, we need to work on our own innovation index and need to have our place at the global table to formulate regulations, figure out privacy laws, and be part of the global conversation on how all of this is measured and what is fair and what is not. We need to be at the global table to talk about how Africa really looks on the ground today, and how it can actually develop.

CULTURAL REVOLUTION

All of this is from a technological point of view, but I also echo sentiments from Funmi Iyanda, Oya media executive director and award-winning broadcaster and journalist, who says we don't just need a digital revolution, but a cultural one too.[90] "A social pan-Africanism existed even before the digital revolution through cross-border trade, but it was often hampered by unimaginative and rigid archaic laws… digital technologies are helping young Africans forge a sense of cultural cohesion that could lead to wider continental integration." I think this is important when we think of how we approach business, entrepreneurship, and even the arts themselves. The fact is that growth in our main industries, including those mentioned above, will undoubtedly happen in large part thanks to our start-ups and the collaborative networks these spring up out of. Every business, these days, is a digital business—or, at least should be one. Even the arts have to re-think what the digital age means. This growth will be further augmented by our own ecosystems, by us putting our innovations together. Our mobile penetration and technological openness show that we do not have to start from the ground up, but only need to foster and nurture what is already happening, here and worldwide. As Tony Blair put it at the World Economic Forum on Africa in Rwanda in 2016:

"Collaboration, openness, the circulation of knowledge, research and information helped found the digital age. They will also be the foundation for further progress today. In Africa, there is a new generation of leadership, which is pushing the continent forward, confident in its future. This optimism has seen them embrace technology, and use it as a force for good. This is right, because if history has taught us anything, it's that pessimists tend to be poor guides to the future.[91]"

---

90   Funmi Iyanda, *Africa doesn't just need a digital revolution – it needs a cultural one, too*. Published at the World Economic Forum's website, April 2016. Available at https://www.weforum.org/agenda/2016/04/africa-doesn-t-just-need-a-digital-revolution-it-needs-a-cultural-one-too

91   Tony Blair, *Why Africa's digital revolution will be powered by partnerships*. Published at the World Economic Forum's website, May 2016. Available at https://www.weforum.org/agenda/2016/05/tony-blair-why-africa-s-digital-revolution-will-be-powered-by-partnerships

IT COMES DOWN TO OUR PEOPLE

This, however, all comes down to the people. A cultural change needs to happen with us. We need to challenge the way we view leadership, entrepreneurship, and innovation. As Fred Swaniker from the Africa Leadership Network continues to say, good leaders do not fall from the sky. We need to be fostering them. We have the brains, we have the passion, we have the character to begin to take on Silicon Valley; to actually partner and collaborate with Silicon Valley in a way that benefits us, in a way where we are bringing our own innovations to the table, and steering Africa in a direction that will be good for us.

I would like to explore this topic further, but first I would like for us to look at certain spots of innovation on our continent — case studies as it were — where we start to see this happening. This can help us start getting to grips with how we need to focus. Thereafter, we can begin to explore how we can really do it — how we can take on Silicon Valley.

"If I have ever seen magic, it has been in Africa."

— **John Hemingway**

✕

AFRICAN INNOVATION CITY

As soon as I touched down at Kigali International Airport, Rwanda, I could feel something phenomenal in the air. Perhaps it was because people kept telling me that Kigali is a truly African city, or perhaps it was the sheer beauty of Rwanda — an African nation with its own, unique African identity. Perhaps it was the smiles and the friendliness of its amazing people. Or perhaps it was the amazing innovation and technology I encountered from touchdown right to where I was going.

I got onto the bus to get into the city centre. I was about to sit down, looked at my phone and noted it spotted a new Wi-Fi network.

"Excuse me," I said to the driver. "Is there Wi-Fi on the bus?"

"Yes," he said to me, smiling. "Free Wi-Fi for everyone."

"Oh, thanks!" I said, sitting down. Well, this was an unexpected surprise. I hopped on board the Wi-Fi and and found it fast and stable.

"There's free Wi-Fi all over the city, in public spaces," said a woman next to me. The initiative, called Smart Kigali, is Rwanda's foray into the "smart city" idea, modernising the Kigali experience and certainly making it an enjoyable one.

I watched through the window as we drove through the clean, winding streets, with rolling hills all around me. Some motorbikes rode past, and I think I spotted some people playing Moto Polo—Polo on motorbikes—but I'm not sure as we turn a corner. Kigali is truly an African gem, and it certainly lives up to the hype. Given Rwanda's tumultuous and horrifying history of about 20 years ago, it's amazing what is unfolding on this part of our continent right now. Kigali is one of the cleanest cities on our continent, lush and green, and even the president participates in a monthly cleanup called Umuganda.[92] It's all part of the city's striving to be a cleaner, greener city, with plenty of environmental initiatives, including turning the Nyandungu wetland into an ecotourism and urban recreation park (expected to be open from 2018).

Kigali's Innovation City has been a government-led initiative to get the whole city connected with fibre and 4G LTE. The plan is to have 95 percent of Kigali's citizen's connected. Such a plan has made the World Bank state that Kigali is the second easiest place to do business. In addition to this, the project focuses on three interdependent platforms: innovation-friendly financial capital, digital innovation, and human capital. "Kigali Innovation City is the Rwandan solution to Africa's development, as it will enable technology innovation communities by allowing them to source highly skilled human capital locally," said the Rwanda Development Board CEO at the launch. "The project was conceived to enable the digital transformation path in Rwanda, and I believe it is a model that can be easily applied across the continent to leapfrog into the fourth industrial revolution.[93]" Innovation doesn't have to be fancy or flashy, it just has to be practical, and Kigali creating an ecosystem that is viable and a perfect fit for its people.

As part of this on-going development and cultural formation, FabLab launched in the city in June 2016. FabLab is a worldwide network in more than 1,000 different countries that make use of digital fabrication technology (joining design and production through computer-aided design and manufacturing, including the use of 3D printers). It was established in 2002 by Sherry Lassiter, together with MIT professor Neil Gershenfeld

---

92   Heather Greenwood Davis, *Smart Cities: Kigali, Rwanda.* Published at the National Geographic, February 2017. Available at http://www.nationalgeographic.com/travel/features/smart-cities/kigali-rwanda-innovation/
93   Press release from the Rwanda Development Board. Available at http://www.rdb.rw/home/newsdetails/article/the-government-of-rwanda-launches-kigali-innovation-city-flagship-project-to-drive-digital-transformation-1.html

and several MIT graduate students. FabLab puts students together and gives them the tools they need to build, tinker, and innovate, such as 3D printers, CNC machines (a process that has computers control machine tools, rather than it being a manual process), mills and cutting machines, such as laser cutters or vinyl cutters. It also provides training and consumables, and all this allows for local members of a FabLab to begin building, inventing and manufacturing.

Along with this, the Fab Academy taps into the network and brings training to those on the ground. "We have a distributed network around the world that shares the same infrastructure," Lassiter says. "We're able to leverage that not only for distributed business opportunities or entrepreneurship, but we're also able to offer distributed advanced technical education.[94]" During this 20-week course, students learn how to design and make pretty much anything they can imagine, using the SOLIDWORKS platform, and get these to the market. Many have started businesses and used crowdfunding platforms such as Kickstarter. From the get-go, FabLab Rwanda began to create smart farming sensors that determine if crops need water, sanitary products for women, and started reaching into drone technology. This all forms part of Rwanda's new "Made-in-Rwanda" campaign, which is about giving locally-produced commodities precedence.

In a similar vein is Impact Hub Kigali, started by American Jon Stever who is also a long-time Kigali resident. These hubs offer flexible office space and connect people to an ever-growing community, with a strong social focus. Impact Hubs are also worldwide, with 15,000 plus members.

Furthermore, education facilities are looking towards creating the same sort of space. There is the recently-established Carnegie Mellon University in Rwanda, an offshoot of the original private research university established in Pittsburgh, Pennsylvania in the 1900's. Carnegie Mellon has a brilliant reputation as one of the best research facilities in the world. The Rwanda campus therefore also allows students to spend semesters at the Pittsburgh and Silicon Valley campuses, connecting stu-

---

94   Michael Molitch-Hou, FabLab Network Spreads to Rwanda. Published at Engineers Rule, December 2016. Available at http://www.engineersrule.com/fablab-network-spreads-rwanda-solidworks-support/

dents to campuses in other countries as well.[95]

These are fantastic opportunities and highlight how Rwanda is actively fostering an innovative culture. But I was on my way to another initiative, and what I was going to find there inspired me in ways I never imagined, but also made me ask some hard questions of what it is we prioritise in our conversations around innovation, especially in our media.

I was invited to attend the launch of the African Institute of Mathematical Sciences (AIMS) Rwanda. I must admit, I was very excited when I got the invite, as I was familiar with the work of AIMS in South Africa. I must say, AIMS Rwanda is truly impressive. And best of all, it's truly Pan-African. After I finished my time there I left asking: why on earth are we not talking more about this sort of thing?

AIMS has done amazing work across Africa and is at the forefront of our scientific and mathematics development. Yes, we have a vibrant scientific side, to the frustrating surprise of too many. I loved my time there, meeting AIMS affiliates and fellows and mathematical scientists. I found myself leaving their presence with bright eyes and a keen mind, seeing Africa in a totally, wonderful new light.

President Paul Kagame of Rwanda summed it up nicely when he said, "We have to move 'beyond potential' and create a workforce that will lead [a] real transformation for Africa. It will only be done through innovative scientific training, technical advances and breakthrough discoveries. And there is not going to be a short cut." AIMS contributes to this by having created a network across the continent via its various centres in South Africa (initially founded in Cape Town in 2003), Senegal, Ghana, Cameroon, Tanzania, and now Rwanda. It not only educates but it also actively promotes mathematics and science in Africa in various effective ways, some of which we will cover below. It is essentially creating a pool of excellent African mathematicians and scientists who will (in turn) apply solutions to our continent's challenges. Yes, many of them actually stay here.

It's doing this in such unique ways that I think can speak to just about every business, entrepreneur, and organisation in Africa. It is actively ad-

---

95   About Carnegie Mellon University Africa. See http://www.cmu.edu/africa/about-cmur/index.html

dressing challenges such as the brain drain, gender equality, cost barriers, and creating ecosystems. Let me elaborate:

1. It has a huge focus on gender equality. Maths and science are notoriously well known for having a small female workforce. But up to 30 percent of AIMS' graduates are now female. It truly makes an effort. For example, if a woman is pregnant, AIMS has a saying that her body may be pregnant but her brain isn't, meaning she can continue studying and working. They make sure that she is well supported, provided antenatal care, and they even set up homes on the campus for family members to help take care of the baby while she is still studying. In line with its high focus on gender equality, AIMS has also just elected its first female research chair, Dr Gisele Mophou. It's amazing to see a female mathematician and scientist at this level.

2. Its Next-Einstein Initiative keeps our brains here. It plans to see 15 research centres established in Africa (it currently has three). In addition to Mophou, the research chairs include the likes of Prof. Mouhamed Moustapha Fall, whose credentials and work has been internationally recognised (some years ago he was being dubbed the 'next Einstein' in popular, international media. I wrote about him in my book *Disrupting Africa* where he is using mathematics to help curb over-fishing). He forms part of the Next-Einstein Forum (NEF) fellows, which is doing groundbreaking work in the field of maths and science here in Africa. The Next-Einstein Initiative, however, also plugs the brain drain by partnering with the Canadian government, the German government, and the U.K. as well as other institutions, so that the research initiatives have access to resources that keep them on the continent.

Typically, what happens with people like Fall is they are quickly snapped up by the likes of Harvard and Oxford, and to be honest, with few opportunities in Africa where you can grow in the mathematics and science fields, what else would you do? However, AIMS' model keeps them here and even helps integrate scientists and mathematicians into other forms of work, where you might not expect to find these sorts of people (more on that below). It's not just about funding them in terms of a salary but it gives them access to resources, provides collaboration between universities across the world, creates an international network of people in similar fields, and keeps the research thriving.

Dr. Rosita Yocgo, research manager at AIMS, says this means their graduates and research chairs get to interact with the best across the world and don't really feel the barrier between being overseas and being here. "The more research chairs we can create the more we will be able to attract researchers that have already gone and are working in the diaspora and be able to convince them to come back to Africa because they will have the same opportunities," she says.

This last point is key. Not only are they looking to plug the brain drain, but also reverse it. I think that is hugely exciting.

3. It is focusing on the future—quantum science. The Rwanda launch coincided with the launch of AIMS' *Quantum Leap Africa initiative*, where it will (for the first time) create an environment that focuses on quantum science, bringing a new dimension to the ecosystem it has been developing for quite some time.

4. It finds creative ways to stimulate a new ecosystem. I've spoken a great deal about a new technological ecosystem for Africa, and AIMS seems to have a very similar vision through what it's doing. This launch in Rwanda is the first time AIMS is formalising the ecosystem it has been developing—an ecosystem within the Science, technology, engineering and mathematics (STEM) fields. By putting learners from all these fields together in one network, they share resources, ideas, and creativity. In times past many of these fields worked in isolation but it's becoming increasingly clear that these fields now intersect, and so the people working within them and studying them should too. At the launch, I could feel the excitement in the air that this was a ground-breaking event; a paradigm shift of sorts with regards to where the future is going.

5. It has a 24-hour learning environment. Lecturers and learners stay on campus, even eating together. This model is producing amazing fruit. It's not just data that people are dealing with but the establishment of relationships is key, and immersing people in the world 24/7 has a way of making it truly alive rather than just something in a textbook. It's worth adding that the lecturers at AIMS have come from the likes of Oxford, Harvard, and other amazing institutions across the world—meaning students have easy, relational access to these bright minds who have pioneered in their fields.

6. It actively creates unique opportunity and work for learners. Rather than giving them tuition and them sending them off into the sunset, AIMS actively works at placing learners in key positions. "We've done this really well," says Thierry Zouhmerman. "Usually, students doing PhD's and Masters in the fields of science and mathematics end up in academia. But we believe the mathematical sciences are applicable to industry and policy-making. Mathematics can be applied to agriculture, energy, food shortage, and so on. So we have a focused programme where we find opportunities for our graduates in industries and / or policy-making so that not all of them end up in academia. Some obviously do but through this initiative, we want to ensure that we can open up their options and viewpoints on how they contribute to the continent."

7. Its tuition is free. This blew my mind. Students go through an 18-month programme that is free. "If you're a really bright student you don't need to have cost as a barrier," says Thierry Zouhmerman. "It's obviously a stringent and rigorous process to get in, but once you're in you get your Masters degree for free." Accommodation is also free.

As I was boarding the plane heading back to South Africa, I got the feeling that AIMS presents a very tangible and viable business model that other organisations and entrepreneurs should model. Think of what we could do if we created ecosystems in various fields and innovation like AIMS has done. Think what we could do if we could find ways to address the cost barriers more effectively. Think about what we could do if we could create environments where people have easy access to experts and people who are pioneering in their field. Think what we could achieve if we all, like AIMS, thought Pan-African from the beginning, making that a central focus.

But I also had a lingering feeling that something else needs to be stated, primarily in the form of questions:

Firstly, why is the media not talking about this amazing work, and showcasing the research and amazing students coming out of this institution all over Africa? Why is it that we're just so silent?

Secondly, why is there not more partnering going on? My own work in innovation highlights that there is a tremendous amount to be gained by partnering via funding and expertise and networking. Surely there should be more of this sort of thing going on?

The Africa Rising narrative is more than a feeling, more than a movement. It's now a reality. And it's coming to our every-day lives. And that excites me. However, nothing will happen unless we are making it happen. If we do not define the culture, it will define us! AIMS is truly shaping the future of our continent—and in ways I never expected. It's making a huge impact and I, for one, am excited. But I think we all have a lot of work to do—and much of it starts with our thinking.

"Every once in a while, a new technology, an old problem, and a big idea turn into an innovation."

— **Dean Kamen**

CHAPTER FOURTEEN

YABACON VALLEY

I find Nigeria a thoroughly exciting country on our continent. And that's not just because I am Nigerian! The overarching and underlying theme I keep consistently seeing with Nigeria's innovators, every time I meet them, is that they are going beyond just innovating but are genuinely looking to completely disrupt the status quo, taking on the big players themselves. It's fascinating and exciting to see corporate players in a particular space being disrupted by startups and innovators of all stripes.

Some people think Lagos could end up being Africa's Silicon Valley, particularly the suburb of Yaba. Here you find institutions such as Queen's College, the Nigerian Institute of Medical Research, the Yaba College of Technology, Igbobi College, the University of Lagos, the Federal Science and Technical College, and the Federal College of Education. So it already has what seems to be a winning formula: connecting young students together. Yaba also has one of the busiest market sites in Lagos, known as Tejuosho Market. It's been quite a fascinating process seeing it rise since about 2011, with banking institutions and startups and plenty of residential renovation to its old buildings, as it becomes a hot spot for the growing Nigerian middle class. Subsequently, there are plenty of retailers that have been moving in—and hotels, too. All this has earned it the nickname "Yabacon Valley", admittedly a controversial nickname that not everyone likes. It has others too, of course, like Yaba Right or

Silicon Yaba or Silicon Lagoon. But for some reason, "Yabacon Valley" has stuck — solidified when The Business Aim, an online platform that focuses on business and startup culture and innovation, published a story on it. Part of what drives people to the area is how it connects to Victoria Island, as well as Ikoyi, an upmarket neighbourhood, and Lekki, a special "multi-functional economic zone" initiated by the State Government of Lagos since 2006. This makes Yaba relatively cheaper to stay in as transport is much less expensive.

Yaba, therefore, has plenty going for it. But Yabacon can trace its history back to 2011 when Wennovation Hub and African Leadership Forum (a not-for-profit started by Nigerian President Olusegun Obasanjo in the late 80's) partnered and began to look at incubating startups. In 2012, Bosun Tijani and Femi Longe, social entrepreneurs and innovators, changed it to the Co-Creation Hub (CCHub). The idea was to "help animate a community of change agents" and it effectively became the first proper startup incubator in Nigeria, located on Herbert Macaulay Road in Yaba. CCHub is a six-storey lab that houses over fifty Nigerian startups. The Lagos State government, as well as several trusts and other investors, got involved. This created a visible tech space, encouraging other entrepreneurs to come on board, and MTN, Google and Nokia began to sponsor the hub. One of the early success stories was BudgIT, a fiscal transparency project headed up by former banker Sean Onigbinde, which received seed funding from billionaire Tony Elumelu. In 2013, Konga arrived — an eCommerce company valued at approximately $200 million at the time (after raising $20 million in Series C rounds) and Africa Internet Group, which has $469 million in four rounds from six investors transferred six of its companies to Yaba in 2014.[96] (BudgIT, in that year, also received a $400,000 grant from the philanthropic investment firm, Omidyar.) Africa Internet Group, now rebranded as Jumia, soon became the biggest employer in Yaba and owns several e-commerce outfits — dealing in cars, travel, online marketplaces, shopping, food, jobs, B2B logistics, and others. "By the sheer volume of coders and support staff employed by Jumia and the African Internet Group in total, Yaba deserved its title of a tech hub," reports Ventures Africa.[97]

---

96   See Wikipedia – https://en.wikipedia.org/wiki/Yabacon_Valley

97   Oluwatosin Adesokan, *The Fall of Yabacon Valley*. Published at Ventures Africa, May

Also in 2014, Andela, a (now) global engineering organisation and talent accelerator, was founded in Nigeria and received $24 million in 2016 from the Chan-Zuckerberg Initiative. This is one of the reasons why, in the same year, Mark Zuckerberg came to visit—his first stop being CCHub — where he said he wanted to learn and see how Facebook can better support tech development and entrepreneurship in Africa. "The energy here is amazing," he said on a Facebook post. During a Q&A with local entrepreneurs, he said, "The thing that's striking [about Nigeria] is the entrepreneurial energy.[98]"

However, it soon became clear that Andela would need to move its base of operations from Lagos to New York, which it did in late 2016. It all made sense for the startup, but it put a damper on the idea of "Yabacon Valley". This, along with the fact that some tech companies are moving out the suburb, and others such as Paystack (an e-payments company with investment from Tencent), Konga.com (a huge e-commerce platform we will look at later in this book) or IrokoTV (arguably one of the biggest innovations to come out of Nigeria) are not based there either, although they do intermingle with the tech hubs and innovators in the area. This means that Nigeria's technology revolution isn't happening in one central space, but seems to be more decentralised. I think is an important point to consider. While we need to learn from Silicon Valley and what's happening in China, we can't seek to emulate everything about both of these scenarios. For one, as I've argued previously in this book, they are miles ahead of us. Secondly, Africa is *huge* and we are made up of about fifty nation-states. How realistic is to think that we should create a central spot in one of these states where it should all happen? Conversely, how realistic is it to think each of our African nations should have their own "Silicon Valley"? Neither of these scenarios is realistic and could end up being a red-herring. While I advocate that we need to have environments where we connect and collaborate and that we need to be building centres and the like, perhaps the idea of having an "African Silicon

2017. Available at http://venturesafrica.com/features/the-fall-of-yabacon-valley/

98   Alex Heath, *It looks like Mark Zuckerberg is having a blast in Nigeria*. Published at Business Insider, August 2016. Available at http://www.businessinsider.com/facebook-mark-zuckerberg-nigeria-2016-8/#he-ate-authentic-nigerian-food-for-the-first-time-and-loved-it-6

Valley"—a particular *place* where it must all happen or come from — is faulty. Personally, it almost bugs me a bit when we keep trying to claim this or that place will be our "Silicon Valley" as it seems to me this just means we want to copy rather than actually innovate.

Rather, we should seek to create community in other ways; or create communities in communities. In other words, we need to be thinking Pan-African. This is clear to me when we actually look at our innovations themselves. For example, one of the innovations I went to meet with in my last visit to Nigeria is a startup called 3line, which integrates billing services and banking into your social media platforms — allowing you to do all your banking via social media. Here is a perfect example of an innovation using Silicon Valley platforms while also being unique in its own. African innovations must speak to local contexts, while at the same time being scalable to a Pan African view, and using technology or platforms already existent within those nations is a great way to go about this.

NIGERIA'S REGULATION

As I've briefly argued previously and will argue in greater detail later in this book, our Pan-African view means we have to rethink regulation and borders. Nigeria, as far as I'm concerned, serves as a great example when it comes to the regulatory landscape. When you are outside of Nigeria there are many challenges faced by the financial services industry due to the regulatory forum. One of the themes I personally have picked up on in Nigeria is that its regulatory environment is quite robust, and is actually helping the financial services industry. Naturally, a lack of regulation can lead to a higher rate of crime as well, but the government is making great strides in this, passing its long-awaited cybercrime bill into law in May 2015.

Here's an example of how the right kind of regulation can lead to financial inclusion and better opportunity for all. The Central Bank has mandated the ability to open a T01 account. A T01 account is a bank account you can open without having documentation, except an ID. It's a very basic account and the easy process allows for greater financial inclusion, giving people an opportunity to start. This is very impressive when you think of trying to get people from all walks of life into the fold. The account can be opened in a couple of minutes and you can plug in social banking from your Facebook account. When you think of the financial implications to the economy, that is phenomenal.

One of the innovators I've met with there is a company called Interswitch, which is probably one of the most impressive tech houses I have seen in a while. The company started operations in 2002 as a transaction switching and electronic payments processing company that build and manages payment infrastructure as well as deliver innovative payment products and transactional services throughout the African continent. It focuses on digital payments and commerce and probably has a very bold vision to compete with the likes of Mastercard and Visa on the continent. That's brave and impressive. One of the ways Interswitch is actively working on financial inclusion is by deploying agent networks across the country called PayPoint agents, which carry out financial services in their neighbourhood on behalf of Interswitch. That includes payments of bills, transfers of funds, cash deposits, withdrawals, and (of course) airtime recharges. Interswitch also operates in Kenya and Uganda, and are forming more local partnerships to expand its reach on the continent. In my view, they are really strong contenders, not just in Nigeria, but from a Pan-African point of view. It seems to me that Interswitch could not even get going in other scenarios where the regulation would be different.

THE LESSONS TO BE LEARNED

Essentially, what I see in Nigeria speaks into two strategies I believe are important for taking on Silicon Valley. Both of these strategies speak into the Pan-African context or a 'borderless Africa'.

This first of these is, as I've mentioned above, the fact that it won't really work to our advantage to focus on a specific time and place and try and make that our own version of "Silicon Valley". This is important, but it requires some mental exercise to fully grasp. It doesn't help to emulate and copy. Rather, we have to take the major lessons we can see happening in the past and apply these to our new world, to a new narrative, and a new mindset. You might recall earlier on in this book that I argued for a mindset that sees our innovators as nations, or countries, of their own.

We can't capture our innovations into borders. We have to challenge our ideas around a borderless Africa here, and create communities within communities, nations within nations basically — an almost invisible 'tech hub' within all of our tech hubs across the continent. I don't mean we need to become homogeneous and scrap those aspects of our individual cultures that make us approach tech and innovation in unique ways, only that we have to connect across borders in unique ways and form communities in that way. This requires Pan-African networks that collaborate with other Pan-African networks, and that tie into local networks and tech hubs and universities and forums on the ground.

The second of these, then, is to challenge our regulations around such matters. Part of this will include our financial regulations. As I showed in chapter four and subsequent chapters, on the "big boys" from Silicon Valley, we are essentially being forced to go borderless anyway. These disruptors already transact as if the borders aren't even there, and often these innovations happen long before we can put the regulations in place. Before you know it, we're trading money on WhatsApp, and government and industry suddenly realise it needs to do something about that. Likewise, our innovators need to be thinking Pan-African from the beginning. We cannot let borders limit our thinking, our vision, and what we should do. Much like Silicon Valley, we need to innovate and ask for forgiveness later — when people have bought into the system and rely on it. That's honestly what they do, and we really need to have a similar attitude. So in the next section, I'd like to explore this topic further and in more detail. But first I would like to show how our best innovators are already doing it, to further bolster the argument.

"You can't hate the roots of a tree and not hate the tree. You can't hate Africa and not hate yourself."

— **Malcolm X**

CHAPTER FIFTEEN

THE LIFE AND TRIALS OF THE COMMON AFRICAN ENTREPRENEUR

In 1971, terror struck Uganda as the then-government was overturned in a military coup, led by Idi Amin. Amin soon threw out the constitution, placed military tribunals above civil law, and ruled with an iron fist. The following year, the previous Prime Minister Milton Obote tried to stage a coup to take over from Amin, but it failed. Amin lashed back by first purging his army of any Obote supporters, and then turning on anyone with an Acholi and Lango ethnic background. The genocide began and it was to last for the next eight years of Amin's madness, a dark and bitter time of evil in our African history we wish we could forget.

In 1972, Amin also turned on anyone from Asian descent, ordering the expulsion of 60,000 Ugandan Asians. Of these was Ashish Thakkar's parents. They fled to the U.K. Forced to leave their home, and being a minority in the U.K., they had to do what they could to raise a family. In 1981, after Thakkar was born, his parents decided it was finally safe to return to Africa, and chose to immigrate to Rwanda. But terror struck again just over ten years later, as Thakkar was 12 years old when the horrific genocides in Rwanda began in 1994. Once again the family had to flee for their lives, and they went back to Uganda, this time as refugees.

Everything the family had built was completely lost. Feeling some of the weight of responsibility on him as a teenager, Thakkar began to venture into business. At 15 he began what today is the Mara Group — a worldwide conglomerate involved in several industries. Of course, back then it was a simple computer parts business. After selling his computer to a friend for a $100 — more than he paid for it — Thakkar realised that all he had to do was just do that again. So he bought another one and sold it, and another one and sold it, and soon started trading. His parents spotted his obvious entrepreneurial spirit and opened up the doors for him to take out a loan of $5,000. He registered his company and used that money to go to Dubai, buy floppy disks and computer parts and products, and sell them back home. He had seen a gap in the market because it was difficult for Ugandans at the time to have access to computers and accessories.

It kept going from strength to strength, and so he eventually asked his folks if he could leave school and concentrate on it. Amazingly, they let him do it, on the condition that he would return if things didn't work out. But Thakkar had even bigger plans. He travelled to Dubai and set up his business there, realising he could be a central figure in the growing computer business at the time. He was right. He was soon selling to companies all around the world. From there, the Mara Group branched into manufacturing and agriculture and telecommunications, hotels and conference centres, and even shopping malls. By 2013 he had established Atlas Mara, which invests in financial services companies and acquires them. Through the Mara Foundation, Thakkar wants to help the next generation of African entrepreneurs start and run their own successful businesses. So far, it has mentored African entrepreneurs in the hundreds of thousands.

REACHING THE DIASPORA

Success came much later for Jason Njoku. He grew up in the U.K with his mother and four brothers and sisters in Deptford, South-East London, self-described as "solidly working class — a council estate kid if ever there was one.[99]" At the age of 12 he moved to a village in Nigeria,

---

99   Peter Guest, Jason Njoku: *South London's Mr Nollywood*. Published September, 2012. Available at http://peterguest.co.uk/journalism/index.php/jason-njoku-south-londons-mr-nollywood/

and left back to the U.K. again at the age of 15. Here he attended the University of Manchester and studied chemistry. During this time, his entrepreneurial spirit started coming out. He used to run club nights to make extra cash, handing out fliers to students outside of bars until 3 a.m. Sometimes it worked, other times no one came, and he and his mates would go home completely broke wondering what they did wrong. Despite this, leaving university in 2005, he truly believed he would be an entrepreneurial success. He started with a magazine for the student community called Brash, after getting loans from friends, but it was just as things were moving from print to digital. "I spent a good three years making every mistake there was to make about how to run a business," Njoku told Peter Guest. "We were very popular, but we just never figured out how to make money." So eventually, they just ran out of it. He started working as a recruitment consultant, but that didn't last long, and so soon he was an entrepreneur again — this time focusing on a blog network and news site. It was focused on law and consultancy and banking, but unfortunately, the timing was also wrong and he could not make money out of it either. Then, after a 2008 trip to Nigeria and seeing the huge popularity of local music, he bought a hundred CD's and was wondering to maybe get into that business, but could never figure out exactly high. To pay the bills he got involved in a T-shirt business and a web design company instead. Everything flopped. Eventually, his failures were so bad he ended up moving back to his mum's house in London — at the age of 29 — an event he calls "humiliating" but a lesson well learned.

However, he noticed something. He saw that his mum's viewing habits had changed dramatically. Growing up, she loved British soap operas and the like. But now she was watching as many Nollywood movies as she could on DVD. His Nigerian friends were all raving about it as well. He wondered about the market for these films and went looking at London's Brixton Market where everyone was buying the DVD's. He tried to find the films online but found nothing, went to the video store to find them there but couldn't — or, at least if they were there, it was impossible to really identify them, even though the films were so popular with the diaspora in Britain. That's when he realised that, despite the popularity of Nollywood, it seemed the distribution around it outside of Nigeria's borders wasn't that organised. He got on the phone with a friend, Bastian Gotter, who was an attendant at a BP (who also became Iroko TV's COO and then CFO), who advised him to go to Nigeria and see what he could do.

There he found the distribution just as disorganised, despite the prolific production of the films. Again, as he told Peter Guest:

> "I did some research into Nollywood, and all anyone talks about is piracy. When you go into the main market, you have to go through the pirates to get to the actual real producers, or people who sell them. I thought it didn't make any sense. So I started talking to people about licenses. I said, I'm thinking of licensing for the Internet. Some of them were trying to sell me the whole license forever for $1,000. I was like: 'that's madness, and I honestly don't think you know what you're selling me.'"

He went back to Bastian Gotter in the U.K. and told him that it was the "steal of the century". And they realised they could fill this huge gap in distribution and marketing in this popular Nollywood market. They launched a channel on YouTube called Nollywood Love, which generated $1.3 million in advertising revenue in one year. Nollywood Love became YouTube's largest Africa partner. It was clear they were onto something huge. So Njoku went back to Lagos and set up iROKO Partners, and in 2011 they launched Iroko TV, which streams Nollywood movies. He also eventually did get into music, streaming it through the iROKING platform in 2011. In 2012, Iroko TV raised $8 million in venture capital from Tiger Global Management. From there, it's become a multi-million dollar company.

SEEING THE RIGHT OPPORTUNITY

I first met Chris Folayan in Paris at the Afrobytes Tech Conference, in June 2017. We had a great time together talking about innovation, and challenges we have as a continent in relation to innovation. I spent a great deal of time in thought at that conference, in my hotel room, or sitting alone at a Paris coffee shop, worrying whether we have missed the boat with Silicon Valley on our continent and if we'll be playing catch up for a long, long time. But Chris helped to get me a bit out of my melancholy through his story and his attitude to African innovation.

He started as an entrepreneur early in life—at seven years old. He had a small tyre reclaiming and recycling business, where he would earn some pocket money for himself and buy stamps and comic books and toys and junk food. He soon established a network of other seven-year-olds who convinced their parents to pick up tyres from the side of the road and deliver them to his house so they could subsequently get picked up by a recycling company and everyone could get paid. Obviously, Chris was a natural business man! He was inspired by his dad who was an entrepreneur and owned an engineering firm. When his dad told him he needs to earn extra money for himself for sweets, that's when Chris began his first business.

When he was older, he had the privilege of completing college in the U.S. While he was there, he would travel home fairly often to see his family and would get requests to bring things back. His friends soon got wind of it too and would send their own requests. He couldn't turn people down, and soon he was taking so much over that they would not let him board the plane, even though he was willing to pay for the extra luggage!

"The list had become so long that I knew there was a strong demand, and when such demands are not met you have an amazing opportunity to do business," he says.[100] So he created an app, in his bedroom, that does exactly what he was doing — bring in items from the U.S. and the U.K. to Nigeria — tested it with his family, and everyone loved it. The word spread and he had to move from his bedroom to his garage, and then into his living room, and after a year into the company's first warehouse. Now MallforAfrica has over 8.5 billion items for sale in its stores.

That app is MallforAfrica, which allows you to purchase from over 200 stores in the U.S. and the U.K. and have the items delivered to your

---

100   Harnet Bokrezion, *How a Nigerian built an African e-commerce empire from his bedroom.* Published at How We Made it In Africa, March 2016. Available at https://www. howwemadeitinafrica.com/mall-africa-thriving-business-linking-shoppers-western-retailers/

door in Nigeria, Kenya and Rwanda. The app accepts payments from VISA and Mastercard, M-Pesa, Paypal, and many others, speaking directly to Africans who use mobile money and those with traditional bank accounts. It even issues its own debit cards, which helps to set international retailers at ease.

In fact, one of the amazing things Folayan has done is break Western mindsets and stereotypes around Africa. "With us," Folayan says, "companies have seen seven-figure increases in their sales. Now they know that MallforAfrica is taking on all risks for them, and by using us, Africa is no longer a region to ignore.[101]"

But the platform also empowers Africans. It helps schools with their books, supplies, computers and educational material. It helps hospitals get the equipment they could not before, as MallforAfrica has so much market clout. "One day I got an email from a lady who was so grateful for the MallforAfrica platform as she was able to order a sewing machine no one else was ever willing to bring or ship to her," Folayan told HowWeMadeItInAfrica.com. "When she received the item she finally started her own small business with the only sewing machine in her small town.[102]"

REFRESHING EDUCATION

Fred Swaniker was born in Ghana, but as a family, they left when he was four years old. Every four years, they would move to a different African country as opportunities came up (his dad is a lawyer and his mother an educator). He studied economics in the U.S. (Minnesota) and was hired by McKinsey in Johannesburg, before he studied further at Stanford and received his MBA there.

"Every four years of my life I moved to a new country in Africa and everywhere I went, I saw that we have a beautiful continent, we have so many resources, so much opportunity but I couldn't understand why we were poor," he told the BBC. "As I grew older, it became clear to me that the main reason why we were poor was because of leadership.[103]" At

---

101   ibid

102   ibid

103   The man trying to train *Africa's future leaders*, published by BBC, January 2012.

Stanford, he came up with the idea of launching an African Academy, but he was under contract with McKinsey to return to employment there when he graduated, or pay the $124,000 tuition fees at Stanford they had loaned him. With two former colleagues at McKinsey, who also helped him launch the academy, and with help from friends and family, he managed to pay off the loan, but it wasn't easy. For two years he had no money and no salary. However, as time went by, more people started funding the launch of the academy — and the more progress they made, the more the funding came.

Part of his reasons for launching the academy was that he had lived and worked in almost ten African countries in his life, and kept seeing the same themes popping up: poor leadership, and parents paying extremely high fees for educating their children overseas. He realised there was no good reason why Africa could not have its own world-class institutions, and there had to be a way he could innovate on the fee structure. The African Leadership Academy (ALA) was birthed in Johannesburg in 2008, launched by himself and Chris Bradford (from Stanford), Peter Mombaur and Acha Leke, who provided the financial backing.

Bradford was responsible for designing the innovative curriculum at ALA, which not only provides academic courses but also African studies (so needed!) and Entrepreneurial Leadership. The latter creates opportunities for students to practice leadership and entrepreneurship skills through simulation and project-based learning. It also innovates on the fee structure — students are given 'forgivable loans' — if they work in Africa for ten years after graduating, the loan is waivered; if not, they pay the tuition fees. It was initially piloted in Cape Town in 2005 before launching as the Academy in 2008. The ALA is one of the continent's only Pan-African schools, admitting 700 students (ages 16 — 19) from 45 African countries at the time of writing. 85 percent of students come from disadvantaged backgrounds. In addition to this, Swaniker has also launched the African Leadership Network (an annual gathering of leaders and network) and the African Leadership University (ALU) — based on similar principles as the Academy — with campuses in Rwanda and Mauritius. His vision for ALU is hyper-futuristic: combining tradi-

Available at http://www.bbc.com/news/world-africa-16342145

tional brick and mortar facilities with digital classrooms to launch 25 African Ivy League Universities across the continent. What Swaniker has successfully done is to disrupt the traditional university education model by offering higher quality education at a lower cost, leveraging the power of Massive Open Online Courses (MOOC). This is breaking the monopoly on knowledge that any one university would have by picking the best content from global universities and curating them into one central source using technology. He is extending his university's traditional infrastructure reach into the digital realm by using technology such as virtual reality goggles to teach. This is innovation in education in truly exciting, futuristic levels.

WHY AM I TELLING YOU THESE STORIES?

I've mentioned some of these entrepreneurs before, both in this book and in other places, so the question you might be asking yourself at this stage is: why am I telling you their stories? The answer is because, as far as I'm concerned, these individuals provide the best current examples of Pan-African innovation, and also provide excellent character studies. From now until the end of this book, we are going to look at how we can actually take on Silicon Valley. We're going to start to strategise. So as we examine the trends around innovation in Africa, and the trends around how Africa is being disrupted by innovations from overseas, it makes sense to also look at the actual people involved and see if we can find any trends that help us understand what actually makes for an African innovator / entrepreneur. Is it a kind of person? Perhaps someone highly driven and ambitious? Is it education that makes the difference? Is it geographical location? What do we see when we look at these individuals, and couple it with other innovators who may not be as successful as they are yet but are certainly rising quickly through the ranks? And if we can answer these questions, you reading this book may be able to find the keys to unlock your own contribution to our continent.

1. EDUCATION

Let's firstly start by dispelling a myth. Education is always a big deal and I support it tremendously — although, there is, of course, *useful* education and *useless* education. The ALA, in my opinion, is the perfect example of education going right. I agree wholeheartedly with Fred Swaniker when he says the following:

> "Good leaders do not fall from the sky. The experience of successful nations, the world over, emphatically points to the centrality of strong education institutions, and particularly robust higher education systems in deliberately training the leaders who take societies to great heights. In the best of these institutions, leaders are not only imparted with the hard skills of leadership, but also socialized on value systems that make them the creators and custodians of social ideals.[104]"

My family was always passionate about the power of education, and my parents sacrificed everything to make sure my siblings and I got the best quality education they could get. If there is anything I'm grateful for, and have a deep-seated appreciated for, is that my parents gave me the best they could with education. This has certainly shaped my views of Africa and given me opportunities. My parents were passionate about raising the next generation of Africa by investing in education, and education in this day and age has a strong position in innovation and entrepreneurship.

But this is all for a separate discussion because I want to encourage those of us who have not had the privilege of education. In terms of what we're speaking about now, I'm sure you noticed that Swaniker studied in the U.S. and later at Stanford, and that Jason Njoku studied in the U.K. You probably also noticed how Folayan had the opportunity to study in the U.S. Perhaps there was something in the back of your mind that said the reason for their success has to be their education; that they have a certain kind of privilege; that it was all because of that one head start. However, you might have missed that Ashish Thakkar had no tertiary education whatsoever when he started what has become the Mara Group at the age of 15. In fact, he even left school

---

104   Fred Swaniker, *Great leaders aren't born – they're made. And Africa is showing us how.* Published at the World Economic Forum website, May 2016. Available at https://www.weforum. org/agenda/2016/05/africa-leaders-new-generation/

to start his company! "Education is good," said Thakkar at an interview with Kenyan StandardMedia. "However, informal education is much more important and valuable in life than formal education. Mentorship and vocational skills training build up an individual.[105]" This is notable and says a great deal about privilege and what a supposed 'head-start' looks like. What Thakkar had was the ability to see things differently and note opportunity, amidst some other basic business instincts. As Jason Njoku said in an interview with BBC:

> "There are a lot of people out there who are smarter than me, who have an Ivy-league education and who have great ideas to start up a business, but something is holding them back and they are voyeurs rather than entrepreneurs. My advice to young entrepreneurs is this: don't wait for the day when you're reading about your idea in the business pages. Do it now. Break free from the shackles that hold you back and start your business today.[106]"

Folayan, for his part, started his own little business at just seven years old. So we have to always understand that there's more to this than education. As I've stated previously, education has always been a big deal for my parents' generation. My mother was a teacher. But it hasn't always worked out exactly as planned. There are so many stories of people receiving a good education, working hard, and finding out now that they have no pension. This is not a story only common to Africa — it's a worldwide issue, which has partly inspired, from a very negative sense, a new generation of entrepreneurs. I believe that this rather gloomy situation is helping us all to see that education is needed, but not always required, and it is not all — you have to couple it with many other factors.

Therefore, the central theme for each of these entrepreneurs — and others as we will see a bit later — is not education, even though that

---

105   Lillian Kiarie, Living the dream: *How Ashish Thakkar became Africa's youngest billionaire*. Published at Standard Digital, July 2014. Available at https://www.standardmedia.co.ke/business/article/2000126574/africa-s-youngest-billionaire

106   Mariam Sowemimo, *Lessons from IrokoTV founder*, who made $30m in his 30s. Published by Tribune Online Magazine. Available at http://tribuneonlineng.com/lessons-irokotv-founder-made-30m-30s/

factors in for some of them. Arguably, it's what they do with their education that really counts. But even so, Jason Njoku studied chemistry in Manchester, something that probably hasn't been a direct help in setting up his Internet movie streaming business! Therefore, we have to dig deeper and scratch under the surface to bring out the true diamonds.

2. EXPERIENCING LIFE IN DIFFERENT CULTURES

This, for me, is a major clincher and something that every entrepreneur and innovator has to consider carefully and seriously. One of the themes that we see coming up with all of these, and seems to come up with practically every successful, or soon-to-be successful, entrepreneur and innovator I meet, is that they have an experience of different cultures.

For some, living in a different country was forced on them due to unforeseen, dire circumstances (as in the case with Ashish Thakkar). For others, it had more to do with opportunity — whether it was their parents' opportunity or their own to study abroad. Whatever the case may be, it seems that it's not so much getting an amazing education but experiencing the world outside of your own is absolutely key and *does* something to you.

I can testify to this personally as well. I've lived on three continents, in five cities, and have visited over twenty countries in total—and the number keeps rising the more I continue my work. I used to assume that most people have the same opportunities or the same life experiences, more or less, but my travels have obviously helped me to see the world as it actually is. This world is *diverse*, yet at the same time we all have one, common human experience—it manifests itself in different ways and through different individual experiences, but humanity finds itself facing the same needs and the same challenges everywhere.

In all the countries I've lived in, like Botswana, Australia and now South Africa, I have always immersed myself completely into the culture there. I would make it part of my identity and say I *am* Motswana, I *am* Australian, or I *am* South African. Growing up, I thought this was an identity crisis, but now I understand that I was actually embracing the people and making them my own. Spending some time outside of your own culture helps you experience different sides to life, and embrace the different opportunities that present themselves to you, and understand different challenges. You get to see it all from a different point of view, including your challenges. One culture might have overcome a challenge while another still needs to, and you get to bring that experience over. You have a more varied view of what culture is like for each individual, and you also understand the idea of the individual much better. When I go to another country, I am really keen to understand their culture and where they are coming from. It impacts the way they view entrepreneurship and innovation, and each culture has their own different nuance to it. Understanding their nuance and the challenges they have helps you dictate innovation and strategy.

Bilikiss Adebiyi-Abiola, who founded WeCyclers in Nigeria, a fantastic innovation that uses bicycles to provide recycling services to households, developed her idea while studying in the U.S. In her city, trash is, according to her, "money just lying in the streets." Rather than seeing the problem, she saw an opportunity. WeCyclers incentivises people to clean up by rewarding them for every kilogram collected and recycled through points sent by SMS. If you know how huge mobile penetration is in Africa, which we have covered in some detail, you can see how this works for Africans. The points are redeemable against goods such as cell phone minutes or basic food items. Rewards have also been funded in partnership with big brands. The fact is that she saw it all differently. While she was fortunate to study at MIT, I believe the experience of getting out of her own borders was paramount in helping her see the opportunities in Nigeria, to see the challenges from a different angle. Connecting with others outside of your culture is absolutely key and, if you ask me, absolutely necessary. If you want to grow as an entrepreneur, honestly, *get out more.*

Emma Kaye, born in Zimbabwe and founder of Bozza.mobi, dubbed Africa's answer to iTunes, Netflix and Spotify, is another example. She got to study in the U.K. and then came to South Africa to co-found an animation company, Triggerfish Animation. In 2008 she founded Bozza. mobi, which is a mobile-first digital marketplace for the Pan-African entertainment industry, allowing artists to directly connect with fans in a uniquely African way by creating a digital distribution platform where

Africa's artists can sell directly to customers across the continent. With traditional distribution in Africa being a challenge, and content piracy a real plague, Bozza.mobi fills a real gap in the entertainment industry. Kaye is a very creative person who sees the value of different cultures. I think this is key.

We don't even need to travel outside of our country's borders, but just need to be exposed to a different situation. For example, Alain Nteff from Cameroon developed the award-winning GiftedMom app only after visiting a rural area and witnessing several mothers and newborns die due to conditions that could have actually been avoided. The Giftedmom app uses SMS and other low-cost technology through the mobile phone to help mothers and pregnant women access medical advice even in rural communities. Had he stayed within his 'world', so to speak, actual lives might not even be saved.

Even Jack Ma admits that getting out of his borders has been key to his success as an entrepreneur building Alibaba:

"Before I left China, I was educated that China was the richest, happiest country in the world. So when I arrived in Australia, I thought, 'Oh my God, everything is different from what I was told.' Since then, I started to think differently."

I could go on and raise some more examples. For me, being around different parts of the world has become normal, and when I lived in different countries I would put my roots down in the culture for at least five to nine years. That helps to form a unique identity, and entrepreneurs must form their own unique identity. I am not a hyper-individualist and it's clear that some of the Western's approach to individualism is not working in the sense that people are becoming islands of their own. But at the same time, you have to develop as an individual to see things differently. I can see now how my moving about has shaped my view on Africa in particular and inspired me to embrace our opportunities despite our challenges — it's helped me to be so positive about who we are.

3. POSITIVITY AND PASSION

I see this positivity and passion with all these individuals above, and I think this positivity is absolutely key in innovating. If you want to innovate, be creatively positive — always understand there's an opportunity in a challenge. Even in Thakkar's case, where his family had been displaced so many times due to dire circumstances, and he felt something of the weight of responsibility for them, you find he seems to harvest a very positive attitude. What others might have seen as disabilities he saw as opportunities.

You have to see the glass half-full without ever being unrealistic about the challenges. No one ever really made a change by being negative. No one has really gotten anything meaningful done without a fair amount of passion for what they're doing. I'm not talking about positive thinking and positive affirmations; I'm talking about a deep conviction about the positive side, and a deep passion for our continent and its future and your place in our story.

As a very analytical person, I often use my analytical skills on any given situation to come to both the positive and the negative possibilities and then choose to progress toward the positive—to do something about bringing the best possible outcome for all. Progress is what is important, not really perfection—and, in the case of Africa, progress is what we are called to be doing. As described by Iyinoluwa Aboyeji, who co-founded Andela which we touched on earlier, a global engineering organisation out of Nigeria backed by the Chan-Zuckerberg Initiative and now with its headquarters in New York, "There's literally no barrier if you're working on the right things and you're passionate about what you're working on.[107]" You need to make this a habit.

4. THE VALUE OF TEAM

Any entrepreneur worth his salt, and any leadership education or entrepreneurial training you go to will always attest to the value of team. We focus on those who hold the vision most clearly and who effectively have

---

107   Muyiwa Matuluko, *Why Andela is paying Nigerians to become World Class developers.* Published at Tech Point, May 2015. Available at https://techpoint.ng/2015/05/20/why-andela-is-paying-nigerians-to-become-world-class-developers/

the guts to take the risk and take the shortfall, and for good reason; but in all these cases the team has been imperative. Even while we can say that Thakkar started on his own at the age of 15, he did not get there without the valuable support (financially and otherwise) from his family. As he himself says, when asked how he manages to run such a large company:

> "I don't juggle, I just pretend to be smart, yet I don't run anything. I oversee my fantastic team of smart, empowered individuals who help me run the organisation. I'm involved in strategy and spearheading growth.[108]"

I love how Chris Folayan even saw the value of team at just seven years old, inspiring and convincing his friends — and their parents — to collect tyres and bring them to his house so he could get them recycled for money. I would argue that this keen and early insight into the value of team has been absolutely critical to his success as an entrepreneur. If a seven-year-old gets it, I'm sure we all can too!

HOW THIS SPEAKS TO BORDERLESS AFRICA

The link here between these trends and the trends we have been examining with Silicon Valley, China, and Africa are astounding. I have touched briefly in parts on the idea of a borderless Africa — how imperative it is that we re-look at our regulation, open up our borders to each other, and think beyond a geographical Silicon Valley but think of making our Silicon Valley a more of a cohesive whole, a collaborative effort of innovators across our borders. Our innovators must think of being Pan-African from day one. In all the cases I highlighted above, and a few others, it's clear that engaging cross-culturally stirs innovation. There is simply *something about it*. It helps for us to see things differently, take it from a different angle, and experience life in a way that we see the opportunities. It also helps to build incredibly strong teams. Fred Swaniker's team is incredibly diverse. Jason Njoku teamed up with his

---

108   Lillian Kiarie, *Living the dream: How Ashish Thakkar became Africa's youngest billionaire*. Published at Standard Digital, July 2014. Available at https://www.standardmedia. co.ke/business/article/2000126574/africa-s-youngest-billionaire

British friend. The Andela team was also very diverse (Iyinoluwa Aboyeji has since moved on to another start-up, Flutterwave, which allows merchants to make and receive payments across multiple platforms). It's clear to me that the easier we make it for us to build teams across borders, the better teams we will build, the more we can innovate in a Pan-African way and in local contexts to truly change the lives of Africans everywhere.

Perhaps you don't have the opportunity to cross your borders and see the world from a different angle, but your city may present cross-cultural opportunities you might never have seen before. I really hope that you see it and do something about immersing yourself in different cultures, different situations. Perhaps spend some time in a different village, a different city - a different culture in your own cultural landscape is all you need.

Now we will begin to examine this revolutionary idea of a borderless Africa in more detail, first looking at how our innovations need to think Pan African from day one.

"Africa has her mysteries and even a wise man cannot understand them. But a wise man respects them."

— **Miriam Makeba**

CHAPTER SIXTEEN

THINKING PAN-AFRICAN FROM DAY ONE

One of the most amazing strengths of African innovation has to do with how our innovators address their local context. They see local problems and come up with local solutions, speaking to us in an African way, and bringing technology in as the base from which to develop and provide the solution. As I mentioned previously, we have to challenge the 'developing world' narrative and ask how a nation should develop in the context of what some are calling the "fourth industrial revolution". African innovation looks different to, say, innovation in Japan—which focuses a great deal on robotics and sci-fi like technology—and for this reason, African innovation needs to be taken on by its own merits. This is why I strongly believe that we really need to develop our own innovation index, rather than relying purely on outside authorities on the subject. Our innovation needs to be rated according to our own context and the homegrown solutions our innovators provide.

But there is a flip-side to this coin. We've been exploring how the "big boys" of Silicon Valley have a keen eye on our continent, and when they come in they create disruption in many of our stable industries. Many times this disruption is unforeseen. For example, I've shown how Uber disrupts the car manufacturing industry more than the taxi industry (because if Uber is cheaper to use than buying a car, and it can be if you split fees or car pool, fewer people buy cars). I also showed how

Facebook could potentially pull the rug from under our telecommunications industries as they look to provide free satellite Internet access. The key point in all this is to show that these Silicon Valley innovators know how to think about local solutions that can also work in a Pan-African context. Have you noticed how each changes the way it does its marketing or payments and adjusts its service with regards to local needs? For example, have you seen that you can pay cash for an uber in many African cities?

China's Alibaba, in particular, is a good example of how this approach really works. As we covered previously, eBay was the big player in China when Alibaba came on the scene, and it owned 80 percent of the market. Alibaba decided to compete head-on and it had an ace up its sleeve: it knew how Chinese think and work much better than eBay, with its head office based in America. Whereas eBay had a clean look and feel—'minimalist' as the saying goes — which appeals to Western audiences with the advent of what was dubbed 'Web 2.0' a decade ago, Chinese like websites that are full of fun and flair, with stickers and smiley faces and a dozen avenues to explore. What looks busy to an American, looks like fun to a Chinese, and Alibaba knew this better than anyone. Also, it boils down to the fascinating subject of language. English uses spaces and capital letters while Chinese writing makes uses of characters — one character can convey a rich meaning without needing to be spelt out in a sentence. To Western eyes, this might look tremendously busy on a website. Furthermore, Chinese just like 'one-stop' shops, and colour conveys meaning in the culture (red might mean good luck, for example).

Nielson Norman Group decided to study how the differences work. In its study, it says impressions formed purely by looking, instead of using, are not a valid user experience. One Chinese participant in its study, testing a Western site, said, "From a pure design perspective, like icons, pictures, layout, the site is great and matches what people, at least young people, love. It's simple, clean, with no ads, and no useless information. But the problem is, while it doesn't have any useless information, it also has less useful information — I can find nothing useful in these simple links. All this introduction of the functionality is just playing with words, with no real meat, no real content at all.[109]"

I think this is important for African innovators to consider. It is true that we want to match international standards of design and functionality, of course, but it also makes me wonder what a true African app *should* look like. While we have a high mobile penetration, and while technology and apps are driving so much of our innovation, I wonder if we considered African design specifically, how many more Africans would jump on board? In the case of Alibaba, its culturally-sensitive design and functionality, as opposed to eBay, made Chinese flock to Alibaba, and in six years it had stolen the market away from eBay significantly—so much so, eBay bowed out the Chinese market. Jack Ma, during this battle, famously said, "eBay is a shark in the ocean. We are a crocodile in the Yangtze River. If we fight in the ocean we will lose, but if we fight in the river we will win.[110]" This is reiterated and explained in more detail in the following comments from Porter Erisman, former Alibaba Vice President:

"All products and services need to be local. And more than any other product or service, an internet business needs to be hyper-local, because it is a reflection of the culture, economy and society it is built to serve. In that sense, e-commerce companies should try to reflect and augment the offline way of doing business as much as possible. For example, in China, where people are less likely to trust a stranger to do a transaction online, we integrated chat software into the website so that buyers and sellers could get to know each other before making a transaction. We also made our payment system an escrow-based system, so that buyers and sellers could store their money in the hands of a trusted third party until their deal was consummated. The images and language on Chinese websites also tend to be more human and playful, to reflect the way people use other websites in China.[111]"

---

109   Yunnuo Cheng and Jakob Nielsen, *Are Chinese Websites Too Complex?* Published at Nielsen Norman Group, November 2016. Available at https://www.nngroup.com/articles/china-website-complexity/

110   See http://www.crocodileintheyangtze.com/index.html

111   Alibaba's Former VP Tells *How Jack Ma Beat Ebay From A Small China Apartment.*

Of course, it certainly helped that Alibaba's TaoBao was free, as opposed to eBay charging for listing on its platform. But all this is simply the basic business maxim that says, "know your market". And really know your market. Sometimes in Africa, I think we assume the market wants what seems to be working overseas — it's a matter of privilege to bring what is 'overseas' here, much like we flock to the Krispy Kremes and Burger Kings of the world. Sure, it's a great experience and makes us feel as if we are living in another world for a while, but we need to balance it off with solid support of local and Pan-African brands.

THINKING PAN-AFRICAN FROM THE BEGINNING

If we as African innovators want to have a lasting impact and if we want to actually take on Silicon Valley in Africa, we need to think about our local context and the Pan-African context very carefully, and at every step of our building. Both are important and both need to be considered. Our innovators need to know the market on both fronts. This means, from day one, our innovators need to be thinking Pan-African, which is not usually the case. Many of our homegrown innovations can actually work outside of their immediate context and be successful. This would all contribute to creating the new kind of ecosystem we are dreaming about.

Here's a small example to show what I mean. South African-based Livestock Wealth, founded by Ntuthuko Shezi, gives you the opportunity to invest in cows through its app. The company manages two farms. You invest in the cattle while they manage the cattle for you. It's obviously an African solution, right? It makes much more sense to most Africans than other forms of investment. You can't export that to most of America. You can't really get that working in Switzerland. But you can definitely export that to most of Africa. I would also argue that there might even be other places in the world that you can export it to as well. In fact, I bet there are.

Livestock Wealth is, therefore, an example of a very clever innovation that we would classify under a 'small' startup. But it could easily go Pan-African. As far as I'm concerned, Shezi and his team ought to be thinking about that from day one. When you look at our most successful

Published at Jing Daily, February 2014. Available at https://jingdaily.com/alibabas-former-vp-tells-how-jack-ma-beat-ebay-from-a-small-china-apartment/

start-ups, that's exactly what they have been doing. Jason Njoku, from the Nollywood streaming service IrokoTV, is a great example of an innovation that clearly had a Pan-African view in mind from its inception. IrokoTV surely competes against the likes of Showmax, Netflix, and even DStv. When Showmax and Netflix arrived on our continent, Njoku didn't seem to break into much of a sweat. On his blog, he admitted that he and his wife use Netflix every week, and he has been a subscriber since 2012.

> "It's amazing. I have blogged and generally been smitten by the company and their internet style market share grab. Where possible, I even try to emulate it. But Netflix irokoTV isn't. There is only one Netflix of Africa. And that is Netflix. Why? People fail to remember that Netflix is an 18 year old company. 18 years they have been refining their skills at getting people to subscribe for content. They are just awesome at it. But Africa is a little different. What Irocko is, and has largely always been known for, is the home of Nollywood. Home and abroad. The strange thing about the mourners of Iroko is they always mention how most of our subscribers are in the West. Yup, US and UK represent ~55% of our subscription base. And it's grown (not break-neck) but steadily over the last few years, in Netflix's back yard.[112]"

He knows he has the core market that matters to his business: Nollywood viewers. He knows that market and knows how to speak to them. Even if Netflix sees an opportunity and pushes more Nollywood content on the platform, Iroko knows the market better — and he has had plenty of time to carve out that niche. Iroko viewers are all over Africa and throughout the world in the African diaspora. From the outset, Njoku knew this and captured an African need so well that IrokoTV not only captures what has been an existing market but is creating new markets for Nollywood where there may not have been before. Not only that, but it is producing Nollywood content and is a key player in the production industry. So when the likes of Showmax come in they have to either partner with IrokoTV or essentially aim for taking second-place

---

112   Jason Njoku, *Netflix in Africa*. See his blog at https://jason.com.ng/netflix-in-africa-b01fea9706da

on the continent. This is the kind of approach and the kind of thinking we need from our home-grown innovators.

Another great example of this is Ashish Thakkar, whose Mara Group now spans over 25 African countries and three continents. It operates in the technology, financial services, manufacturing, real estate and agriculture industries:

> "People keep talking about bringing Silicon Valley to Africa, and I like and appreciate this message, but it doesn't excite me. I do not want to bring Silicon Valley to Africa, I want to take Africa to Silicon Valley. We need to be innovative and global. Why keep using Facebook, Twitter and all these American products when we can create great things like Safaricom's M-Pesa? Those great innovators started in gory garages, what's holding us back?[113]"

I like this vision. It shows that we can't limit our "Silicon Valley" to our borders, but have to create a different kind of Silicon Valley in Africa — one without borders and yet exists within our borders and across our borders. We have to think of our approach to this differently.

Underneath Thakkar's core vision with the Pan-African, Mara Group is to make Africa a worldwide, tangible player in just about every market. He is actively working on solving our "last mile" of logistics problem, and also understands something about how the African continent's image abroad is often way off compared to how things on the ground — which is stirring him to consider starting our own 'innovation index' that will measure innovation according to our criteria and context. Whenever I speak to him, I am stirred by his vision and how relentless he is at achieving it. All of this is in a Pan-African range of view. When speaking to CNN about growing African economies, Thakkar is straightforward about the need to think Pan-African:

> "Pan-African collaboration is extremely important. I think things like

---

113   Lillian Kiarie, *Living the dream: How Ashish Thakkar became Africa's youngest billionaire*. Published at Standard Digital, July 2014. Available at https://www.standardmedia. co.ke/business/article/2000126574/africa-s-youngest-billionaire

regional integration, inter-African trade does need to increase and is increasing. I mean, the progress in the East African community has been amazing. The manner in which they've harmonized so many different laws and policies and mindset and priorities within that region has been fantastic. So, we need to see more of that take place on the continent. The fact that we're 54 countries, yet we're a billion people is an advantage and a disadvantage. I think to strengthen our weakness in that collaboration across the continent is crucial.[114]"

Some people joke that Mara Group is the African version of Virgin. It's not far off. But the vision is to soon see the joke work the other way— that Virgin is simply the British/American version of Mara. I think this is an important distinction that we have to think about; it shows us how we even need to change our language about these things. When we speak about the vision of our company, we need to always be speaking of how we are going to extend throughout Africa, like Chris Folayan who speaks about expanding MallforAfrica in such a way that it encourages and grows intra-African trade.

Fred Swaniker, the founder of the African Leadership Academy, the African Leadership Network, Global Leadership Adventures, and African Leadership University, is a brilliant example of a man who is seeing the Pan-African future from an educational perspective and finding ways to connect us together through our borders in a Pan-African way. His mission is to create the next generation of African leaders, with a vision of seeing 25 universities across Africa, each campus accommodating ten thousand leaders—all the campuses together, therefore, "educating and developing 250 thousand leaders at any given time." He is not just looking at what's going on now but is thinking about what things will look like in 50 years time.

The Africa Leadership Academy, based out of Johannesburg, and the infrastructure it is creating has a vision to compete with Ivy League type of institutions, investing heavily in African youth and fostering leader-

---

114   Alex Court and Holly Brown, *Self-made tycoon: 'Africa is doing amazing – it's our turn to shine'*. Published at CNN, April 2015. Available at http://edition.cnn.com/2015/04/16/business/ashish-thakkar-africa-is-doing-amazing/

ship to prepare not only them but the continent for the future. His vision is exactly what I think our innovators ought to be keeping in mind: create the next generation, create the future.

What is fundamental about the African Leadership Academy's strategy, I believe, is that each student is meant to create a viable business which can then be scaled and live on its own. That's how you start to create this network we've been talking about in this book. For example, if you were selling hair products on campus, or an app that helps people study, the ecosystem and collaboration is fostered at the Academy—and you take that network with you. The same logic applies to the African Leadership Network, which essentially gathers bright African leaders under the age of 50 and puts them together. It usually meets once a year in a designated city in Africa. The more the group meets and collaborate in a relaxed setting, the more we can see ecosystems spring up.

But what I find the most interesting is how the team tracks impact. For example, if I met someone in Mauritius as someone who is part of the African Leadership Network, and out of our meeting we decided to partner and delved into a project that created a certain amount of jobs, a certain amount of leaders, or spun off into other startups, Swaniker and his team track that impact. I don't think anyone has tracked this sort of thing before. Usually, I find that a lot of our conferences tend to work counter-intuitively. We put everyone in a room and hope for the best, and we have no way of seeing if it really did anything, if those people connected, or if anything at all came from it. There are times when people just don't connect and can't find a way to partner, and then the hub or the conference or the event was nothing more than us listening to powerful speakers and then grabbing a beer and going back to our hotel room, left to work everything out for ourselves. Meanwhile, if we connected with the right people, we might just find the right partnership to bring our breakthrough in whatever challenge we're currently facing; or we might find a new project that will break open something we never imagined before.

Technology as we know it has not existed in Africa for a long time and is only a couple of decades old. Things like the mobile phone only came here about ten to fifteen years ago. Internet and data are also, of course, relevantly recent. Sure, we have had our own innovations historically, but when you start to compete or compare Africa to the rest of the world, tech innovation is really new. If you do a comparison on the time frame between Silicon Valley who had about seven to eight decades, and we who have had about two decades, you can start to appreciate how far we have come in a short time frame and how innovative we actually are. That is encouraging and absolutely key. But we need to appreciate this massive learning curve for us.

I don't think we really do. We are always keen and open to investigating other innovative solutions that come from the outside, as opposed to our own. We have to have a significant mind shift about this: one that as opposed to looking at a need-based approaching and focusing on future innovation. We need to think that in thirty years time we will leave a legacy for the next generation, so that when they come in they actually have a platform to innovate from — infrastructure, a mindset and cultural and historical thinking that they can lean on, as opposed to just a new technology. Once we start to think like that, it sets a pace for us in the African innovation setting. We need to start thinking Pan-African, not just country based or community-based. And that is how we will find the next Einstein or Zuckerburg.

I know in my last book I spoke a great deal about many of the innovators and innovations above, and they tend to get a lot of airtime in general. Perhaps you're saying to yourself, "I'm pretty tired of hearing about these guys by now. Is there nothing new?" Well, that's the point. We have to keep repeating the same successes when we take a Pan-African view because actually, we don't have enough innovators thinking like them. See it, then, as a challenge. We need you as an innovator to elevate your thinking and your view of innovation, and think homegrown and Pan-African at the same time, all the time. In my view, this is critical if you want to have a lasting impact, which I believe you do. Silicon Valley saw this a long time ago. It's time we do the same—before Silicon Valley scoops up our industries for themselves. We're poised, right now, to do some amazing things—but we have to be bold and big about it.

But there's more to it than this. We need to think of our businesses and innovations in a Pan-African way, but we need to also think of the *team* we have available as beyond just Africa. In other words, we need to think about the African diaspora.

"Teams are crucial because they combine the differing talents of different individuals, and they make the whole better than the part."

– Hakeem Belo-Osagie

CHAPTER SEVENTEEN

INCLUDING THE DIASPORA

Given my background as an engineer, I have a very analytical way of thinking. This leads me to approach almost everything by way of logic and to try and glean as many hard facts as I possibly can. Many years ago, I was an African who thought our continent was a difficult place with no opportunities, and that I and my logical approach had very little place in it. That is one of the reasons I initially moved to Australia, to study there. This narrative and view of Africa wasn't purely something I had cooked up myself but was actually something I had grown up hearing and therefore believing. A lot of my parents' generation really believed life was better lived elsewhere, and the best thing to do is get an education and go to the first world and make a living there.

I did that but found it wasn't all roses. In fact, it's not really any easier in a first world country at all. This I can guarantee anyone who is reading this book and thinking of immigrating. So we can tick that box and debunk that myth. When you look at your average African living in the States, UK or Australia, more often than not, they have a very basic life. They're not living it up or living the "American Dream" — work hard, come home to your white picket fence, enjoy your hobbies on weekends. Looking back, even if that was my life, I have no idea how I would survive it — it would probably bore me to the verge of clinical depression. Rather, give me projects, give me a business, give me vision. I want to pioneer something. I don't want to just soak up a salary and eat food and go fishing and drink beer on weekends. Some of us Africans in first world contexts actually have two or three jobs just to make ends meet. They work menial jobs even though they have significant qualifications, Masters or PHD's. This is what life is like outside our borders for many of the diaspora.

If I look at things from that angle, it doesn't make sense. Most Africans in the diaspora will tell you that living in a first world is not the dream that is sold to you. What is the alternative then? The alternative is to stay in Africa and face the difficulties of our own context. But in my view, the difficulties we face here as individuals are not necessarily worse than living in a first world country. And often, the difficulties we face there are more emotional in nature, as you find yourself truly struggling with your identity.

We have, of course, a much larger poverty problem. I'm not down-playing that because that's not really what I am speaking of right now. I am speaking to entrepreneurs and innovators, and I want to say it's an even playing field here in Africa for an African. There are very few exceptions to the rule where an African has done much better outside our continent than they could have here, but I believe that with the right view and the right opportunities in Africa you can actually do far, far better than you would in a first world country.

Secondly, the reality is that you can look at Africa as a half-full glass or a half-empty one. It really is your choice. I go through my moments too where I read the news or I see some negative development, and I think to myself that it doesn't make sense — I don't understand why it has to be so difficult. Why can't we all just work together? Why can't we just put our skills and our brains and our money and our opportunities together and create a better Africa for ourselves? We struggle with corruption, xenophobia, state capture, and (often) purposeless leaders who don't seem to know why they were elected in the first place. All this can be very demoralising if you look at the glass half-empty. But I have to realise that no one ever really made a change by being negative but rather by seeing new opportunities. There are certain days when you also read the news or track some new development and you realise that you *have* to look at it half-full because there is so much opportunity — opportunity not just for people visiting us but for us Africans ourselves. The only people who can capitalise on our opportunities properly are Africans. If we don't wake up and smell the coffee, we will, unfortunately, miss the boat.

One of the questions that many Africans ask me is, "Why did you come back from Australia to Africa?" My answer is usually, "Why not?" The reasons are simple. I would never have accomplished even one tenth of what I've accomplished here on this continent, especially since I decided to see things half-full. I would never have written a book about African innovation, become a media contributor, having had my own radio slot, or had the amazing privilege of meeting the passionate, smart, leading innovators and entrepreneurs that I have — many of which I call friends. I would have had no impact overseas because I was actually a minority. Sure, maybe I would have had a stable job and would have built model airplanes with my kids every weekend, living comfortably, and telling my kids to play it safe like I did… and probably getting very restless. Being in that sort of context, you buy into the culture and the life, but the truth is that your heart beats the red African soil, and I have something to add to this continent, and that is why I came back.

If as an African you choose to view the glass as half full, you can have an impact, guaranteed. The way I approach Africans who have a negative view is to work on logical facts and go through a logical process — presenting all the facts. I try to demonstrate, just as I'm trying to do through all my writing and speaking. I am trying to showcase opportunities — that there are people and leaders and tech and innovations all happening under our nose; that people are doing something about where we are, so why not join them? When you present those facts it's really up to the individual to accept or disprove it. In my view, with time there will be enough tangible optimism around Africa that it will spill over to the side of more optimism than negativity. It will eventually be that the negative individuals will become the exception rather than the rule.

I think one of the major areas in which this thinking is critical is when we consider the African diaspora. Many of those in the diaspora are longing to make a difference for our continent, but they often don't know exactly how they can do it without physically being here. Others need to be shown that the story of this continent is not at all what they think. I believe we need to think better about this and find better solutions for them and for us together.

THINKING ABOUT HOW WE VIEW HOME-GROWN INNOVATORS

In my continued journey with promoting African innovation, including recently having gone on a tour connecting with innovators, I've noticed an interesting trend. It seems to me that foreign innovators who have identified an issue on our continent and discovered a solution and come here to implement the solution, tend to garner a bit more respect than many of our homegrown innovators. This respect comes in the form of general perception, how we speak about them, and how we fund them. Homegrown innovators tend to need to work a little bit harder to get the same sort of response and respect from us.

Perhaps some say that there aren't enough credible homegrown innovators on the continent, which may be true in some instances but not in all. Plus innovation, at least of the kind we're seeing across the world today, is relatively new for us. But I think part of why we give foreign innovators the respect we do is because they come from a background of experience and knowledge, whereas we're still trying to find out way through things.

But we can use this general trend in a positive way to tap into the diaspora because in many instances they are garnering the background knowledge and experience overseas that we seem to respect so highly. So why not make use of that? The diaspora can contribute so much to the development of our continent and within innovation—but the problem is we are sometimes just not creating opportunity, or talking to them, or finding them and feeding them the knowledge they need to see how exciting Africa has become, and the potential. In general, we don't seem to include those in the diaspora as part of our narrative, as part of the change.

I think many diaspora Africans would love to participate in creating a new narrative for Africa, and in innovation more specifically. Some probably think that the only way they can do that is to move here, take a massive risk, set up shop, and get involved. But I don't think so. I think what's lacking is other alternatives. We have to think more remotely. For example, why not invite those who are working for Facebook or Amazon to work on something we are doing even while they are there? With the Internet, they don't always have to be here. It doesn't even have to be a high-level executive, but even a simple coder in the diaspora could contribute to an innovation we are working on here.

We ought to be headhunting them and creating opportunities for them to participate in our ecosystem—opportunities where they don't need to necessarily move back (but may in the long run). We ought to be finding them, educating them, and showing them what our innovators are doing. And then asking them: Well, how do you think you can contribute to these innovations? How do you think the experience you've gained can help us here?

The 'brain drain' is a very real problem and instead of just lamenting about it we have to work at reversing it or even taking advantage of it by tapping into those garnering experience overseas. Most people who are part of the 'brain drain' assume they don't really have options — especially if they specialise in something niche or have a unique skillset. But this does not need to be so.

I myself know the tugging at the heart that occurs when you're out there. I spent ten years in Australia creating jobs. One day it suddenly dawned on me that if I could do that in Australia why couldn't I do it at home? That made me finally begin to work out my own views of Africa, to where I am today where I believe our innovation can really change everything about our continent in a hugely positive way. So I came back.

But when you're not on our shores there is a sense that you have to figure out life for yourself, and you end up living in something of a bubble. I found this same sense with many of my African friends in the diaspora. Without being involved in the community that is Africa we lose not only a sense of our own identity but that connectedness we need to see how we form part of our story, past, present and future. And we don't pass our story down to the next generation, creating a disconnectedness from who we actually are.

That's why we need to find ways to connect our fellow Africans all over the world to us, and in today's connected world there are so many new ways of doing this. What we need to do is just change our mindset about how the diaspora can contribute, and I'm sure we'll then begin to find ways to include Africans everywhere to participate.

And when I say Africans everywhere, I also mean Africans of all kinds. In building a Pan-African team of innovators across Africa to come together and take on Silicon Valley, we need to also challenge our cultural perceptions around who can contribute. In the next chapter, then, I'll get a bit controversial and challenge our particular views around the contribution of women in the fold.

"The seeds of success in every nation on earth are best planted in women and children."

— Joyce Banda

CHAPTER EIGHTEEN

THE AFRICAN GIRL-CHILD AND INNOVATION

Innovation is bringing information to the next generation like never before, thereby empowering the African girl-child and giving her equal opportunity. We all can be a part of this. In fact, if we don't, we will miss a valuable and integral part of how we can actually take on Silicon Valley, or work with Silicon Valley in a way that is to our benefit.

So far we've covered a lot of ground. We opened up to look at how Silicon Valley started and how it is looking at Africa. We did the same with China. We explored pockets of innovation in Africa that help us draw important lessons, and we explored the necessity for Pan-African innovation. At this stage, you might be wondering where it's all going, and how I'm going to pull it all together. This book is all about examining trends. The truth is, there are myriad trends and it might be difficult to summarise and pick out an 'action plan' with all the angles we have to consider. Perhaps right now you're feeling challenged and encouraged, but are still not sure what to do next. I don't want to leave you without action points. We can't let all of this remain complex but need to simplify so we know what next step to take.

To help with this, I want to close in the next few chapters with the story of our innovators themselves. In my last book and in other places where I've been published, and at conferences and the like, I've spoken about innovations that are changing Africa and that carry tremendous potential — innovations that truly change lives. Many of my favourite innovations such as WeCyclers from Nigeria, which addresses the collection of trash; or the Vula App, which I've also spoken about in a previous chapter; or the portable WiFi solution from Kenya, BRCK; or M-Kopa Solar; or the African Leadership Academy, which I've already spoken about, have grown and expanded since I first encountered them, and I would love to talk more about them in themselves. But that would be repeating myself. Instead, I want to come at it from a different angle. Each of these has a person or persons behind them and I want to ask, who are they?

In addition to examining the technological and entrepreneurial trends of today's 'fourth industrial revolution, we need to also examine the personal or psychological trends. We need to effectively piece together what makes for a successful African innovator. The trends we might uncover here are important in highlighting how we need to think and approach entrepreneurship and our African innovative spirit.

Growing up, I didn't have access to a lot of technology. Many middle-class kids began to be exposed to technology through video games (Nintendo, PC, Sega Megadrive) or simply via noticing that their parents were starting to work on computers. My parents at the time, however, couldn't afford video games or the like or didn't think there was any value in it, and probably never thought I would be interested in it. I wasn't really, to be honest. I remember playing video games at some of my friend's houses, but I never really thought about having that at home.

This is interesting to me, given that I am so passionate about technology now. It feels like a disparity to me — not having it growing up and now being surrounded by it. The time I realised I actually enjoy technology was in university. As a university student, I had to get my own computer and I did not have enough money to buy one. In those days, we didn't have smartphones and tablets, and laptops were pretty expensive and often impractical. What we had were component PC's, what some might call 'box-type' computers. The benefit of this was, of course, that you could buy the parts separately and slowly build it up. You could go out and buy the case with the power supply, then buy the motherboard the next month, and then get your hard drive, get RAM and so on. So I saved a bit and bought the components — getting some RAM from friends; and I remember buying my motherboard from Incredible Connection, a computer retail store in Botswana. I was probably about 17 or 18 years old at the time. I really enjoyed doing this because not only was I able to build my own computer, but I was even deemed cool by lots of people at the time to be able to do that—so I got myself the all-important school popularity points. Only people with money could afford a computer, and those without did not have the skillset to build their own. So the whole process made me feel like I was getting a step ahead. I knew of technology of course, as we had a TV and tech-type products at home, but when I built my first computer it was an invaluable experience. It's then that you can see what the power of technology can do and you can see that translating into my passion now.

There are multiple stories I can draw out of that, but one of the most notable for me was my first University project in Botswana. It was based around being able to track locomotives using GPS technology. We were able to track them on an interface that had been designed off the programming language, Java. That was very cool and at that stage it was revolutionary. Now we have Uber and Google maps, but I saw this sort of thing in its beginning stages. I remember my final presentation at University where everyone thought it was very impressive. That probably was my first foray into the impact of technology on my life and how it would change things going forward for me and for our entire world.

This realisation of how technology will change our world continues when we think about some of our traditional challenges faced by actual people. How did our best and most successful innovators, as people, address these challenges? One of my most interesting looks into this subject was at the World Economic Forum (WEF) on Africa 2017, where women were honoured for their contribution to innovation on the continent. In my own work in the African innovation space, I found it a rather troubling one day about two years ago from the time of writing this book when I realised that out of all the innovators I've interviewed, spoken about, written about in my book and articles, very few of them were actually female. This insight, to my own shame, had to be pointed out to me by a female media contributor whom I was writing a piece for. From that day I set out to try and equal the scales, as it were and put effort into finding more female innovators.

However, I was soon to discover it just wasn't that easy. It's not as if women are unable, of course. What it comes down to, in the end, is what it comes down to in all fields of work, opportunity, and entrepreneurship in Africa: the plight of the African girl child. This is a subject that I've grown more passionate about as I've grown in my love for our continent and as I've realised more and more just how much of a pioneer my mum was. Like many African fathers, mine had to work for extensive times outside of our country. So it was up to my mum to take care of the details at home. While working as a teacher herself, she raised five really good kids—four of them girls—who succeeded in their studies, went on to do masters, and are all working now. This in a time when opportunities for women are far less than they are today. Imagine having to raise three to five kids and at the same time be innovative and at the top of your game, as it were. That is very difficult and many times women have to prove even more to their male counterparts as to why they should be allowed to the table — meaning, they often have to work much harder than I do.

I think the biggest gift my mum gave me was time management. I have a phrase I use all the time which is, "Five minutes early is always on time." I apply that to my work ethic. This goes well back to my childhood days. I have memories of my mum actually leaving us at home because weren't on time. She was a teacher at our school, so if she would drop us, we would have to be on time to get in the car to get to school. If she left us at home, she still expected us to be on time. She would often come and check in class if we arrived on time and you can imagine there would be some very fine disciplinary action at home if we did not. That ethic has stuck with me from childhood growing up and is one that I still apply today. I think it's a very good ethic for anyone to apply, especially for entrepreneurs or innovators because you are then true to you word.

My mum taught me to have a very deep respect for women and to appreciate what they bring to the table. Her example created this respect. To see what my mum and my sisters have accomplished is quite phenomenal. I was chatting to a female innovator not too long ago who, while catching up on how things are going in life in general, told me her baby was due in a few days. My mind was sufficiently boggled. I couldn't comprehend that she was still working and as bright as ever a few days just before having her child. Even more so, a few days later after she gave birth to her child, she was still communicating with me via email, trying to set up a meeting.

We need to really change our attitudes and our viewpoints around female innovators. Not only should they be at the table with men, they should be firmly recognised for what they bring to the table, and what they have had to go through to get to the table. The WEF on Africa 2017, which took place in Durban and which I was privileged to be a part of, convened regional and global leaders from business, government and civil society to agree on the priorities that will help Africa achieve inclusive growth. With all the above in mind, one of the highlights for me was seeing six top female entrepreneurs honoured at the event. All of the entrants had to have run a business that's less than three years old, with at least one year of revenue and had to have had an innovative technology or business model. Each of them contributed to the think-tank on giving entrepreneurship a boost in Africa. Here's more about them:

Aisha Pandor, co-founder of SweepSouth

I met Pandor about two years ago when she launched the ever-growing-in-popularity SweepSouth app. SweepSouth, based in South Africa, allows for you to book a domestic cleaner through its app, indicate how many rooms you need to be cleaned, what special requirements you might have, whether you have cleaning products or not, and other options. It's kind of like Uber for cleaners, with the cleaners having the option to work flexible hours and find the best opportunities; while the platform's algorithm looks to match its 'SweepStars' (its cleaners) with the right customers. You can request the same cleaner again and they can rate you as a customer. This is doing two things. Firstly, it's ensuring that domestic cleaners are paid fairly for the hours they work. Secondly, it's helping to elevate the status of cleaners in South Africa in the mind of our society. It's a very simple solution to a problem in South Africa that I believe will bring fantastic change to an industry long in need of an overhaul.

Temie Giwa-Tubosun, founder of LifeBank:

LifeBank uses its platform to get blood to the right place in Nigeria in the right time. It uses a predictive modelling system to make sure health workers are supplied with the blood they need. It mobilises blood donations through its app and then connects hospitals and health centres with their needs. It plans to expand into several more major cities of Africa very soon.

Charity Wanjiku, co-founder of Strauss Energy Ltd.:

Strauss Energy (Kenya) integrates energy generating technology into basic building materials: roof tiles, glass, pavement, walls, roads, and in stadiums and warehouses, etc. It makes use of Building Integrated Photovoltaics (BIPV) to do this, which are energy-producing solar cells fitted into functional parts of any construction. Strauss Energy is able to undercut other solar tiles by 30 percent, and unlike solar panels, BIPV is more cost efficient, durable, and more aesthetically pleasing.

Oluwayimika Angel Adelaja, founder and CEO of Fresh Direct Nigeria:

As a social enterprise, Fresh Direct focuses on protecting and boosting local farming and production, especially amongst the youth, using new technologies that will help Africans compete on a commercial scale. One of its technologies is stackable container farms, which assist urbanites to farm and harvest high quality produce. It amazes me that these stackable container farms aren't in every city everywhere already, to be honest. The technology uses less water and, of course, land than conventional farming but is able to produce a yield that's 15 times greater. When you go and check out what can be done with these sorts of farms, it's truly space-age, exciting stuff. We can literally have farms for a fraction of the price all over our cities—I really believe it's a unique breakthrough.

Darlene Menzies, founder and CEO of FinFind:

South African-based FinFind assists start-ups and SME's to get financing, by matching them with (to date) 200 lenders and 300 loan offerings. It does this easily through its website. It also explains financing, links businesses with accountants and advisers, and, on the lender side, effectively provides a consistent stream of leads.

Esther Karwera, co-founder of Akorion:

Akorion's tag-line is "ICT for Agriculture". Based in Uganda, it has developed software that collects real-time data (GPS data, production data, inputs demand, product supply, mapped cultivated land, biodata) for farmers, and connects them with financial institutions, suppliers, insurance companies, markets and exporters. Smallholder farmers can sell direct to agribusinesses, creating better opportunities for them at a better price. It even helps farmers to know the right nutrients for their soil and adjust accordingly. It has built up a network of 42,000 farmers in Uganda at this time and is helping in terms of rural unemployment in a big way.

These are only the tip of the iceberg. Other women, such as Ory Okolloh and Juliana Rotich, digital activists who co-created Ushahidi, a crisis-mapping tool that was developed to help curb violence in elections and has extended into the States and Europe and Australia for all sorts of other uses (firefighting, civil rights, and others) are examples of women making a huge difference through innovative technologies. And women are, of course, working in other fields such as education and job creation. There is Dr Gisele Mophou, who I spoke about in a previous chapter, the first female chair of the African Institute of Mathematical Sciences (AIMS) in Rwanda. As you can see, each and every one of these women is pioneering and innovating in important fields and industries, working hard to help and shape an amazing future for us as Africans. I for one found the honouring of these women at WEF encouraging, and am excited to see what can happen when we get over our preconceived biases and give such women the respect they deserve, ushering in a new generation that will give new meaning to the phrase, "African girl-child".

"Failure is a good thing."

– **Hakeem Belo-Osagie**

CHAPTER NINETEEN

— × —

THE MISSING LINK: PRIVATE EQUITY

In my work with innovators on the African content, a trend I've picked up, again and again, is a struggle for funding. Many innovators may have done well in their country and are in the position to successfully replicate their success and expand to other nations, but they are corralled by a lack of access to the right kind of funding.

According to the Disrupt Africa African Tech Startups Funding Report of 2016, startups in Africa raised funding in excess of US$129 million in that year, with the number of startups securing funding up by 16.8 percent compared to the previous year.[115]

As stated by Tom Jackson from Disrupt Africa, these numbers show real growth in the amount of funding available to tech startups. In fact, he says that there would have been other funding taking place outside of what they surveyed. However, according to other analysts, more startups are folding because of lack of access to funding.[116] A further report from VC4Africa highlights how startups are largely dependent still on the founder's capital. This isn't necessarily a bad thing until you see how low venture capital (VC) funding and angel funding sit pretty low on the scale

---

115   Tom Jackson, Number of African tech startups funded rises 17% in 2016. Available at http://disrupt-africa.com/2017/01/number-of-african-tech-startups-funded-rises-17-in-2016/

116   Memory Mataranyika, *SA grabs lion's share of Africa's startup funding*. Published at Fin24 Tech, February 2016. Available at http://www.fin24.com/Tech/News/sa-grabs-lions-share-of-africas-startup-funding-20160223

of funding available — just 12 percent collectively. Here's the diagram:

AFRICAN START-UPS ARE RELIANT ON FOUNDER CAPITAL
SOURCE OF START-UP FUNDS

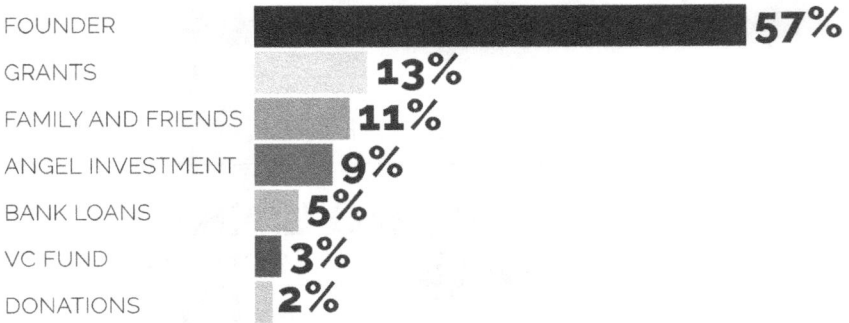

FOUNDER	**57%**
GRANTS	**13%**
FAMILY AND FRIENDS	**11%**
ANGEL INVESTMENT	**9%**
BANK LOANS	**5%**
VC FUND	**3%**
DONATIONS	**2%**

This trend, Quartz reports, might also be explained by the fact that only a handful of investors operating on the continent have made profitable exits so far.[117] When you think of the life-cycle of an innovative company, it usually starts from seed funding, where family and friends and the innovator themselves are putting in the funds to see it take off— which is what we see above. From there the company is looking for VC funding, where it has a prototype product or service that has done relatively well, or the business has a few stable clients, and the company wants to expand nationally or into another country. If the business grows (or survives!) through that phase, it moves to private equity – it's now a sustainable business and can grow into a genuinely profitable business nationally or multi-nationally. The last phase, typically, is then to be listed or partner with a bank for financing.

It's in the VC funding phase, however, that there seems to be a consistent problem on our continent. I think this is a real challenge that we need to address. It might be helped if angel investing increased as well, but that's beside the point. The VC phase, in my opinion, seems almost non-existent here, and this is a huge gap for innovators. This means a lot of innovators have to look beyond our borders and approach the likes of

---

117   Yomi Kazeem, *African start-ups are securing more investment—but there's still room for growth*. Published by Quartz Africa, May 2016. Available at https://qz.com/691106/african-start-ups-are-securing-more-investment-but-theres-still-room-for-growth/

Silicon Valley, but this comes with all sorts of problems and misunderstandings about the African context, resulting in mismatched expectations from investors and a model that just does not work here.

In an attempt to get to the bottom of this problem and see what we can do to rectify it, I've conducted anecdotal research of my own and gotten on the ground by speaking to innovators and several VC and private equity funds on the market. Through this I've picked up two consistent trends:

1. Innovators have unrealistic evaluations, usually tempered by the fact that they have spoken to a Silicon Valley-like VC firm. The problem is the way these overseas companies and investors work does not actually work here. Their approach to innovation funding is different. For example, they will typically employ an Uber-type approach: build an asset, throw lots of money at it, and hopefully in six to ten years time the asset is so big that someone will buy it out. During that process, a lot of cash has really been blown, but the reality is that the sheer scale and number of innovators in Silicon Valley makes this worthwhile. For every ten innovations on the table, one will take off and do very well, becoming the next Airbnb or Uber or whatever else, and the sale of that asset will justify not only the investment into it but the investment into the other nine that have done only relatively well, or are still growing, or haven't even done well at all.

Here in Africa, however, we just don't have enough innovators to justify this sort of model of funding – or the right amount of throughput to do so. There are other factors at play that we have to consider. Tom Jackson is the former editor of HumanIPO, an online tech news site, which had to shut down due to disappointing advertising revenues. One week before the closure was announced, he agreed to a frank interview with consulting firm GrowthAfrica on what happened. ""A lot of people in Africa do not have the option of trying a second time," he said. "Unlike techies in Silicon Valley, maybe they have not worked at [consulting firm] Accenture for six years. After failing, perhaps your African entrepreneur has to get a job because he does not have the resources to have a second go."

Silicon Valley's 'failure culture' — where failure is celebrated and glorified — is an important point to consider. Failure is built into the whole system and culture. There is a whole support system for innovators and entrepreneurs where they know they can fail and learn and try again. This kind of luxury, however, we don't have. All of this means we are usually not mentally prepared for entrepreneurship. We don't have the cultural or family support around us because our parents may not subscribe to that way of thinking. Even if your parents buy into the idea that you are going to be an entrepreneur, there is no financial support to provide your way through. This is the fundamental issue most entrepreneurs face in our context. They have no one to back them up emotionally, mentally and financially—or even just someone who says, "Here you go, here is a bit of cash. Go for gold!" While aspects of our culture romanticise about entrepreneurship, we don't have the safety net and foundations in place to make our entrepreneurs truly successful. Our entrepreneurs really face the same challenges most of our artists do: a lack of real support that goes beyond cheering, networks to tie into, and opportunities. Our parents' generation have no pension to play with and our generation has no financial independence, so already off the bat, we struggle.

When I compare all this to Silicon Valley and the system they have set up, where there is access to cash, a support system, mental preparation, networks, and a way of thinking that you can assimilate, I get why it's working. They even build failure into the system, turning it into a positive. Former entrepreneur turned academic, Vivek Wadhwa, goes so far as to say that Silicon Valley's culture of glorifying failure is what sets it apart. He claims that Japan, for example, has tried to replicate Silicon Valley by building fancy tech parks, subsidies for research and development, and even built a the Okinawa Institute of Science and Technology (OIST) research university, but still haven't managed to achieve what they set out to achieve. No matter how much money they throw into it, it just doesn't produce the same result. Why?

"In any country, innovation and economic growth come from startup ventures. But most Japanese don't want to take the risk of starting a business. Indeed, the social stigma and financial repercussion of failure are so great that the founders of failed businesses become social outcasts; no one will work with them again or fund them; and all too often they end up committing suicide.¹¹⁸"

Sound familiar? I bet it does. Meanwhile, back at Silicon Valley, they've invented the "fail fast, fail often" mantra. In 2009, a whole conference that glorifies failure was launched in San Francisco — the Failcon, which now is also in Tel Aviv, Bangalore, Barcelona and other cities. In Silicon Valley, entrepreneurs regularly give speeches and write books about the value of failure. If you've failed, you're a success — because the belief is that failure means you learn, and you build on that to not fail the next time. Or the next.

Obviously, all the hype has produced some problems with significant criticism. Author Rob Ashgar from Forbes is scathing. After quoting Richard Branson who quoted the playwright Samuel Beckett, saying "Ever tried. Ever failed. No matter. Try again. Fail again. Fail Better," Ashgar states the obvious: "Branson can't afford his pilots to fail again or fail better or fail forward or, frankly, fail at all. Ever.¹¹⁹" He has a point, obviously. The failure rate of Silicon Valley startups is said to be at 90 percent (which is quite normal for most types of industries) and some think that there are too many entrepreneurs who simply never rise above failure, all the while glorying in it, whilst close relatives who invested money in them lose badly. But yet it seems to me that the general culture of risk-taking and the support failed entrepreneurs get is on the whole much healthier than our culture right now. In our culture, to fail means you are no good, and you have even tarnished the image of your family.

So as an entrepreneur with no support system, you are afraid to fail. Creativity requires a safety net of sorts—a knowledge that if something fails, it's going to be generally okay. But most of our entrepreneurs and innovators can't find themselves in this sort of creative space because of

---

118   Vivek Wadhwa, *Japan: To Fix Your Economy, Honor Your Failed Entrepreneurs.* Published at Tech Crunch, October 2010. Available at https://techcrunch.com/2010/10/17/japan-to-fix-your-economy-honor-your-failed-entrepreneurs/

119   Rob Asghar, *Why Silicon Valley's 'Fail Fast' Mantra is Just Hype.* Published at Forbes, July 2014. Available at https://www.forbes.com/sites/robasghar/2014/07/14/why-silicon-valleys-fail-fast-mantra-is-just-hype/#52947e3624bc

the way we view failure and risk. Those who end up going for it, very many times foster a "me against the world" attitude. I know this—I've experienced it as an entrepreneur myself. Now you have to prove that it's not going to fail and you can do this. But any entrepreneur worth their salt knows that this is not the way to go, as it is almost a recipe for disaster.

In fact, by the time an innovator has overcome all the many hurdles we have to overcome both culturally and practically if they've had any form of success, they find themselves flat-out tired. You've been hustling and struggling for a very long time, and so when success finally comes it can be hard to maintain it. If you compare this to Silicon Valley again, entrepreneurs have renewed energy around innovation because of the different cultural set-up. Because there is an entire support structure, whereas here the best we can say is go get some sleep!

However, this is changing, and we have to be the ones to continue to change it. I like the way Chris Folayan from MallforAfrica puts failure into perspective. When asked what his favourite job interview question is, he says it's "tell me about your failures."

> The answer to this is important because it tells me how the candidate takes risks and will admit when things didn't work out. People always like to discuss their successes, while I'm more interested in their failures and how they overcame and learned from it.[120]

According to the GEM Global Entrepreneurship Report from 2014, the business continuation rate in Africa is the highest in the world. It sits at 14 percent, while Latin America comes second at 5.4 percent and North America at 4.1 percent. Despite this, the report shows that Africans are increasingly optimistic. As per *This Is Africa Online*:

> "Individuals living in African economies tend to be the most optimistic about their perceptions of potential opportunities and their own skills

---

120   *Meet the Boss: Chris Folayan, CEO, MallforAfrica.* Published at How We Made it In Africa, January 2017. https://www.howwemadeitinafrica.com/meet-boss-chris-folayan-ceo-mallforafrica/

for entrepreneurship. They have the strongest entrepreneurial intentions, and their fear of failure is the lowest in the world.[121]"

It seems to me, therefore, that we are starting to assimilate something of the 'failure culture' from Silicon Valley. At our various hubs and conferences, we're starting to speak more about it. Again, *This Is Africa*:

> "As part of the movement to start a more honest conversation about the ups and downs of entrepreneurship in the region, startup failure events are springing up in cities all over Africa. In Johannesburg, South Africa, Sandiso Ncube hosted a discussion of entrepreneurial failure at JoziHub – a networking and workspace devoted to social entrepreneurship—in July.
>
> "It coincided with the launch of two books on learning lessons from entrepreneurial failure by Mr Ncube and his business partner Tshidiso Radinne: "A 10 minute guide to lessons entrepreneurs learn the hard way" and, humorously, "I slept in my car for entrepreneurial reasons: Why entrepreneurship is like drug addiction".
>
> "Meanwhile, Impact Hub Johannesburg is launching a series of so-called "Fuck Up Nights" [typical African honesty!]. At the first event, which took place at the end of June, a panel of entrepreneurs who had all experienced failure at some point in their self-employed careers spoke candidly about when they have made mistakes, hit brick walls and lost money as a result.[122]

My scepticism, however, is that our VC funds don't want to wax lyrically about failure culture and speak about the emotional benefits of that sort of thing. Why would they? We shouldn't expect them to. Rather, they want to see results—and, as said above, we just don't have the scale of innovations for VC funds to take as many risks.

So what do we do? What works here, in my opinion, is what I call a 'convertible' model. This is where a company is funded according

---

121   Sherelle Jacobs, *Talking Failure: Africa's new startup trend*. Published at This is Africa, July 2015. http://www.thisisafricaonline.com/News/Talking-failure-Africa-s-new-startup-trend
122   ibid

to agreed milestones and targets, and maybe later down the line, the investor has an equity stake in the business. But many innovators have approached the likes of Silicon Valley and have come back with what is essentially a crazy valuation, expecting the same sort of approach they take, and then are let down when they hit the reality of what's happening on the ground here.

I think a good example of this comes from Allon Raiz who owns Raizcorp. Raiz is intimately familiar with failure. When his first child was born he had to borrow R22,000 from two different people so the hospital would release him. When he brought him home and watched him sleeping in his crib, the reality of the moment hit him. "I just collapsed on the floor in tears. I thought, 'What am I doing? What AM I doing? I can't even pay for my own baby to come home.'"[123] At the time Raizcorp was not going well. He had been told that an incubator could not make money, ignored the advice, and now was finding he was wrong. And it wasn't the first time he experienced this sort of failure. When he was in his 20's a multi-billionaire saw potential in him and offered to back any business he began. He started a New York Sausage Factory in Pinetown, Durban, but it completely crashed. "I'd been given everything. A private school education, a tertiary education, funding, a mentor and the privilege of starting a business of my choice," he told Entrepreneur Magazine. "I had what most young, aspiring entrepreneurs can only dream of. How could I, given all of those things, fail? And yet I did.[124]"

However, in the long run, Raiz was not wrong about whether an incubator could make money. Raizcorp is now one of the few profitable incubators in the world—and is Africa's only unfunded for-profit business incubator. He is regularly asked to contribute to think-tanks and hubs and conferences around the world, such as the World Economic Forum, the African Development Bank EMRC Annual Conference, South Africa's Human Resource Development Council Entrepreneurship and Education Technical Task Team, and the President-led Competitive

---

123   Entrepreneur Magazine, *Raizcorp: Allon Raiz*. Published January 2013. Available at http://www.entrepreneurmag.co.za/advice/success-stories/entrepreneur-profiles/raizcorp-allon-raiz-2/

124   ibid

Investment Climate Strategy (CICS II) in Kampala, Uganda.[125]What is it that Raizcorp is doing differently, and why do I also believe it holds a key to our VC funding problem?

The key lies in Raizcorp's trade-marked Prosperator methodology. What Raizcorp has done is figure out how to incubate businesses from inception through to growth, by providing an incentive to investors to support the idea from start to finish. As a return for investing and providing infrastructure to the company, and so on, you can either receive equity or cash back. Receiving equity, in the long run, would often be much better, but the fact that you can go for cash makes it less risky. This concept can also be applied to corporates. Nothing is stopping a corporate from saying to someone it employs who has a good idea that it will incubate the idea in its own ecosystem and in return for that it receives a share in the business. That's a win-win situation, not a monopolistic one. And from an investment point of view, I believe this is an approach to take. If you compare this with likes of Silicon Valley, by looking at how it started with Frederick Terman at Stanford incubating ideas, investing in them, and creating the necessary environment, it's a very similar approach. It's a different market and a different approach to how things often work today, but ultimately it's the same concept. And it can be applied across our borders.

2. VC firms in Africa expect profitability very quickly. This second trend is quite obvious and is also why I'm sceptical about a 'failure culture' here, even though it's needed, and I welcome our conversations on it and think comments by Chris Folayan and others are brilliant. Plus, it's not just the innovators who need to get comfortable with failure, but our VC funds as well. But I think it makes a lot of sense that VC funds what to see profitability happen quickly. I would be thinking exactly the same. If your business isn't leaning towards profitability very quickly, it's difficult to justify a constant investment. This is big money and if that money is put elsewhere, even into a bank, there are guaranteed returns.

I find that it boils down to whether or not innovators have a viable business model. Now note this: I did not say whether they have a viable *innovation*. What I am talking about is a business model. My experience has

---

125   ibid

been that there is actually a lot of funding going around, but there are not enough viable innovative businesses. Let me explain what I mean so you don't think I'm contradicting myself. I have a database of innovators that I think are viable and that I would like to fund. Last year I went through about six of those innovators that I thought were really profitable. When I scratched the surface, I found out that they have really good technical expertise (or working towards it) *but not enough business acumen or commercial savviness to run a full business.* That in itself is not attractive enough for investors. As an investor, you want to put your money where there are profit margins.

While I've spotted these two trends I've also spotted two other things I find fascinating – and hugely encouraging.

1. VC funds actually want to play with innovators. And, of course, the innovators need the funding. So what's the problem then? It's quite simple. They're just not connected to each other. They are just not talking. There's a serious case to be made that VC funds need to engage earlier with innovators. Aside from the funding, they can also provide necessary expertise – give the innovator access to markets and networks; insight into how to grow; info on tech funds in the continent; and buttress all that with the actual funding.

The era we are in now is one that is fostering entrepreneurship and innovation worldwide. I don't think we can replicate Silicon Valley because we don't have the cash to throw at innovators, and the entire mindset and set-up are very different. How Silicon Valley was started was very different, and to import that model here, I can guarantee will not work. However, we can learn from everything we've assessed up until now. *What I believe our model should be, is to enable the infiltration of the cultural approach into innovation.* We have to set up a system that protects innovators and entrepreneurs. We may need to give them a safe working environment like a corporate where you get a steady paycheck and medical paid etc., but at the same time fostering innovation and entrepreneurship.

When they go into this system the reality must not be stifled. We need to adopt a rather complex model, but at the same time, it needs to be simple in its approach. Like we saw at Stanford, what we need to do is bind all this into the education system, and build up the culture with a fresh generation well before they get into the corporate world. That model is called INTRApreneurship and that is the model I use, because I am fascinated by it. If you look at any innovator who will do well, all they are trying to do is remove the historical negatives and the cultural negatives, so you can go to your parents and say you have a steady job and a paycheck.

Once you remove all the stresses, I can almost guarantee that an entrepreneur's creativity fires off like a cheetah that has finally decided on its prey. In my travels I've often been asked if the next Einstein will be from Africa, but the truth is they will never pop up if they are worrying about their next meal, because life gets very small when we have to worry about all the details. So if you remove all stresses and foster an environment for them, they are absolutely going to be able to engage their mental faculties. Silicon valley was set up because Terman had an idea to create a premium university and tie it into industry. If we apply the same sort of thinking, we can see how this also remains relevant. It's not necessarily about how do we help entrepreneurs, but how we remain relevant and how we remain relevant is by fostering innovation and entrepreneurship. I think this is a model we need to explore as it works for both parties.

2. Public entities really do want to participate. The South African Revenue Service (SARS) serves as an example. There's an open secret on SARS' Income Tax Act called Section 12J which is actually an amazing opportunity for investors that many have no clue about, even though it was introduced by the South African National Treasury in 2009.

Section 12J allows an investor to put money into VC company funds and receive a tax exempt certificate. In other words, if you invest a million dollars or if you invest R100,000, it's tax free. It's an ideal situation for small investment groups, corporate executives in a high threshold tax bracket, and, of course, companies investing into innovation.[126]This is a very clever way in which SARS is stimulating investment into startups, and innovation falls very neatly under this bracket. A question I'm asking,

---

126   Find out more info about it at SARS (link: http://www.sars.gov.za/ClientSegments/ Businesses/Pages/Venture-Capital-Companies.aspx) or listen / read an interview at Moneyweb at http://www.moneyweb.co.za/moneyweb-radio/save-tax-venture-capital-investing/]

however, is how do you take this sort of model that SARS is pushing and replicate it, where investors hedge their bets due to an incentive such as tax relief, creating a pool of funds that plugs the gap between innovators and VC funding? I don't have the answer to that question. Yet. But I think we have the right starting point here. I also think that we have one major tool that we can employ right now and will make a huge difference straight away and it's this: *To simply just talk to each other.*

I like how Allon Raiz, speaking to Moneyweb after buying a private school in Johannesburg, put it: "We can squeal about the lack of entrepreneurs in our economy, or we can do something about it." This is true. From funding to education to cultural formation, to challenging our own selves, we have to do something about it. Both innovators and investors have a part to play. We have to foster and create our innovations in a way so they get to a point where you can actually fund them. Part of that is to think Pan-African. Part of that is to bring in the diaspora. Part of that is to remember our women. And the other part is to develop a viable business model. That's done by networking and collaborating and connecting with others who can help you — hence, it is critical for any innovator to get involved with a network. I believe that once our innovators can show a viable business model, the funding will be on the up — but it requires a change of thinking from our innovators to see themselves, and to see what they're doing, differently and positively.

"If you don't have ambition, you shouldn't be alive."

– Aliko Dangote

—————————————×—————————————

CHAPTER TWENTY

TECH TRENDS

We've now covered significant ground in analysing the big boys of disruption coming from both Silicon Valley and China. We've looked at how each could affect Africa in negative and positive ways, and we've looked at some of the historical trends to see if we can glean common threads that drive innovation that will help us take on Silicon Valley. We've also looked at some key insights into entrepreneurship that will help us think about our cultural presuppositions more clearly, and we've discussed the need to think Pan-African and the brilliant strategy in including the diaspora.

It seems good to me, at this point, to examine one other thing: the technological trends of Silicon Valley. We need to look at the aesthetics, functionality, consumer wants, and philosophical approaches that Silicon Valley has to technology. This will help us understand how Silicon Valley innovations actually work, and what makes them so successful. They aren't overly complicated, but they do require us to think carefully about them, and find out how to apply these in our own context with our own unique African style and approach.

In doing this, we are asking the questions: how do Silicon Valley's innovators create markets? What is it that makes us so attracted to them, from a tech point of view? I believe there are six main trends to note here.

1. DATA IS KING

All of these innovations know the customer intimately. They collect information, use analytics, compartmentalise, and personalise your account. They make informed decisions based on real-time customer information.

Have you ever noticed that when you search for an item on Google it doesn't take long before you see ads on social media related to what you were searching for? For most of us, we don't have the knowledge or the time to bother finding out what cookies Google has installed in our browser, or to go into each of our accounts and change our privacy settings, and so on. Well, think of this scenario. Google knows you intimately. They know your life cycle. They know when you're looking for a school loan, when you buy your first car, when you're about to have a baby, and what your main interests are. It's not difficult to find out: all they have to see is what you're searching for. They know that you're probably having a baby because you seem to be shopping for a pram online. They know you're thinking of moving because you're looking for houses. They know you're planning on travelling to Europe because you seem to be googling pictures of Europe, looking at airline prices, and so on. They also know which bank you use and they know which restaurant you eat at and so it carries on. This intimate knowledge about you is king. So it's not so far fetched to think that when searching for a new car you could get a message from Google, in some way or another, saying something to the effect of: "We notice based on your search history that you're looking for a car. Here is a pre-approval for a loan for a [insert name of your favourite car] at [insert name of your closest dealership]."

Recently, it was uncovered how Uber even uses psychological tactics to keep its drivers driving. As reported by the New York Times:

> "[Uber] is engaged in an extraordinary behind-the-scenes experiment in behavioral science to manipulate them in the service of its corporate growth — an effort whose dimensions became evident in interviews with several dozen current and former Uber officials, drivers and social scientists, as well as a review of behavioral research.

To keep drivers on the road, the company has exploited some people's tendency to set earnings goals — alerting them that they are ever so close to hitting a precious target when they try to log off. It has even concocted an algorithm similar to a Netflix feature that automatically loads the next program, which many experts believe encourages binge-watching. In Uber's case, this means sending drivers their next fare opportunity before their current ride is even over."

Note the mention of Netflix. All these innovators are looking to understand how humans work, how you personally work, and try to cater for you. Even music apps like Deezer want to cater music for your tastes, but don't think that doesn't mean that this sort of info won't be used to generate income from you in some other way — for example, they note you listen to a lot of jazz, and then let you know about a jazz gig coming up close to your area. QQ Music from Tencent already pretty much goes this route.

Most of us don't feel taken advantage of when that sort of thing happens as it just helps to promote good service, and we feel the convenience. I for one would love to know about gigs in my area, be told about specials at the closest Ethiopian restaurant, and have these apps inform me of anything that lines up with my tastes. They know that most of us are like that and therefore data is king. If you collect the right data you can innovate in more ways and branch off in new directions. Any innovator, then, starting off needs to, from the start, figure out how to collect relevant data from the beginning so that it will be easy to provide more value-added services down the line.

2. NO CALL CENTRES

Have you ever called Google, Uber or Amazon? Neither have I. Why? Because their systems always work! There's no need for me to get hold of a call centre.

This is a fundamental test for any organisation of today. The size of your call centre determines the operational efficiencies of your organisation. In my opinion, having no call centre is the epitome of customer experience. There is a direct correlation between the size of your call centre, whether it's in banking or telecommunications or whatever else, and the customer experience. The less calls you get the more likely the better your customer experience. Note how Google is never down. But think of the bank and financial services industry. As a customer I don't wake up in the morning and think, "Man, I really want to get on the phone with a call centre today." Do you wake up and think, "I can't wait to call the bank"? Of course not. Who *really* wants to call the bank? The only time you call the bank is when you can't find info or Internet banking is down, or something has gone wrong with your card, and so on.

The key to innovation these days is to simplify the experience, and that's why consumers prefer a digital experience these days, if they can have one. While I prefer talking to a human, I also don't want to talk to one through a call centre. But if an app guides me through the right process without me needing to call, I would prefer that. The big boys have shown us that it can be done. And when it does come to some sort of help-line it's generally (as in Amazon's case) an instant messaging service — which I, for one, prefer. If you've ever used it you'll find the experience is quick, effective, and friendly.

Call centres create a lot of employment, and as the world's biggest innovators move away from them (or never even bother with them) it's worth thinking about what that will do to our economies. Call centre systems are prime candidates for innovation: there is really a need to do things differently there. Our homegrown innovations need to take this into account and find better ways to speak to their customers.

3. PAYMENT DISAPPEARS

With Uber, iTunes, Amazon, Google, and most successful innovators these days, you never really think of the payment. When you log in the first time you get asked for your credit card details, but after that you never bother with it again, at least until your card expires. Leave your uber drive and payment happens—you don't even need to push a button.

Payment has fundamentally disappeared in the customer experience and so customers have gotten used to this convenience. They expect it. To have to put payment details in every time to do a transaction, or having to log in and confirm with a complicated password, is just not what people expect. The most extreme version of this is Amazon's "one-click" buy system. It literally just does everything in the background for you, and if you ordered something by mistake, the help process is so brilliant and they will refund you so quickly that it doesn't feel as if you were put out at all.

Simply put, a new world order is emerging where the best intelligence on data is king. Our thinking needs to evolve to follow this approach, as customers want convenience. For industries on the continent to start to compete they have to think of that. For our financial services industry to compete, it has to find ways to make payment disappear. It has to almost actually disappear from the customer's mind, move to the back of the whole experience. The banking services need to disappear. This is a bold statement to position with the banking industry, but if we want to compete that's the reality of where things are.

4. THEY'RE NEVER DOWN

I find it fascinating how, if we get on our phone or desktop and fire up the Internet and go to Google, and told by our browser that there is a connection problem, we *never* think, "Oh, Google must be down" but always assume, "My Internet must be down." Why is that? Because we know Google is *never* down. Facebook is much the same. When it crashed in 2015 for 40 minutes, it was international news. Facebook had to apologise in a way we would never see from most of our online companies. In my history I only remember once in December, 2014 where WhatsApp was down over Christmas (I think it was only 30 minutes) and it was simply due to massive congestion. After that, never again. When you think about it, WhatsApp is just a communications platform, and yet we get so antsy about it. Yet we actually do not need Facebook or Google nearly as much as we need our bank. When you need to make a transfer or pay someone, you really do need to know your banking app will never be down. Yet, when it is, you don't usually express surprise. Frustration, yes, but not surprise! That's problematic. Why is it that Uber and Google and Amazon can get this right, yet we can't?

It's a question worth pondering. It may have less to do with technical expertise or resources and more to do with our philosophy around tech. What makes the innovations we've analysed from the "big boys" of Silicon Valley and China so disruptive is they're *always on*. This means that, for the majority of us, we'll go to Google first because we know it's reliable — even if we aren't consciously thinking of it that way. If Google decided to get into the banking sector, you would probably be happy to give them a try — for, after all, they're never down. You know it doesn't matter where you are in the world and what time it is, that if you can get online, you will find them.

5. THEY DISRUPT SUBTLY

This is massively important. Note how in many of the potential disruptions we covered in the preceding chapters, there have often been no massive press releases, big announcement, and lots of hype. Things just happen and one day you find a new service, and then they start talking about it. Even when they do announce to the media beforehand, it's usually the media who are left to draw conclusions. The innovators don't like to give their game plans away too easily — they're just looking to maintain an innovative public image.

Like Uber. One day I woke up and just found out it was in South Africa. The billboards and launch only came later. The same thing happened with WhatsApp calling, and later, WhatsApp video. While some media houses were talking about it as they were trying to glean inside information from their sources, on the whole it was all rather low profile. When Amazon provides new services it just happens and because it's so efficient, and has such a good reputation, it grows by word of mouth — still the most effective form of advertising.

The reason I flag this is because by the time a new innovation becomes a norm in the industry, it's too late because these Silicon Valley disruptors have already entrenched it in the economy; it's already become part of the fabric of society. Regulation then is too late. Even if you decide to regulate for all the right reasons, it becomes incredibly bad PR for you as a government. That's subtle disruption. It's effectively saying, "Hey, we've done it. Now what are you going to do about it?" And in many cases, very little can realistically be done about it.

6. THEY DISRUPT ON A MASSIVE SCALE

The big boys of innovation that we've covered have their eyes on the world. They look at a global issue and try to provide a solution for it, and then make their disruption locally relevant. As we discussed, Facebook obviously looked at the lack of Internet coverage in Africa and saw an opportunity. If they started to find a solution by going to each of our fifty odd nation-states and work with each of them, it would have been too difficult and taken another hundred years, perhaps. They would have been stuck in the mindset of needing to partner with telecommunications operators, rolling out pilots, conducting research, working with each local regulation, and so on. But instead they start massive and partner with a satellite provider to just beam Internet to the whole continent. It's a much simpler solution and much bigger.

The same goes with Amazon disrupting logistics and the remittance industry. It started with a global view, realising that the "last mile" of logistics is a global issue, and so it worked on fixing that. Now its solution can help Africa in a big way. It is able to provide relevant solutions to the industries and the countries you work in. If we go country by country it becomes difficult to disrupt and compete. We can, however, compete with large multi-national disruptors if we have a Pan-African reach.

SO WHAT DO WE DO?

These innovative disruptors, which we have highlighted in the first half of this book, will fundamentally change the landscape, just as Henry Ford did to the transportation industry, relegating the horse and carriage to a recreational sport. So the real question is: *Do we fight this or are we prepared to ride the new wave?*

My view is that we do both. At a macro level, I worry about the real disparity in our economies that we will feel as whole industries get cannibalised, disrupted, or have the carpet pulled out from under them. It will happen too quickly and we won't be able to recover in time, making it easier for others to take advantage of where we are at. Our industries – telecommunications, financial services, retail, health, education etc. — need to act as if these changes are imminent.

In addition to this, we need to start thinking of industries that would emerge out of this massive eminent disruption. Important questions need to be asked such as, how and where do we up-skill? How do we position ourselves? We need to move from a needs-based approach to a forward-thinking one. The disruption that is coming is coming whether we like it or not, like a raging river in flood. It's up to us to build the right channels up front so that we can guide the river and avert the damage when it comes, because it will.

It starts with the innovators themselves. With you, reading this book. And so, in the next chapter of this book, I want to inspire you to think deeply and positively about who you are and how you define yourself - to explore what it means to be an African innovator.

"Your work is going to fill a large part of your life, and the only way to be truly satisfied is to do what you believe is great work. And the only way to do great work is to love what you do. If you haven't found it yet, keep looking. Don't settle. As with all matters of the heart, you'll know when you find it."

— **Steve Jobs**

CHAPTER TWENTY-ONE

THE INNOVATOR CODE

Where does Africa Rising start? What is the point of entry? It starts with our innovators themselves. It starts with you.

In cataloguing our African transformational stories, I've begun to see certain themes with our innovators – a thinking and passion and positivity that our best innovators share. In a previous chapter we looked at the themes of our innovators' lives; in this chapter, we will look at the philosophy that seems to drive practically every innovator making a difference.

This is what I call the "innovator code". And when you go through this list, think of everything we have covered thus far and how it all ties in.

1. African innovators won't let others define who we are.

Even if they can't actually verbalise it or realise it, this is a matter-of-fact between innovators. They not only see things differently but also refuse to let Africa be defined and boxed by others. As I discussed previously, we cannot simply take the standard old story of 'industrialisation' at face value. We can't be defined by this story because it is largely the story of the current 'industrialised' nations. While we can learn from it and 'industrialise' where appropriate, we live in a different world with different challenges and different technology and a different history.

2. African innovators are visionaries.

I like this quote from Fred Swaniker at a TED talk:

"Too many times we think only of the challenges we have in Africa, but there's one thing that's good about being African and it's this: we don't have legacy, we can be the first to try new things," he says. "We don't have to copy models from other parts of the world that are actually now broken. Rather, let's re-invent and build things for the 21st century.[127]"

With the African Leadership University, Swaniker's vision is to create 250,000 leaders at any given time, with each campus having 10,000 leaders learning. In 50 years, the ALU would have created three million transformative leaders for the continent. If that isn't vision, what is? Can you imagine the number of jobs that would create? By 2050, we are poised to have the biggest workforce in the world. But if they don't have jobs, we will become the world's biggest liability.

3. African innovators believe in the African people, and genuinely believe we can change the continent.

South African, 30-year-old Dr Imogen Wright is a reflection of this. She has created a software solution that enables healthcare workers, in a much lower-cost way than ever before, determine how well an HIV positive patient will respond to Anti-retroviral (ARV) drug treatment. Her company, Hyrax Biosciences, builds online tools that analyse the DNA of the Human Immunodeficiency Virus (HIV) and other bacteria to look for drug resistance. What has traditionally been a very expensive exercise now means any doctor with Internet access, in theory, can prescribe the right drugs across Africa. "I get out of bed for the woman in a rural area who feels sick today and doesn't know why, because she's resistant to her HIV medication and it was too expensive to do a resistance test at the clinic. That woman shouldn't be sick when we have the technology to keep her healthy," she says.[128] This shows me that, as an innovator, she

---

127   See Fred Swaniker's TED talk, *The leaders who ruined Africa, and the generation who can fix it*. Available at https://www.ted.com/talks/fred_swaniker_the_leaders_who_ruined_africa_and_the_generation_who_can_fix_it/

128   See Imogen Wright's bio at Women in Tech, available at http://womenintech.co.za/blog/imogen-wright/

is passionate about what she does – it's not just a job or a path to a successful career or a means to pay the bills. It's not just something she does on weekdays so she can get to her hobbies on the weekends. It's not the American Dream: it's bigger than that. She really believes that what she does will change lives.

Or what about Dr Eddy Agbo from Nigeria, a molecular biologist, who has created a new 25-minute test for malaria that costs only around $2. Until now the only way to test for malaria has been via blood samples which take days before results. Agbo's solution is a simple urine test – much like a pregnancy test. With the World Health Organisation (WHO) telling us that Africa accounts for most global cases of malaria (88%)[129]we can see that Agbo has created a low-cost solution that meets an African problem where Africa is at.

Innovation is not necessarily invention. We don't need something complicated, expensive, or hyper-futuristic. All of these innovations are using simple technology to solve on-the-ground African challenges. The challenge is for innovators to collaborate, to find innovators in other industries that can make their product work better. We need supporting infrastructure: health insurance innovations, stock management solutions, government support, and so on. For example, Agbo's test is brilliant, but how do you order it and get it to rural areas? Can it be bought through an SMS or digital payment service? Can it be supplied via a microinsurance scheme?

Innovators value people. This 'African people' focus is a consistent theme. While they're proud of their achievements, it's because they know their work makes a difference. They're not celebrity types who are building a brand or career, but they're the kind who just want to do what it takes to bring change for the good.

4. African innovators are practical dreamers.

The epitome of this statement is Dr Moustapha Fall, who was born in a little village called Keur Samba Kane, two and half hours from Dakar, Senegal. He is a renowned African mathematician, has published dozens of research papers in international mathematics and physics journals, and

---

129   See the World Health Organisation stats at http://www.who.int/malaria/media/world-malaria-day-2016/en/

has a myriad of professional qualifications. Moustapha believes mathematics can help you understand your surroundings, therefore, allowing problem-solving of important challenges ranging from optimising resources in construction to conserving forests and other natural resources. The biggest plight of coastal towns and villages in Africa is population growth, whilst fishermen still cast their nets in the same waters that they did years ago. Using a mobile app, the fishermen record the number of fish they caught for the day as well as how long they were at sea. The results over a period of time are analysed statistically and then modelled using applied mathematics and theory. Whether the final outcome of the research is largely commercializable across Africa is still undetermined, but what is clearly obvious is they are serious about trying to improve the African life.

Fall is a practical dreamer. You can see this in how he speaks passionately in a conference presentation about his dreams: "Helping our kids move from science through culture and curiosity is the key to the development of science in Africa," he has said. He wants to make mathematics accessible to all Africans by showing the practical applications of mathematics to real African issues.

Do I dare say that we will find the next Einstein from Africa? I keep getting asked this question from Lerato Mbele, an anchor at BBC. And I never have any genuine answer for her. But as a continent, we should know who the next Einstein is and support them. We are looking for those Thomas Edison's who can think outside the box, and it takes a creative genius to do that. I really want to find them and I want to go back to Lerato at some stage and say that we have found the next Einstein. Out of all the people in Africa, the next Einstein must be here. For example, the Awethu Project, which invests in startups, has found minibus taxi drivers that have psychometric test scores that sit in the world's top one percent, according to Yusuf Randera Rees, Awethu's CEO.[130]Do we dare to participate in the space exploration race? Do we dare to dream the practical dream? The answer is a resounding YES! However, we will do this in a uniquely African way. This is the practicality of the African innovator's dream.

---

130   *Moneyweb Inspiration Factory: Yusuf Randera Rees.* See it on YouTube at https://www. youtube.com/watch?v=rczulmFP6_E

5. African innovators are rebels who value creativity

"I'm a rebel at heart," says Emma Kay, the founder of Bozza.mobi. "I'm an entrepreneur, even though I have a background in investment banking!" African innovators aren't afraid to completely switch careers, industries or countries in search of their dreams. In fact, it seems to be the precursor to them fulfilling their ambitions.

The late Everett Rogers, an American communication theorist and sociologist, wrote a groundbreaking work called *Diffusion of Innovations*[131] in 1962. In it, he showed how innovators and early adopters tend to possess the same characteristics: (1) being able to identify problems; (2) are able to think creatively; (3) sense opportunities; and (4) envisage the potentials of the future. (By the way, it was Rogers who coined the term 'early adopter').

GROWING A NEW GENERATION WITH NEW EYES TO SEE

What we need are innovators who understand what's needed for change, know how to work with people, have a great grasp of history and context, hope for the future, and possess creative chops to get us there. If we can create true leaders – not people with just a degree in management, or people who know how to play politics – we can transform the continent. We need to have the long-term in mind. That's Africa Rising – a new generation with a different sense of their own abilities and the potential of our people. Moreover, it's a generation that won't just adopt industrialised strategies but will look to create African solutions to African problems.

In my work to date, I've pushed the narrative of African solutions to African problems, but in this book, I've adapted it a bit to say what we actually need are Pan-African innovations to African problems. I've found this view validated and illustrated extremely well in a study by the Harvard Business Review, "Africa's New Generation of Innovators.[132]" What follows are the key takeaways to this important study, which I believe summarises so much of the research that's out there, and certain-

---

131   See Wikipedia: https://en.wikipedia.org/wiki/Diffusion_of_innovations

132   Read the study at https://hbr.org/2017/01/africas-new-generation-of-innovators

ly helps to put the data onto what I and many others have been feeling for some time.

IT BEGINS WITH A STRUGGLING MIDDLE-CLASS

While I myself have highlighted and written about Africa's 'good consumer story' and rise of the middle-class, it appears that many investors and multinationals have felt disappointed by the growth of this class on our continent. Two recent cases prove the point. In 2015, Nestle announced a 15 percent retrenchment strategy across Africa and reduced its product line by half. "We thought this would be the next Asia, but we have realised the middle class here in the region is extremely small and it is not really growing," Cornel Krummenacher, chief executive for Nestle's equatorial Africa region told Reuters.[133]Barclays Bank announced in 2016 that it will begin to exit out of the continent as part of a general exit strategy from emerging markets that did not develop as quickly as they originally thought. In addition to this, corruption, a lack of infrastructure, and a skills shortage are amongst the other gripes. But the lack of middle-class growth, at least at the speed that was expected, was the biggest driver.

However, Harvard's study shows something profoundly interesting, and that is local entrepreneurs and other multi-nationals are enjoying tremendous growth and success. So the question is, *why?* As per the Harvard Business Review's study:

> "We believe the answer lies in the difference between "push" and "pull" investment. Push strategies are driven by the priorities of their originators and generate solutions that are imposed on markets and consumers. Pull strategies respond to needs represented in the struggles of everyday consumers. The difference in outcomes could not be starker."

What are these differences? When multinationals enter a new market,

---

133   *Meet the Boss: Chris Folayan, CEO, MallforAfrica.* Published at How We Made it In Africa, January 2017. https://www.howwemadeitinafrica.com/meet-boss-chris-folayan-ceo-mallforafrica/

they intend pushing their current products onto the (emerging) middle-class. They bring their entire operating style and cost structure with them and set their prices in effect to limit market penetration just to that middle-class. When more competitors arrive, of course, there will be lower margins and lower growth. That means, of course, that in the end they were not pioneering in a new market but were targeting, as Harvard's study puts it, a "finite base of existing consumption, fighting for every point of share in a highly competitive environment."

However, with "pull" development, the market is assured. There is a sufficient demand. Again, from the study:

> "When innovators develop products that people want to pull into their lives, they create markets that serve as a foundation for sustainable growth and prosperity. Our research focuses on ventures that address the unmet needs of everyday consumers instead of seeking high-margin opportunities by chasing the middle class. They purposely follow the lowest-margin opportunities, relentlessly managing costs by integrating as many elements of the activity chain as possible, from raw materials sourcing to final distribution. They pull needed infrastructure and talent into the company and integrate around potential nodes of corruption—choosing to build self-reliance rather than to depend on existing options. Their investments are guided by a desire to increase affordability and accessibility, and the resulting price and cost discipline fuels higher growth, expanding the market by targeting nonconsumption. Higher growth boosts employment, as ever more workers are needed to make, sell, and distribute products and services."

The study then goes on to provide other real-world examples, claiming that pull strategies driven by market-creating innovators are behind the prosperity that has emerged in Taiwan, South Korea, Singapore, and Hong-Kong (the "four Asian tigers"). There, the leading companies focused on low costs over high margins and created markets by "targeting non-consumption". The Tolaram Group, originally founded in Indonesia, and enjoying success in Nigeria, is another real world example. I would encourage you to read the study for yourself to see all the finer details.

But another example the study mentions is M-Kopa, which, for me, is a great example of the power of humanitarian causes partnering with commercial projects and is actually one of my favourite companies at the moment. It has successfully and profitably created solutions in the low-cost home electricity field for the poor. Based in Kenya and launched in 2012, it took just four years for the company to bring its 'pay-as-you-go' solar energy model to 300,000 homes in East Africa by the beginning of 2016. It connects about 500 homes a day. Along with this, it had sold 40,000 home-improvement and technology products by January 2016, such as energy-saving stoves.

I recently asked one of the founders, Chad Larson to describe to me where they are as a business. Chad said, "You move from an idea to scaling it and then to other countries, and you'll take all the funding you can get. But now as a company, we're selective about who we work with. We want to partner strategically." When a company has matured to that degree, you know they're starting to function on a different level. It's amazing how a home-grown Kenyan company has innovated to such a degree that it has created a new, growing market, continues to invent unique products, and is now starting to cherry-pick who it is it wants to work with. This is not just innovation, it's maturity. The Harvard Business Review outlines this success by saying that, "Although the World Bank calls Kenya's economic growth 'modest at best,' M-KOPA is creating a market out of hundreds of thousands of people—left behind by centralised infrastructure projects — who are pulling the company's solution into their lives." This is it, exactly.

AFRICA KNOWS AFRICA, AND SILICON VALLEY KNOWS THIS

Finally, the Harvard Business Review study ends with this gem:

"At once the most challenging and the most essential trait shared by the market-creating innovators we have studied is their ability to target nonconsumption — to sense the unmet needs that potential consumers struggle to satisfy, and to develop solutions and business models that can meet them. These innovators adopt a different perspective on the world — they look for what isn't being consumed. This trait may come more easily to entrepreneurs steeped in the local culture, but we believe it can be learned."

And this, I believe, is not only the trend we see working in Africa and other emerging markets but is actually how Silicon Valley works. Since the beginning, they have created markets that never existed before, and they continue to do so through their innovations. Or, they create new ways of doing business in existing markets, therefore cannibalising traditional modes of business and infrastructure.

Can you see what this is showing us? *We are doing it.* We are already going in the direction that has proven to be a success so many times in the past, but we are simply doing it our way, in our context. In some cases, we are doing it purely by accident. Perhaps this is because this is actually the way the world works. As the quote says above, this trait — of sensing the unmet needs of potential consumers — comes more easily to entrepreneurs steeped in the local culture. Silicon Valley has long understood this principle and that's how it's biggest successes work — these companies have known for a long time, not only logically but experientially, that this is how you create markets. And if we want to take on Silicon Valley and / or work with Silicon Valley to our benefit, we need to take ourselves seriously—and take the way we are innovating seriously.

Once we have learned the truth of this, that Africans need to create African solutions, and (it turns out) Africans will actually invest in those solutions and pay for them and consume them — and this economic activity will actually grow a middle-class — we can begin to emulate it quite deliberately. Harvard offers four strategies in which this can be done: (1) Spot the 'struggling moment' (in other words, see the problem); (2) Be alert to workarounds (in other words, 'life hacks' — find new ways to manufacture, distribute etc. Recall the example of China's *shanzhai*); (3) Learn from law bending (note how consumers are willing to bend laws in some cases to get something they want, for example the filesharing service Napster in the late 90's, where people could download MP3's of songs — something the market was not providing because it was so new but yet people clearly wanted, even though they never knew it before, and thus were willing to bend the rules to get), and (4) identify abundant or slack resources (find how to incorporate both human and natural resources into a low cost solution. Airbnb and Uber are examples as they rely on a sharing economy model).

This study from Clayton M. Christensen, Efoso Ojomo and Derek van Bever at Harvard Business School, I believe, helps to bring together the thought process we have gone through, and the many of examples I've cited, throughout this book. We've seen exactly how Silicon Valley makes use of these methods, how it is working in China, and how it is starting to work in Africa. The good news then is this: we are on the right path. Let's keep at it.

This is Africa Rising. And it's how Africa Rising must evolve. We need to think strategically. We need to think long-term. We need to partner in different ways. We ought to be discussing private investment. And we need to realise one very important philosophical point: there are plenty of examples of those already doing it. The problem is we're just not talking enough about our successes that are actually changing the narrative, but this narrative has wings, and it's taking off.

"It is the time of the African lion to rise, and for Africa to take the lead."

— **Ashish Thakkar**

CHAPTER TWENTY-TWO

×

ACHIEVING THE DREAM

My goal is to leave a legacy of African innovative thinking. I hope I have begun to achieve that, but there's still more work to do. If anything, I want to leave you with the encouragement to know that there is nothing stopping us from competing on the level of Facebook, WhatsApp, Alibaba, Google, Uber, Amazon and the likes. We have all the elements in play like African satellite providers; we have telecoms companies which have the data and the customer base, and we have a regulated frame of that already enabled; we have the intelligence and the developing networks; we have a rising group of people who want to support Africa as Africans; and we have an amazing story.

As opposed to just writing about it, I want to foster that change. This book and all my writing and speaking is one way in which I want to do this. But I also want to put key players together in an ecosystem that will ensure we can foster change together.

We need to be ourselves — as individuals, as Africans, as the continent of Africa. No longer do Africans want to blend in with the old story, but rather we want to blend out, forging a new way. The old story of industrialisation, the so-called path of development, is a good one — but it's not *our* story. Elements of the story will surely resonate and be relevant. But Africa Rising means Africa is rising, not a pseudo-Europe or America. The Silicon Valley story is a good one, but it's Silicon Valley's story, not ours. China's story is a good one, but it is not ours.

What will our story be?

We have to ask some simple questions. Is there some sort of natural law that means development and progress can only follow one path? The answer is, of course, no. Through collective creativity, Africans can find a different path. If we take our own path of development seriously, the Africa Rising narrative, we will achieve the dream of Africa we are looking for.

One of the things I do before travelling to a new country is I read about the history of the country on Wikipedia or other online sources, and I always make a point to visit a museum or something along those lines, to educate myself about the people I am rubbing shoulders with. When I read Wikipedia, I always see the same trends about Africa: mention of slavery, colonialism, or war and it always reads of oppression. I am not saying that those things did not happen, but there is quite a bit of history around Africa that is not captured. And it would be good for these entries to show what is happening *now*.

In writing this book, I decided to look at what Wikipedia says about the U.K. and the United States, and from the beginning, it's very different. It talks about their historical icons and rich heritage of thought and victories, and it's all very positive.

This is a hard pill for me to swallow because we are not painting that sort of picture of ourselves. It makes me wonder what type of information the future generation will be reading about. Would they still read about slavery and colonialism? I hope they do, of course, as it happened and we must learn from it; but it's not all that has happened, and it certainly isn't all that is happening *now*. We have moved on in many respects, and we are an amazing people who are rising up beyond it. We have our own heroes and historical figures who have impacted us and the world. Why aren't we including them in the way we speak and write about ourselves — and how we let others write about us?

It's sad to realise that on Wikipedia you are allowed to add and edit entries, and I ask why we actually just aren't doing that? This has bothered me greatly. One thing I would love to see is that we, as Africans, use these sorts of platforms to change the narrative. Everywhere we can, we should take that sort of opportunity. It is very easy, as we can just contribute to platforms like Wikipedia and change what the historical views are and define what the future generations will read.

However, this isn't all just about having passion. I was a late bloomer in terms of passion around Africa and I only realised that when I had time to formulate my own views on what Africa should look like. I realised something when I spent some time in Australia. I saw it not only with myself but other Africans there too, and I think it's applicable across the diaspora. I realised there is a sense of loss of direction when you're out there, that you have to figure out life and how you fit in all by yourself.

I'll never forget the day I shared this innate feeling of being lost with a fellow African friend, and he agreed emphatically.

"I feel like I am going through life with one eye on the road to make sure I don't crash," he said, "and I have my other eye on the map, trying to figure out where on earth I'm supposed to go."

I've never forgotten that and it impacted me in ways I didn't expect. I realised that traditionally as a young African male, he would have had elders, uncles, family members or male figures around him who would help him in his life to adulthood, and when you're out there you miss that step. In Australia, we were so far away and felt so out of touch, and what you focus on is making a better life for you and your kids, to the detriment of the story of Africa. We forget to pass on the stories of Africa and we lose that sense of community that the next generation needs.

So for the Africans who are going from one country to the next, or from town to the next, or from one continent to the next, we should not lose the element of what makes us African, by passing down the stories from one African to the next. This is important because if we lose this, we lose an element of who we are. That's why someone like myself who lived in Australia for close to ten years would say I feel so disconnected from Africa and when I finally got it, when I finally realised who Africa really is, I got so fired up for our continent and that flame and passion has never died.

Something I recommend for most African families is that we need to go beyond just providing education and providing for our family, and we must always ensure we do not lose that root and connection to the motherland. It is a hard thing to do, especially if you are negative about Africa, or have to deal with the real challenges of xenophobia or challenges of race and colour. We have got to figure out a way to continually pass on our good stories and our stories of hope and victory. That is who we are, we are a continent of storytellers and we pass on stories from one generation to the next to pass on that passion and love for Africa. In the context of passing on stories, I am passionate about passing on the stories of African innovators and writing about the thought processes that will hopefully shape the next generation. It is important as we move from one form of communication which is verbal story telling, to an online platform that we make sure the element of storytelling remains.

OUR INNOVATORS ARE THE FUTURE

Since the idea of this book came to me, I've spoken at numerous conferences and workshops. Every time I speak, I learn. I learn from the people who speak to me about their ideas or are inspired by my talk. I learn from Africans from all over the globe who contact me via social media because they want to contribute to the African innovation story. I see themes. I see trends. I've tried to outline these in this book to the best of my ability. But one theme I can't quite quantify is the passion and energy resonating from every-day Africans about contributing to the African narrative. There just seems to be an underlying energy or excitement bubbling underneath. The closest word I can use to describe this is Ubuntu, that well-known African philosophy that tells me I'm not actually a person without you, without others. This book is to inspire all the Africans out there, passionate about Africa, who want to contribute to our beautiful continent. Your talent is required. It's time for us to leave a legacy of African innovation for the next generation to come.

In 2016, Bill Gates spoke at the 14th Nelson Mandela Annual Lecture in South Africa. He noted how when he asks students in Ethiopia if they thought about what they are going to do when they graduate, they look at him as if he is crazy even asking such questions because they know what they're going to do. They're not weighing their options. They came to university to get trained so they can get on with it and make Ethiopia into a prosperous country.

> "They saw themselves as members of a community with needs, and they were going to dedicate themselves to serving that community by meeting those needs. I see that sense of purpose whenever I come to Africa, and especially whenever I talk to young Africans. I think this is unique. I meet with students all over the world, and they aren't all so committed to giving back. Students here believe in themselves, and they believe in their countries and the future of the continent."

I believe that is what Africa looks like. And we need to foster this generation of emerging leaders, entrepreneurs, and innovators. Gates continued down this line, challenging us to do everything in our power to build the future Madiba dreamed of. "What can Africa be, what can the world be – and what must we do to make it that way?" he asked. This is what innovators ask. And I love his positivity:

> "If there is one thing I'm sure of, it is this: Africa can achieve the future it aspires to. That future depends on the people of Africa working together, across economic and social strata and across national borders, to lay a foundation so that Africa's young people have the opportunities they deserve."

Kudos, Bill.

EPILOGUE

I write this epilogue as the book is about to go to print. I ask myself one fundamental question. Why have I written this book? Is it just so I can say I have another book under my belt? To achieve the elusive dream of becoming a best-selling author? To see my name in print?

No. The answer is simpler than all that.

I want to talk to every African, despite their creed, colour, gender or race. I want to talk to every African who is just as passionate about our continent as I am, and I want to convince those who aren't as passionate about Africa that they should be. Because there is good reason to be. My editor, Ryan Peter tells me my writing style is "conversational journalism". As an engineer turned author and afro-tech optimist, this is the first I've heard of the term. It does, however, embody what I'm trying to do when I write this book. I wish I could talk to every single African, both here on the continent and spread far and wide in the diaspora, who are longing for a new narrative for our continent and who are yearning to actively participate in it and write our new story.

I remember my Skype conversation with Wayne Conradie, the South African photo-journalist based in Norway, whom after proceeding to apologise profusely for cold contacting me via social media, spent 45 minutes telling me about how passionate he is about our continent. I know nothing about photo-journalism but I remember driving home that day smiling.

I remember Kudzai, a Zimbabwean living in Australia who sent me a message asking me how she can invest in African innovators after reading my previous book. I credit chapter 17 to her as our conversation helped me to crystallise all my thoughts around that so much better.

I remember my Uber driver, John from South Sudan who picked me up when I was in Washington D.C. Our conversation was so riveting that I had to look him up on Facebook after he dropped me off. His passion for his country was so evident on his posts and was clearly reflected in our conversation.

I remember a conversation with quiet Alvin, whom I met in Rwanda, where I was so inspired by his focus and dedication to his craft – social media marketing. I wouldn't be surprised (and fully expect) if I read about him running an impressive social media campaign for our next generation of leaders. I wish I had his focus when I was his age.

I remember dinner with Kaakpema, Ugandan-born but based in Silicon Valley. We had a three-hour conversation about how we can change the future of innovation and I told him he already is that voice for the African diaspora in Silicon Valley.

I remember breakfast with Tshepo, in South Africa who ended up putting together my social media campaign for this book with the #KNOWYOURCHANGE hashtag. Even more impressive is his vision for African Jazz and how he is getting our young jazz artists recognition on the global stage.

I remember dinner with Nigerian, Oyin and Ghanaian, Charles in Paris around how they are disrupting the diaspora market – giving Africans a genuine opportunity to participate in the growing ecosystem on the continent. The French waitress asked us as we paid the bill "What are you guys doing?" Charles' response – "We are changing Africa". And the most impressive thing about that conversation was, we all three fully believed we can and would disrupt Africa!

And I realise the themes with all these conversations is how **they inspired me**. Talking to Africans who are passionate about our continent is truly inspirational.

So I put a challenge to Africans reading this to tell me their stories.

I challenge African economists to think about what the impact of Silicon Valley on our continent would be. It should weigh the positives and negatives of Silicon Valley disruptors – Uber, WhatsApp, FaceBook and Google, highlighting the revenue streams and job creation opportunities as well as the disruption to industries it impacts, and then project the impact for the next couple of decades. Not only would I be truly humbled if an African economist puts this together, I guarantee I will write and promote it!

I challenge African journalists to get out there, get on the ground, and write our stories — to tell the stories of how we are changing as a continent, and how we are innovating for ourselves and can take on Silicon Valley.

I challenge you to think differently, to work differently, to see everything in a new light, and to know this: we can do this. We can take on Silicon Valley. Because "we are it". There's no miracle generation that will solve our problems. There's no one else who is going to do this for us. It's up to you and I, and that's it. If we don't do this, the next generation will be asking us hard questions, and what will we say?

I'm proud of the "Disrupting Africa" movement that has started. If you're passionate about our continent and are already or want to be part of the change, we are friends already. Let's talk. Let's collaborate. Let's connect with others. Let's tell each other our stories and take these stories to the world.

Let's keep disrupting Africa!

ACKNOWLEDGEMENTS

As an engineer turned media contributor and Afro-tech optimist, I'm acutely aware of the fact that I've needed people to get where I am. I believe in team. Otherwise, I wouldn't have the skills to write this book. Understanding and looking internally to why I do this fills me with so much purpose, but that on its own is not sufficient to deliver an outcome.

I have a deep appreciation for my wife, Nkhesani for always creating the environment to "do me". The biggest contributing factor to my ability to telling the African innovation story is having the ability to do so, and I'm eternally grateful for your love and support. Thank you for the opportunity to participate in the Disrupting Africa movement.

I never understood my desire to absorb and glean knowledge—sometimes reading two books a week, and now becoming a bonafide author. Looking back it was my mother, Mrs Chineze Oranye who I am to thank most deeply for this. She exposed me and my siblings to global knowledge and that has always been an invaluable tool in my journey. This book is a dedication to you for your love and investment in me.

To my dad, Mr Chike Oranye for literally sacrificing all he had to make sure we got the best education. I appreciate your role in getting me to this point in my life and providing the learning experiences necessary to be the man I've become. To my four sisters, Nwando, Ifeanyi, Ogugua and Nkem, for always cheering me on. I am proud of the women you've become. You represent the epitome of what our African female innovators and entrepreneurs have become to me. Thanks for always making me laugh in our conversations. Always the best times.

To my editor, Ryan Peter. Thank you for feeling the passion and buying into the vision. Thank you for putting up with the many calls and messages about my ideas and for continually refining the book until I was happy with the message. This book means something to our generation and I'm thoroughly blessed for your contribution in helping me clearly articulate my message.

Many thanks to Victor Kgomoeswana who took a chance on an unknown radio voice. What a story it has been since our first meeting!

An ode to you and a promise to pay it forward. To Antoinette Prophy for setting up the meeting, thank you. This is us disrupting Africa!

To my publishing team, Shane, Clare-rose, Lee and Tshepo. Fascinating that I didn't how powerful a team I had until I started penning this. It's no mean feat to publish a book and I am indebted to you for your effort.

Over the past year, there were those who saw something in me and helped me advance my cause. To Neil Novick, not only for believing in me but investing your time and advice in ways you probably haven't even realised. Some talk the talk, but you walked the walk. Thank you for helping me crystallise my "why" even further.

To Craig Lyons and Allon Raiz who continually share their time. I'm honoured.

To Lincoln Mali. I will continue to practice the "Bring Yourself to Work" concept.

To Dominic Lai, for investing precious time-in a 25-year old kid in Australia. Your lessons have been invaluable and I've kept my promise to pay it forward to numerous individuals. I always leave them with the same message you gave me to "pay it forward to the next generation."

I've had the privilege of meeting some amazing people who have made this book possible. To the innovators who share their time and their experiences, which have enabled me, see the trends I've written about in this book. To the amazing people from all over the globe who contact me to share their stories and inspiration after reading my first book. This is our time!

And finally, to you reading this book, thank you. And a double thank you if you contribute to moving the needle of innovation for the continent. Together, we keep disrupting Africa!

ABOUT NNAMDI ORANYE

Nnamdi Oranye, a regular media contributor who is featured in multiple publications including CNBC Africa, Mail & Guardian, BBC, Carte Blanche and others, is passionate about how technology and innovation have the power to truly change lives in Africa. His many travels and business experience across the continent have greatly contributed to his huge optimism for the continent and its bright future. He features frequently as a presenter and chairperson across conferences internationally, contributes regularly to think-tanks on the subject of innovation, and has been named amongst the 100 most influential names in Africa's telecoms, media and ICT industry by the AfricaCom100 Research Board.

He is also the author of "Disrupting Africa", Africa's first book to chronicle the lives of innovators and entrepreneurs changing the African landscape.

Go to **about.me/nnamdioranye for more details.**

www.ingramcontent.com/pod-product-compliance
Lightning Source LLC
Chambersburg PA
CBHW071539200326
41519CB00021BB/6537